THE
ACQUISITION
AND
DEVELOPMENT
OF LANGUAGE

PRENTICE-HALL

CURRENT RESEARCH IN

DEVELOPMENTAL PSYCHOLOGY SERIES

John C. Wright, Editor

PRENTICE-HALL, Inc., Englewood Cliffs, N.J.

THE
ACQUISITION
AND
DEVELOPMENT
OF LANGUAGE

PAULA MENYUK

Research Laboratory of Electronics
MASSACHUSETTS INSTITUTE
OF TECHNOLOGY

To my parents
Helen and Leon Nichols

13-003087-2

Library of Congress Catalog Card Number: 79-135023
Printed in the United States of America

Current printing (last digit):
10 9 8 7 6 5 4

PRENTICE-HALL INTERNATIONAL, INC., London
PRENTICE-HALL OF AUSTRALIA, PTY. LTD., Sydney
PRENTICE-HALL OF CANADA, LTD., Toronto
PRENTICE-HALL OF INDIA PRIVATE LIMITED, New Delhi
PRENTICE-HALL OF JAPAN, INC., Tokyo

THE PRENTICE-HALL SERIES
IN DEVELOPMENTAL PSYCHOLOGY

JOHN C. WRIGHT, Editor

PRENTICE-HALL
CURRENT RESEARCH IN
DEVELOPMENTAL PSYCHOLOGY SERIES

JOHN C. WRIGHT, Editor

THE ACQUISITION AND DEVELOPMENT OF LANGUAGE
Paula Menyuk

HUMAN INFANTS:
EXPERIENCE AND PSYCHOLOGICAL DEVELOPMENT
Burton L. White

CONTENTS

2

THE INFANT'S CAPACITY TO ACQUIRE LANGUAGE

3

THE ACQUISITION AND DEVELOPMENT OF PHONOLOGY

4

THE ACQUISITION OF SYNTAX

5

THE DEVELOPMENT OF SYNTAX

6

THE ACQUISITION AND DEVELOPMENT OF SEMANTICS

Students of child development traditionally have been interested in language development for two reasons. First, the study of the acquisition of language potentially can tell us a great deal about the physiological and intellectual functioning of the child as he matures and, second, the use of language is considered to have a tremendous effect on the child's relationship with himself and to his environment. Despite this interest, and many years of research, not a great deal was known about what the child learned when he learned a language. A linguistic description of the structure of language has caused a new upsurge of interest in the study of language acquisition because it promises to shed much further light on our understanding of the child's acquisition and use of language and its relation to other aspects of his development. This linguistic description has been termed transformational or generative grammar, and its goal is to account for all the generalizations about language of which the native adult speaker has knowledge, such as (1) what is a sentence and what are the functional relationships expressed in sentences, (2) what is a word and how is it used in certain contexts, and (3) what is a speech sound and how is it used in certain contexts. This knowledge is presumably what the native speaker uses to derive the meaning of an utterance and to express intended meaning. Linguists have termed this knowledge "competence" and they attempt to describe this competence by structural descriptions of the possible sentences of a language.

In recent research on language acquisition it has been hypothesized that this linguistic knowledge is what the child acquires over the developmental period. It has been further hypothesized that structural descriptions of the utterances produced and understood by children at various stages of development will describe this knowledge and lead to a better understanding of the relationships between this acquisition and developing physiological and psychological functions. Therefore, this book deals primarily with the experimental results of studies undertaken to examine the *structure* of children's comprehension and production of language.

The first chapter introduces some questions which are pertinent to the study of language acquisition and some explanations and descriptions that have been offered to account for the process. The second chapter discusses physiological and behavioral studies of the infant's readiness to acquire language or of what he might know about language during infancy. In chapters 3 through 6 the child's development of phonological (speech sound), syntactic, and semantic categorizations and compositions is discussed. Most of the research dealt with is concerned with describing and explaining why some structures are used before others and the possible relationships between early and late development. Therefore, it is focused on the child's acquisition of the linguistic system and what this can tell us about his physiological and intellectual development. The seventh chapter is concerned with the study of the effect on linguistic and cognitive behavior of marked individual differences due to physiological state. Chapter 8 deals with studies of the effects on these behaviors of group differences due to differences in the language in the environment. This latter research focuses on the question of the effect of language behavior on cognition and communication. The final chapter discusses the various theories that have been proposed to account for language acquisition, and, thus, presents a review of research questions that have yet to be answered.

This experimental approach, employing structural descriptions of the language that is understood and produced at various stages of development under various conditions, is quite new. Therefore, many questions remain to be answered. It is hoped that the students who read this book will find these current research efforts a good reason for engaging in the task of obtaining answers to these questions and a good beginning for further exploration.

Grateful acknowledgement is given to the faculty and research staff of the Speech Communication and Linguistics groups in the Research Laboratory of Electronics with whom many of the issues raised in the book have been discussed. Special thanks is given to Mrs. Hedy Kodish for her translating, typing, and retyping of the manuscript, and to Norman Menyuk.

This book was written while the author was a staff member at the Research Laboratory of Electronics, Massachusetts Institute of Technology. The research was supported by the National Institute of Health (Grant 2R01 NB–04332–07).

PAULA MENYUK

SOME QUESTIONS
ABOUT LANGUAGE
ACQUISITION

THE STUDY OF THE CHILD'S acquisition of language has engaged the interest and fancy of those who have wanted either to better understand the development of children or to better understand the nature of language, and this study has been going on for centuries. Georgina Masson (1957), describing the scientific interests of an emperor, reports "According to Salimbene, in an effort to establish what is the mother tongue of the human race, the emperor had some children brought up from birth in complete silence in order to ascertain what language they would speak. The experiment was a failure, and all the children died." One might state that the emperor asked a foolish question and certainly ran a poor experiment. Despite the fact that research, of one kind or another, has been going on for many centuries, answers to the questions, Why do children acquire language? and How do they acquire it? have yet to be provided in detail.

For many years it was assumed that the structure of what was acquired (the language) was understood and that a list of the sounds, words, and sentence types produced by children at various stages of development would be an adequate description of the process of language acquisition. However, although a body of facts had been collected which indicated gross developmental changes, it was clear that such a description of linguistic behavior did not include what the child knew about language or could use in comprehending and producing utterances at various stages of development since language is not composed merely of lists of sounds, words, and sentences. Further, researchers found it very difficult to correlate the above descriptions and observations with descriptions of the child's changing physiological and psychological competences; the most they could come up with was the general observation that as the child grew the size of the lists grew or the proportions of usage of items in the lists changed. Therefore, not only was there no adequate description of why or how a child acquired language, but also there was no adequate description of what he acquired which might then lead to explanations of why and how.

A linguistic description of the structure of language which has had considerable influence on current research in language acquisition is the transformational or generative model of grammar. It has had this great influence because it attempts to describe adequately what is acquired, and many experimenters have assumed that an adequate description of *what* is acquired at various stages of development can lead to interesting hypotheses about *why* and *how* language is acquired.

This chapter will present a summary of some of the outstanding questions about language acquisition that current research is attempting to answer. These questions will be considered in the light of the observations that have been made about gross developmental changes in linguistic behavior and about developmental changes in physiological and psychological functioning during the language acquisition period. A brief discussion of the main theoretical positions concerning the relationships of language and thinking will also be presented. The models of language termed generative grammar and psycholinguistic descriptions of language processing that have been derived from the linguistic model will be briefly described. Finally, the methods by which the models of language and language processing have been applied in current research in language acquisition will be outlined. The observations that have been made will be reexamined in detail in the light of current psycholinguistic descriptions, and theoretical positions and descriptions of the linguistic and psycholinguistic models will be expanded in subsequent chapters as specific aspects of language acquisition are discussed.

DEVELOPMENTAL CHANGES DURING THE LANGUAGE ACQUISITION PERIOD

Descriptions of language acquisition and development have indicated certain observable facts. The infant produces a number of sounds (grunts, cries, gasps, etc.) because of his physiological state. He then begins to produce a number of sounds that are different in acoustic composition from those produced previously and the nature of the situations which appear to provoke them is also different. Spectrographic analysis has shown that the units of utterance during this period show the same duration as do the units of utterance of the adult, and, at about the ninth month, adultlike intonation patterns and imitation of adult intonation patterns have been noted (Nakazima, 1962). This period, during which children produce strings of utterances marked by intonation and stress, although they produce no clearly identifiable morphemes, has been labeled the "jargon" period by some experimenters.

Following this period some observers have noted a marked decrease in vocalization (Jakobson, 1962) and then the appearance of words. This fact has been cited as an indication of the lack of association between the periods of development that come before and after word production has begun. The words produced at this stage may not always be words which can be found in the lexicon (dictionary) of the language, but they are considered words by virtue of the fact that the same phonological combination (speech sound sequence) is used consistently by the child in the presence of a particular stimulus object or situation (Murai, 1963/4). These are not word approximations such as "muk" for the word *milk,* but such sequences as "tutu" for *teddy bear* or for any soft toy animal in the child's environment. Furthermore, the child presumably comprehends some aspects of the meaning of words he may not be producing. When asked to do so, he can bring some objects to his mother or identify them by pointing. By the second year of life many conventional words are being used. Along with these pre-conventional and conventional words, various intonational patterns are being used. Words and phrases are marked with declarative, emphatic, and question intonations (Menyuk and Bernholtz, 1969), and utterances such as "up." "up?" and "up!" are being produced.

In the third year of life the child uses short sentences which have been termed "functionally complete" (McCarthy, 1930)—that is, the listener understands what the child is saying although the utterance is not grammatically complete. For example, a child aged 2 years, 10 months produced the following sequence of sentences: [1]

1. I need a sponge
2. That wash thing off
3. Everybody can't have turn
4. But I didn't have any turns
5. I want do that when I finished
6. I want those
7. I see animals
8. This one riding on horse
9. I want some
10. You can't take

---

[1] These sentences were in the language sample obtained from a pre-school child in a population described in Menyuk, 1964.

Although many of these utterances are not grammatically complete, they can, for the most part, be understood.

It has been found that pre-school children produce sentences which are incomplete (not understandable), functionally complete, simple, simple with phrase, compound, complex, and compound-complex (McCarthy, 1954). In terms of the above descriptions, therefore, pre-school children are using all the sentence types used by adults. Within a given sampled time the frequency of usage of the more complex of these structures increases as the child matures, as does the variety of the sentence types used. Mean sentence length also increases with age.

In addition, it has also been found that, in the normal development of language, deviations from completely grammatical speech sound sequences and sentence types occur in the utterances children produce. Different kinds of deviations from completely well-formed utterances occur throughout the developmental period. These differ in structure from the nongrammatical utterances produced by adults. For example, a child might say "He do it too much times," whereas an adult might say "He, he really is a pest, just did it too many times."

One other observation about the language acquisition process should be stressed. It was noted earlier that the child produces and uses for communicative purposes words which are unique—which are not imitations or even approximate imitations of words he hears in his environment. He also produces and uses for communicative purposes sentences containing syntactic structures for which he has no model. For example, he produces such utterances as "n-touch" and "anudder one shoes."

All the descriptive studies of language acquisition and development tell us that the behaviors outlined occur and in the order described. It has been reported that not all children go through a clearcut single word phase or clearcut jargon phase, just as all children do not go through a crawling phase or do not crawl in exactly the same manner before walking. However, in normal development, all children go through a babbling period before they produce sentences, just as all children turn over and sit up before they walk. In addition, these language acquisition processes are largely resistant to distortion. If the child is severely mentally retarded or grossly physiologically impaired in some ways (such as being deaf or brain damaged), these processes are disturbed and language incomprehension, mutism, or specific language deviations may occur. The only environmental deprivation which seems to be directly related to deviance in the acquisition processes outlined is complete isolation from the speaking community for a critical period of time, and even here the evidence is apparently not conclusive (Lenneberg, 1967).

During this period of language development the child is developing motorically. Lenneberg (1966) has listed the time correlations between certain changes in motor performance and certain language changes. It should be kept in mind that these correlations are merely comments on when types of performance—motor and linguistic—occur. They indicate that both performances have a *fixed* developmental schedule of change, but these co-occurences do not imply dependency. Indeed, some children who cannot walk or use their arms or hands in a coordinated manner do, nevertheless, develop language.

When the child at 4 months is producing nonphysiologically induced sounds (cooing and chuckling), his head is self-supported and the tonic and neck reflex is subsiding. During the babbling period (6 to 9 months) the child also sits alone and pulls himself to a standing position. At 12 to 18 months he produces a small number of words, follows some commands, and responds to "no." He also, at this stage, stands momentarily alone, crawls, and takes some steps when held. When his vocabulary grows from approximately 20 to 200 words at 18 to 21 months, and when he points to objects that have been named, comprehends simple questions, and forms 2-word phrases, his stance is fully developed and he walks clumsily. At 24 to 27 months he has a vocabulary of 300 to 400 words, produces 2- to 3-word phrases, and also runs and can change his position from kneeling to sitting. At the stage at which the fastest increase in vocabulary is observed (30 to 33 months) and when he is producing 3- to 4-word sentences, he also has obtained good hand and finger coordination. At 36 to 39 months the child's vocabulary increases to about 1,000 words or more, he uses well-formed sentences containing certain grammatical structures, and he runs, walks stairs by alternating feet, jumps, and can stand on one foot momentarily and ride a tricycle.

Piaget has described the period of about 0–2 years as the sensory-motor period (Flavell, 1963). During the last 6 months of this period the child starts to make internal symbolic representations of sensory-motor problems and to deduce problem solutions before attempting a solution by trial-and-error behavior. Because of this acquired competence he can, among other things, imitate models not immediately present, engage in pretense play, infer objective causes when only effects are seen and vice-versa, and reconstruct memories of past events. It should be remembered that during the period of 18 to 27 months the child has progressed from producing words to producing 2- to 3-word phrases, and has progressed from taking a few clumsy steps to running. At this stage ". . . the child has passed into a new era in which this symbolic capacity, much more than other actions, becomes the important instrument of cognition" (Flavell, 1963, p. 150). During the first 2 or 3 years of the pre-operational subperiod (from approximately 2 to 5 years) the child applies his representational ability, defined as the ability to differentiate signifiers from significates, to an increasingly larger range of phenomena. It is during this period and well before the end of it that the child achieves basic mastery of the syntax of his language (Menyuk, 1963).

Some other developmental changes in physiological and psychological functioning have been observed during this period. Physiological changes are occurring in the overall size, proportions, and control of the vocal productive mechanism from birth until puberty. In addition, it has been observed that memory storage capacity increases with age. For example, children are able to recall longer and longer sequences of digits as they mature. However, a number of studies have noted that the nervous system is limited in its capacity to collect, collate, and store stimulus information (Miller, Galanter, and Pribram, 1960). Given the limitations of the nervous system for memorizing all instances of stimuli and storing them for later use, a capacity to organize the primary data in a structural manner for a later retrieval has been inferred. Obviously maturational changes in memory occur not only in capacity for storage but also in organizational ability.

What is obvious in these discussions of increasing competence in sensory-motor and cognitive functioning is that the child, during this period, achieves greater and greater facility in differentiating and integrating sensory inputs, storing this information, and putting these integrations to use. In terms of language development we know that the process of increasing complexity in language usage, in terms of size of vocabulary, sentence structure, and speech sound structure, occurs and that by about the end of the fourth year of life the basic sentence types postulated as being used by the adult are being used by the child. We know that systematic approximations to complete grammaticalness occur before and after basic mastery of the production of the various sentence types described has been achieved. In other words, the child produces both grammatical and nongrammatical sentences simultaneously. In addition, we are very generally able to say something about the sensory-motor and cognitive development of the child before the fourth year of life which may be related to his language acquisition. We hypothesize that language cannot be simply a function of memorization of lists of sentences because of the memory limitations of the nervous system and because all speakers of the language must be capable of producing an infinite number of sentences of the language. We know that the child achieves basic mastery at an early age and after a limited sampling of the possible linguistic data.

How are these aspects of development related to each other? What we need to add to this general knowledge is a description, in detail, of this process of increasing complexity—how it is initiated and its developmental course. To understand the facts of language development we would like to describe both the set of utterances understood and produced by the child at any given age during the developmental period and the processes of change in the set of utterances understood and produced at various ages. In studying the language development of children we would not only like to describe the facts of this development, but we would also like these descriptions to offer us possible explanations for the facts described and to reveal relationships between the child's physiological and psychological capacities and his language acquisition. Most of the current research in the language development of children has been concerned with obtaining this detailed description of the structure of what the child understands and produces at various ages as well as with obtaining an explanation for this developing structure.

LANGUAGE AND THINKING

In summarizing Piaget's position on the relationship between language and cognition, Flavell states the following:

> Piaget . . . stresses the enormous role which . . . [a] linguistic system plays in the development of conceptual thinking. Language is the vehicle . . . of symbolization, without which thought could never become really socialized and thereby logical. But thought is nonetheless far from being a purely verbal affair. . . . In essence, what happens is that language, first acquired through the auspices of a symbolic function which has arisen earlier, will reflexively lend tremendous assistance to the subsequent development of the latter [Flavell, 1963, p. 155].

Vygotsky takes a somewhat different position (1962, Chapter 4). He states that thought and speech have different roots and that the latter is not a simple continuation of the former. There is a pre-linguistic stage in the development of thought and a pre-intellectual stage in the development of speech, and for some time these processes develop independently. At some stage of development, however, there is a meeting of thought and speech when thought becomes verbal and speech rational.

A great deal of theorizing time and research time have been expended on arguments about the relationship between language and thinking. Although these arguments are important and interesting, no attempt will be made here to cover, in depth, the research that has been undertaken in an attempt to resolve them, since this would require and has produced volumes. Instead, the main positions that are held and some representative research and the conclusions drawn from it will be discussed. Figure 1–1 presents a graphic representation of these main positions in a very simplified manner.

The various positions represented under the headings A, B, C, and D of Fig. 1–1 are the following:

A. The sensory-motor processes of the human nervous system, which allow differentiation and classification of inputs, lead to the development of primitive symbolic functioning. This, in turn, leads to conceptual thinking

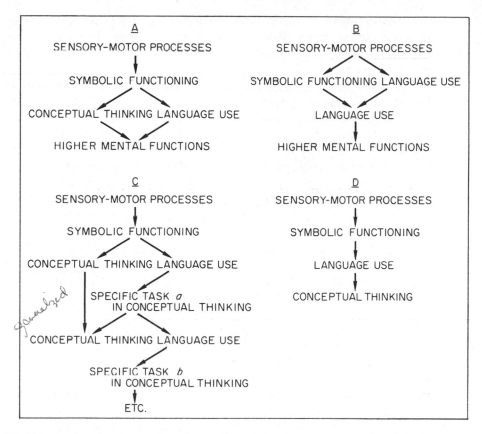

FIG. 1–1   A schematic representation of some theoretical positions concerning the relationship of thinking and language.

and language usage, which are more or less independent of each other. However, language, when acquired, contributes to the development of higher mental functions.[2]

B. Sensory-motor processes lead to the development of perceptual symbolic functioning and the development of language. These processes stand apart in the early stages of development, but language usage then continuously influences later development.

C. Sensory-motor processes lead to the development of perceptual symbolic functioning which then leads to language usage. Each process develops independently, but there are specific cognitive tasks in which language is always employed.

---

[2] "Higher mental functions" is a term used by Luria, 1966.

D. Sensory-motor processes lead to the development of perceptual symbolic functioning which then leads to language usage. Language usage continuously effects conceptual thinking and the development of higher mental functions.

One aspect of these positions will be touched upon in a forthcoming chapter. The argument of whether language processes should be considered to be unique—that is, anatomically and physiologically unique—or the same as cognitive processes will be discussed in Chapter 2, which deals with the child's capacity to acquire language. A second argument concerns itself with whether conceptual thinking is dependent on language or language on conceptual thinking or whether the two processes are independent. The various types of experimental testings of this question and the various conclusions that have been drawn from this experimentation will be considered now.

In two experiments in which children had greater difficulty in matching an action to a statement when they had to move an item which was the object rather than the subject or actor in the statement (Huttenlocher and Strauss, 1968), the experimenters concluded that comprehension requires correspondence between the form of the linguistic description and the extra-linguistic state of affairs. One might also argue that the perception of "state of affairs" has been shaped by the linguistic form—that is, by the expectation that subjects act but objects do not. Since the situation could not be manipulated in the experiment, the linguistic form had to be. This latter kind of argument has been carried to its extreme in the "Whorfian hypothesis" (Whorf, 1956). Whorf states that we organize the world and react to it in particular ways because of the linguistic system in our minds. The following conclusions might be drawn from this statement: (1) a particular linguistic system (that is, the grammar of a particular language) should affect the way in which various stimuli are perceived and problems are solved; (2) the level of acquisition of a linguistic system should effect the way in which stimuli are perceived and problems are solved; and (3) absence or deviancy of a linguistic system should seriously attenuate performance in cognitive tasks. The experimentation that has been undertaken, therefore, has taken three directions: cross-linguistic studies, studies with children of various ages, and studies with children having little or no language. Some exemplary studies will be discussed.

African and American children (aged respectively, 4 to 8 years and 3 to 5 years) were given a transposition of size task (Cole, Gay, Glick, and Sharp, 1968). An asymmetry exists in the language (Kpelle) of the African children. Members of their linguistic community often say "big" (yer) but seldom "small" (er). This asymmetry does not exist in American English. The stimulus array consisted of 10 squares which increased in size in equal steps from the smallest to the biggest. Training took place on middle squares 5 and 6, and the children were asked to tell the experimenter which one the experimenter was "thinking of." Half the subjects were always told that the smaller square was the correct choice, and half were told that the bigger square was the correct choice. The training period was continued until there were 9 sequential correct responses. Half the subjects were then tested on a comparison of 2 adjacent squares from 5 to 1 (those decreasing in size) and the other half were tested on adjacent squares from 6 to 10 (those increasing in size). The experimenters found that at the start of the training period African children were biased toward guessing that the *bigger* square was the correct one whereas American children showed no such bias. During the test period, however, there were no differences in the performance of the two linguistic groups. In a post-test period the verbal response asymmetry appeared again. The authors conclude that the readily available categorization determined the choice. These results indicate (1) that children can learn or have the capacity to learn how to categorize stimulus arrays in a manner which does not fit in well with the readily available categories of their linguistic system; and (2) that when approaching a problem they will first use the readily available categories. It appears, then, that language can bias conceptualization in ways that are dependent on the structure of the language, but that the child still maintains his capacity to conceptualize along dimensions which are divergent from those of the language in appropriate situations.

It is possible that the structure of conceptual thinking is not dependent on a *particular* linguistic system but may, however, be dependent on the universal aspects of language. All languages describe relationships and provide a categorization system. These aspects of language might, therefore, provide the means by which the child can classify the logical relationships and categorizations of phenomena. It has been found, with adults, that when they are asked immediately to identify a color among a set of colors to which they have been briefly exposed, the codability of the color (a readily available category) does not affect performance. However, when they are asked to identify a color after some delay, codability sharply affects performance (Brown and Lenneberg, 1954). The results of this experiment, as well as others, indicates that language is important for an aspect of conceptual thinking—memory—and thus might contribute to the performance of children engaged in cognitive tasks in which memory is an important factor.

In a study with deaf and hearing adults and deaf and hearing 6-year-old children, Lantz and Lenneberg (1966) found that communication accuracy or the ability to formulate distinctive linguistic categories for colors was consistently related to performance in a color recognition task. Hearing adults did best in the recognition task and deaf children did worst. None of the differences obtained could be explained on the basis of differences in perceptual discrimination.

Outside of tasks which call upon the labeling system of a language for accurate repetition, other tasks which might call upon other structural aspects of the language for accuracy of performance have not been examined. Moreover, the results of experiments on the contribution of the language labeling system to cognitive tasks confuse rather than clarify the issue of whether or not readily available categories are necessary in certain cognitive tasks. For example, although the linguistic categorization system is available to the child, he does not use it in some instances. He may linguistically categorize (make a verbal response to) the stimuli in the task, but he may not use these categorizations in performing the task.

Children aged 4 and 7 years were first given the task of learning to select a stimulus from a set of stimuli which varied simultaneously in two dimensions (large black, small black, large white, small white) (Kendler, 1963). Both dimensions (brightness and size) could be used for a correct selection, but each child had to select only on the basis of one dimension. The children were also required to describe the correct stimulus in terms of one dimension. For example, if the correct stimulus was large/black the children could state that it was either large or black. In the second task the children were required to select the stimulus which was the reverse in one dimension of the previously selected stimulus. For example, if the previously selected stimulus was small/black, a reversal response would be to select either a stimulus that was large or a stimulus that was white. If the child had in the first task described the size dimension, then rewarding a reverse response in the size dimension (large versus small) would render his verbalization relevant to the task. If, on the other hand, the child was rewarded for a response in the brightness dimension (white versus black) his verbalization was irrelevant to the reversal task. Thus previous verbalizations could be either relevant or irrelevant to the reversal task if they occurred. In some instances there was no verbalization. It was found for both age groups that faster reversal shifts were produced when relevant verbalizations occurred than when irrelevant verbalizations occurred. With the younger age group relevant verbalizations appeared to produce a faster shift than no verbalization. However, for the older group there was no difference in the mean number of trials needed to learn the reversal shift between the relevant verbalization and the no verbalization condition. The experimenter concluded that in the no verbalization condition the older children were making covert verbal responses and using them in the reversal task. We cannot tell whether or not the younger children were making covert responses in terms of these data. However, when the verbal response was irrelevant, the mean number of trials needed to learn the task was significantly greater for both younger and older children. The interesting result in terms of this discussion is that younger children took longer to learn than older children even in the relevant verbalization condition. That is, verbalization of the type defined as critical in accomplishing the task did not lead to equality in the performance of the groups. Despite the fact that the response was available to these 4-year-old children, from their everyday language, for covert use in the no verbalization condition, they were not utilizing their linguistic categorizations in the same manner as the older children. Having or producing a linguistic category is obviously not the only factor which may affect performance in this cognitive task. Changes in cognitive performance because of age (whatever these are) seem to have as great as or a greater effect than verbal labeling on performance.

This study also showed that whether or not the response was produced had a marked effect on the performance of the younger children. This factor was examined in a study which attempted to parcel out "mediational deficiency" from "production deficiency" (Flavell, Beach, and Chinsky, 1966). The experimenters described "mediational deficiency" as that condition in which a response is made but does not mediate performance, and "production deficiency" as that condition in which no response is made. Children in kindergarten, second, and fifth grade were given the task of recalling in a certain order a number of pictures among a set which had been previously pointed out by the experimenter in both an immediate and a delayed recall situation. Observation was made of random lip movements, lip movements which appeared to be subvocal speech productions, and actual word productions, both silent and aloud, during the encoding and recall tasks. There was a substantial increase in spontaneous verbal productions from kindergarten to second grade and from second grade to fifth grade. There was also an increase in scores obtained by children from kindergarten to fifth grade. On the surface, it would appear that actual production of a verbal response to a visual stimulus aids in the recall of this stimulus, but the experimenters point out that it has been observed that children's nonsocial speech (produced during problem-solving tasks, etc.) has been observed to become more internalized as they mature (Vygotsky, 1962). In addition, there are obviously many other variables outside of the production of the response which might account for the increase in scores. These variables might account for both the increase in scores and the increase in verbalization as independent developmental changes. One of these variables might be the nature of the task.

The results of an experiment examining children's recall of a maze solution into which verbalization was introduced indicated that production of a verbal response need not enhance children's recall (Rosenbaum, 1967). Children in grades 1 through 6 were either performers or observers in the task. In the verbalization conditions children who performed the task called the number of the correct response in the maze while the observers listened and watched or the observers called the number of the correct response. In the nonverbalization condition both performers and observers were silent. In general, the following conditions produced the best to worst results in maze solution by each type of performer:

1. Observers who did not verbalize—verbal condition
2. Observers who did verbalize—verbal condition
3. Observers—nonverbal condition
4. Performers who did not verbalize—verbal condition
5. Performers—nonverbal condition [3]
6. Performers who did verbalize—verbal condition

One conclusion that might be drawn from these results is that verbalization helped those who did not actually do the verbalization but interfered with the performance of those who did. The experimenter concludes that verbalization was thus able to interfere with performance because it was in fact irrelevant to the task. However, in the previous experiment, verbalizing while encoding or decoding did not impede performance but, rather, appeared to enhance it. Certainly, one can state that there is a nearer relationship between pictures and names than between numbers and lights, and that this difference in the tasks brought about differing results. However, these differing results again make clear the very marked effect of the type of task on whether or not verbalization enhances performance.

There have been many studies examining the cognitive abilities of deaf children compared to their hearing peers. The results of 31 studies examining 8,000 children's performance on nonverbal I.Q. scales is summarized by Vernon (1967). These tasks involve memory, abstractions, reasoning, concept formation, etc. In 13 of the studies the deaf population was superior to their hearing peers, in 7 there were no significant differences in performance, and in 11 they were inferior. In the latter instances the differences were "small." Despite these findings 35 percent of the deaf population never achieves functional literacy and only 5 percent develop average skill in verbal language by adulthood.

A number of comparative studies of the performance of deaf and hearing children in various cognitive tasks have been undertaken.[4] Some of these studies failed to show differences which a "mediational deficiency" theory

---

[3] The exceptions are third to fourth grade performers who did better when verbalizing in the verbal condition than they did in the nonverbal condition.
[4] For example, see Furth, 1964.

would predict (Youniss and Furth, 1963). In those instances in which differences in performance occur, it has been hypothesized that diminished general experience (deaf children often lead restricted lives in an isolated community) and different strategies of cognitive task solution resulting from this lack of experience may account for the results. Lack of language per se or lack of available verbal categories, then, may not account for differences in the performance of deaf and hearing or for the differences in the performance of young and old children. These differences may be due to differences in cognitive strategies. However, these cognitive strategies appear to be more or less efficient depending on the nature of a particular task, and some tasks appear to be more successfully performed when verbal categories are a part of the cognitive strategy. It might also be argued that when deaf and hearing populations perform equally well in certain cognitive tasks, this is due to the fact that the deaf have a linguistic system which shares certain characteristics with the linguistic system of the hearing population. When deaf children perform better than hearing children in certain cognitive tasks, it might be argued that these are just the tasks in which linguistic categories interfere with performance. Thus, experimentation with a population which supposedly should resolve arguments obviously does not.

At this stage of the research endeavor some tentative conclusions appear to be reasonable. The processes of cognitive and linguistic functioning appear to be channeled separately, but to meet in particular task situations. Language acquisition and development is obviously dependent on sensory-motor processes, and if these processes are what is meant by cognition, then, clearly, language usage is dependent on cognition. These processes, however, also obviously underlie further cognitive development or "higher mental functions." No conclusions can be drawn about whether language provides the bins and structures for the sorting and use of experience, or whether the sorting and use of experience provide the bins and structures for language. Perhaps, put this way, it is basically an uninteresting question. A more interesting question might be what is the nature of the cognitive tasks which appear to be dependent on language.

LINGUISTIC DESCRIPTIONS

We have considered some of the facts that have been described about observable linguistic behavior and some of the facts that have been observed about the sensory-motor and cognitive capacities of the young child which may be related to observable behavior. We would like, now, to consider some of the facts that have been observed about languages. All languages are composed of speech sounds, syllables, morphemes, and sentences, and meaning is largely conveyed by the properties and particular use of these units. There are underlying regularities in these units and in their relation to each other so that, for example, the same utterances are judged to be grammatical, nongrammatical, agrammatical (not a sentence), or ambiguous by most native speakers of the language. Also, certain sentences are grouped together as being similar in meaning by these native speakers. In addition to the above generalizations, it has been noted that there are restrictions on the syntactic structures found in all languages (Greenberg, 1963).

Observations of the structure of the language and the linguistic behavior of the adult indicate that during the developmental period the child must learn certain aspects of his language. He must learn the functional relationships expressed in the sentences of his language and the classes in his language which carry out the task of expressing these functional relationships. For example, he must learn the difference in the relationship expressed in the sentences "I hit him" and "He hit me." He must learn the difference between grammatical and nongrammatical sentences such as "He goes there" and "He go there," and that sentences such as "Machines dance" and "Baby boys flap their wings" are nongrammatical but in a manner different from "He go there." He must learn what are sentence paraphrases such as "John loves Mary" and "Mary is loved by John" or "He isn't the one" and "He is not the one." He must define the classes in his language in terms of the roles they play in sentences. He must understand that noun phrases can be subjects or objects in sentences and that verb phrases are predicates of sentences. He must learn that noun phrases may be composed of determiner + noun ("some boys"), and verb phrases may be composed of verb + noun phrase ("play the piano") and, thus, derive the classes *noun, verb,* and *determiner*.

He must learn what are grammatical markers of gender, case, tense, person, and number in his language and learn to apply them appropriately. He must learn the properties of the speech sounds in his language and distinguish between words such as "bit," "pit," "mit," etc. Underlying this performance is obviously the capacity to segment the stream of speech into the units sentence, phrase, word, and speech sound. In summary, the child must learn the syntactic, semantic, and phonological rules of his language. He must learn these rules so that he can understand and produce an infinite number of possible sentences in his language.

Linguists have provided structural descriptions of the possible sentences of a language. These structural descriptions include syntactic information, semantic information, and phonological information or are, in other terms, the structural descriptions in the grammar of the native speaker of the language. This is the knowledge that is used by the native speaker to understand and produce sentences.

The following are some simple descriptions of the aspects of the stream of speech which the linguist claims the speaker must have knowledge of to understand or produce a sentence.[5] Appendix A should be examined for a description of the syntactic symbols used and the key to the phonological symbols can be found in Appendix B.

Syntactic information

Syntactic rules describe the functional relationships in sentences and, thus, define the classes of the language. The syntactic component of a grammar is composed of base structure rules, transformational rules, and morphological rules. Underlying each sentence of the langue is a kernel string. Base structure rules generate kernels by rewriting rules of the following kind:

$$S \longrightarrow NP + VP$$
$$NP \longrightarrow Det. + N$$
$$VP \longrightarrow V + NP$$

By implicit definition the subject of the sentence is the noun phrase of the sentence, the object of the sentence is the noun phrase of the verb phrase, the predicate of the sentence is the verb phrase of the sentence, and the main verb is the verb of the verb phrase.

Each item (N, V, etc.) in the underlying string has syntactic, semantic, and phonological properties and there are, in addition to rewriting rules, rules which impose selectional constraints on the co-occurrence of items in the string due to their properties. Thus the sentence "The beauty is everlasting" would be marked as nongrammatical since there is a selectional rule which states that a noun which is abstract ("beauty") never appears in the context Art. + N.

In addition, the base structure string also indicates the transformational rules which will apply. For example, the following rules for the expansion of pre-sentence indicate that the sentence can be a Q, Imp, Emp, or Neg or any combination of these except a Q-Imp.

$$S \longrightarrow (Pre\ S)\ NP + VP\ (Adv)$$
$$PreS \longrightarrow \frac{Q}{Imp}\ (EMP)\ (NEG)$$

---

[5] See the following for detailed descriptions of (a) syntactic rules, (b) semantic rules, and (c) phonological rules: (a) Chomsky, 1965, and Katz and Postal, 1964; (b) Katz and Fodor, 1963; (c) Chomsky and Halle, 1968, and Postal, 1968.

Figure 1–2 is a description of the underlying structure of the sentence "The boy hits the ball." A bundle of syntactic and semantic properties and phonological features marks *each item* in the string. Thus, the item "boy" in Figure 1–2 would have the properties noun, singular, animate, human, male, etc., and be composed of the speech sound features which comprise the sequence /b/ /oy/.

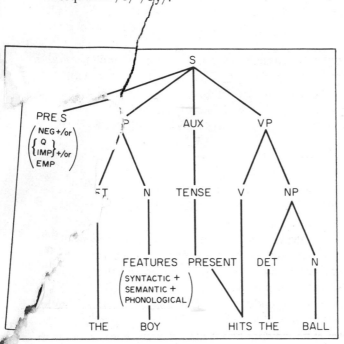

FIG. 1–2 A partial description of the underlying base structure of the sentence "The boy hits the ball."

Transformational rules are rules for operations on underlying strings to derive various sentence types. By addition, deletion, permutation, and substitution within or among kernels, various sentence types are derived. Morphological rules are rules for the application of grammatical markers such as person, number, tense, etc. The following is a description of the changes that may occur in the underlying kernel with the application of transformational rules:

1. Underlying string: The boy present hit the ball
2. Negative placement: The boy present not hit the ball
3. Do Support: The boy present do not hit the ball
4. Q Aux Inversion: Present do not the boy hit the ball

5. Affix hopping: Do + present not the boy hit the ball
6. Contraction: Do + present + nt the boy hit the ball
7. Morphological rules: Do + present + nt ⟶ Doesn't
8. Surface string: Doesn't the boy hit the ball

Transformational rules may operate on two as well as one underlying kernel. Figure 1–3 is a description of the underlying structure of SI and SII.

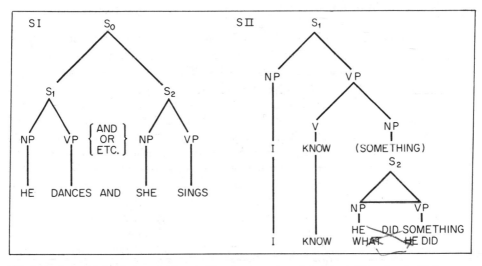

FIG. 1–3 A partial description of the underlying base structure of conjoined (SI) and embedded (SII) sentences with examples.

Strings may be conjoined or embedded within one another in the following manner:

SI—Conjunction

S_1	NP	VP	NP					
	I	see	the boy					
S_2	NP	VP	NP					
	I	see	the girl					
SI	NP	VP	NP	*and*	NP	VP	NP	
	I	see	the boy	and	I	see	the girl	

SII—Relative Clause

S_1	NP	VP	NP
	I	see	the boy

S₂	NP		VP	NP			
	The boy		is	a scout			
SII	NP	VP	NP	WH + NP	VP	NP
	I	see	the boy	who	is	a scout

By using the operations of conjoining and embedding, indefinitely long sentences could theoretically be generated. ("The boy who sat on the stool which was broken by the man who . . .")

Semantic information

The semantic component of the grammar consists of a dictionary or lexicon and projective rules. The dictionary defines the morphemes of the language by enumerating the properties of these morphemes. In terms of properties, "boy" is animate, human, male, young, etc. Projective rules interpret the meaning of items and the underlying syntactic structure of the string and impose restrictions on the co-occurrence of items in a string. Thus sentences such as "These mothers have children" or "He is pregnant" would be nongrammatical. To interpret the meaning of "The boy hit the ball" one must have knowledge of the properties of "boy," "hit," and "ball." The definition of "ball" may contain not only the features N, inanimate etc. but also *distinguishers* such as *social activity* and *physical object of globular shape*. However, the meaning of "ball" in this sentence can be disambiguated by projective rules which indicate that the verb "hit" (V trans.) can only co-occur with "ball" (physical object). Perhaps, then, syntactic properties and selectional restrictions indicate the possible co-occurrence of syntactic classes whereas semantic properties and projective rules indicate the possible co-occurrence of members of the class. The distinction between the role of syntactic rules and the role of semantic rules in placing restrictions on the co-occurrence of items in a string has not been clearly formulated.

Phonological information

In the lexicon of the language each morpheme is described not only in terms of its semantic properties but also in terms of a set of matrices of distinctive features. These matrices of features describe and distinguish from each other all the phonemes of the language. Phonological rules are then applied depending on the underlying structures of the sentence and of the morpheme. For example, in English, plural and tense markers are dependent on the speech sound component which ends the morpheme. A *partial* listing of the rules for pluralization in English contains the following information: Nouns which end in a vowel add /z/ to pluralize; nouns which end in a voiced consonant also add /z/, but nouns which end in an unvoiced consonant add /s/. Thus the plural of "boy" is boy + z, the plural of "band" is band + z but the plural of "muff" is muff + s. The underlying phonological representation of sentences is directly related to the surface representation via the matrices of features, syntactic rules, and phonological rules.

Distinctive features are the articulatory and acoustic characteristics of the set of speech sounds of the language. The actual distinctive features which do, indeed, differentiate speech sounds in languages are in the process of being determined by empirical studies. A possible matrix of features for the initial consonant in the word "boy" and the word "ball" (/b/) as represented in the lexicon is compared to a matrix of features for the initial consonant in the word "pick" (/p/), the initial consonant in the word "sick" (/s/) and the initial consonant in the word "tick" (/t/) in the following example:

Features	b	p	s	t
consonantal	+	+	+	+
obstruant	+	+	+	+
coronal	—	—	+	+
anterior	+	+	+	+
nasal	—	—	—	—
continuant	—	—	+	—
strident	—	—	+	—
voiced	+	—	—	—

It should be noted from the above example that each matrix of features differs from each other matrix of features in at least one feature but that some features are shared among the sounds. For example, the speech sounds /b/ and /p/ are alike in all features except voicing, the speech sounds /b/ and /s/ differ in several features, but all the speech sounds in this set share the feature —nasal. It seems logical to suppose that speech sounds should share a set of features since they are produced by the same vocal mechanism and heard by the same ear, so that only a restricted set of variations can be possible. It is also logical that speech sound components should differ from each other in at least one feature. We can then admit into the language a great number of words which are phonologically similar but are still unambiguous, such as "pit" and "bit," "nip" and "nib," etc.

This still leaves many ambiguities in terms of homophones, and for the resolution of these ambiguities rules other than phonological must be relied upon. Some linguistic descriptions imply that the syntactic base structure and transformational rules shape the sentence, semantic rules lead to interpretation of the sentence, and phonological rules translate underlying structure into surface structures and are essentially rules for input to the vocal mechanism (Chomsky, 1965). The variability of dimensions of the vocal mechanism of particular speakers and their motor facility places constraints on the actual output. Therefore, one person's production of "boy" will not exactly match another person's production of "boy." We have, thus, both ambiguities and inconsistencies in the primary linguistic data. It is familiarity with the grammatical rules of the language which allows disambiguation and resolution of surface ambiguities and inconsistencies. Thus sentences such as "He has a very slow gait" and "He has a very red gate" do not create difficulties in understanding even when spoken by different speakers who vary in age, sex, and personality.

PSYCHOLINGUISTIC DESCRIPTIONS

It is possible that a system of syntactic, semantic, and phonological rules such as those described above does in fact describe the linguistic knowledge or competence of the native speaker of the language. This theory implicitly makes a claim about the nature of the human organism. The human organism doesn't simply have the capacity to learn and generalize from the acoustic data, but, rather, has the capacity to search for and store abstract aspects of the linguistic system since there is nothing in the acoustic signal which segments and structurally describes an utterance in terms of its underlying composition and meaning.

Some psycholinguists concur with the view that such a description describes the competence of the native speaker, but they also add that the native speaker uses this described competence or knowledge to understand and produce sentences. Figure 1–4 is a rough indication of the model of performance as it has frequently been conceived of by some present-day psycholinguists.[6]

By following the arrows from top to bottom in this model the routine would be as follows: I want to say something (Dictionary and Semantic Rules); How shall I say it (Syntactic Rules); How shall I produce it (Phonological Rules); How shall I articulate it (Production Mechanism); I said it (Utterance). By following the arrows from the bottom to the top the routine would be either recreated in a process of "analysis by synthesis" or reversed in a process of "synthesis by analysis," and thus understanding

---

[6] For a more thorough description and explanation of a psycholinguistic model, see Wales and Marshall, 1966.

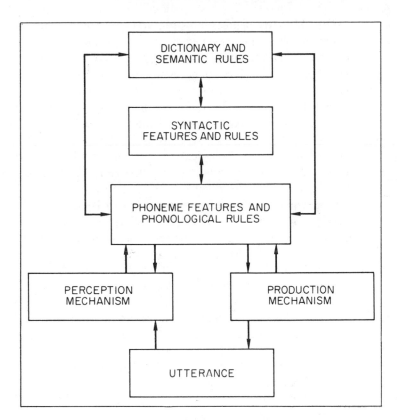

FIG. 1–4 A psycholinguistic model of the production and comprehension of utterances.

of the utterance is achieved. It should be noted that there are also arrows indicating cross references between semantic rules and syntactic rules, between semantic rules and phonological rules, and between syntactic rules and phonological rules, indicating that perhaps tentative hypotheses are reached which are then checked by reference to parts of the system before the final stage of comprehension or production is reached.

As can be seen, this psycholinguistic model of performance does not appear to be very different from linguistic models of the structure of language. Other psycholinguists are disturbed by the fact that such a model does not seem to be very realistic in terms of the time used to process utterances. The capacity to detect and recognize abstract features, store them in some manner, and use them to understand and produce utterances is obviously dependent on such capacities as perception and memory. Recent research in psycholinguistics has addressed itself to studying memory and perception when the structure of the linguistic stimulus is systematically varied. Various degrees of structural complexity are represented: active versus passive sentences, negative versus declarative sentences, etc. Various degrees of grammaticalness are represented: anomalous sentences versus nonanomalous ("The plane flew the man" versus "The man flew the plane"), sentences versus nonsentences ("The boy ate the apple" versus "apple the ate boy the"). Types of ambiguities are represented: surface ambiguity ("I'm holding a [pear] [pair]") versus deep structure ambiguity ("Flying planes can be dangerous"). These studies are undertaken to determine the "psychological reality" of linguistic descriptions. It is felt that in this way the relationships between the structure of the language and the human being's capacity to use this structure will become clearer and a realistic model of performance can be derived. It should be noted that most of the recent psycholinguistic research with adults has been concerned with the understanding of sentences rather than with their production while the reverse is the case in research with children.

And, indeed, it has been found that the time needed to process utterances or the difficulty experienced in this processing is not always a direct reflection of the linguist's structural descriptions of the derivation of sentences and their degree of complexity in terms of the number of rules needed to derive them (Fodor and Garrett, 1966). The conclusion has been reached in some instances that linguistic structural descriptions may indeed be stored in long-term memory and thus represent the native speaker's competence, but that for immediate processing of sentences the listener may use other strategies which are different from deriving a complete structural description of the utterance. These strategies do not involve the use of all the relevant rules, but, for example, may involve finding the main verb in a sentence and determining the types of structures this subclassification of verb can take as subject and object (Fodor, Garrett, and Bever, 1968).

In addition to arguments concerning the use of linguistic structural descriptions in actually understanding and producing utterances, there has been some concern about limiting descriptions of linguistic behavior to the description of the structure of the utterances produced and understood by native speakers of the language. Besides linguistic rules, other kinds of rules—involving such factors as the setting and the cultural predispositions of the subjects—may be affecting responses in a given experimental situation (Hymes, 1964). It is suggested that these factors may affect the way in which the linguistic competence of the users of the language is habitually employed, and perhaps a study of them will yield a more adequate model of performance.

Alternative views of the adequacy of linguistic descriptions in providing a description of the language user's use of language are: it is adequate; it is adequate in describing the user's competence or knowledge of the language but not his performance in processing language; it adequately describes only one aspect of linguistic behavior. It should be added that some psychologists have expressed the opinion that the rules described may be rules about language but are not rules of behavior (Palermo, 1966). It is clear that the relationships between linguistic <u>competence and linguistic</u> <u>performance</u> have yet to be precisely defined. However, it is by experimentation that these relationships will be defined rather than simply by theoretical assumptions.

APPLICATION OF DESCRIPTIVE MODELS
TO LANGUAGE DEVELOPMENT

Recent research in language acquisition and development reflects the same types of theoretical positions as those held about adult language use. The research to be reported has taken several directions: (1) the study of the relationships between the acquisition of the linguistic system (the grammar of the language) and the physiological and psychological capacities of the infant and young child; (2) the study of the acquisition and development of aspects of the system (phonology, syntax and semantics); (3) the use of aspects of the system in various cognitive tasks; and (4) group and individual differences in the acquisition of the system due to physiological and environmental factors. As can be seen from this list, research directions do indeed reflect theoretical assumptions about the factors affecting linguistic competence and the relationship between performance and competence.

A large preponderance of current research has addressed itself to linguistic descriptions of the utterances produced and, to a lesser extent, understood by children at various stages of development. Longitudinal and horizontal studies of the utterances produced and understood by children over some developmental period have been undertaken, and the phonological, syntactic, and semantic information or knowledge which children appear to have acquired at various stages of development have been described. By varying the structures of the signals either phonologically, syntactically, or semantically in experimental situations which require discrimination or identification or recall, an effort has been made to describe the relationship between physiological and psychological capacities such as perception and memory and particular linguistic performances. The study of the course of acquisition and development when marked physiological and environmental differences from some norm exist has been undertaken by descriptions and comparisons of the structure of the language produced and understood by children who are <u>physiologically deficited</u> with that of those who are not, and by comparisons of the language of children from <u>different socioeconomic and racial backgrounds</u>. The use of language in various cognitive tasks has been examined, implicitly, by the nature of the experimental tasks given to elicit information about the comprehension of language. For example, when children are asked to identify a picture exemplifying a sentence or to manipulate objects to exemplify a sentence or to follow an order, not only is their comprehension of the sentence being tested but also their ability to use this comprehension to carry out a specific task.

This is a brief description of how linguistic and psycholinguistic models have been applied in current research to the study of language acquisition and development. The aim of many of these studies is to give a detailed account of what is acquired at various stages of development rather than simply to indicate that output increases and complexity increases as children mature. An effort is made in some of these studies to explain as well as to describe the changes in behavior that are observed. It is hoped that answers to such questions as: In what ways are physiological and psychological development intimately related to language development? What is the nature of the cognitive tasks that appear to be dependent on language? and what are the relationships between linguistic competence and linguistic performance? will be obtained.

2

THE INFANT'S
CAPACITY
TO ACQUIRE
LANGUAGE

THERE HAVE BEEN SEVERAL distinct approaches in hypothesizing about the child's capacity to acquire language. All assume that since only man learns to speak and use language, this capacity is biologically distinct—that is, it does not "exist" in other species. This distinction is viewed in varying ways. One view is that the difference between man and other animals consists of the fact that other animals have much more elaborate inborn behavior but man is born with a greatly superior capacity to learn. Eccles states, "The human cortex surpasses that of all other animals in its potentiality to develop subtle and complex neuronal patterns of the utmost variety (Eccles, 1966). Some state that different organisms learn different things but that the principles which govern learning are alike for all organisms. That is, there is no question that not only physiological shapes (wings, antennae, gills, etc.) but physiological functioning—that is, the structure of seeing, hearing, smelling, etc.—and the manner of responding to what is perceived are species-determined—i.e., they result from the differences in the physiological structure of the various species. However, arguments do exist about whether or not differences in manner of generalizing and hypothesizing about what is perceived pertain between animals and about whether or not all learning is shaped by environmental conditions or is innate.

"Is language specific to the human species?" is the first question that one might put. It is generally accepted that language, in the form in which it is practiced by people (speaking, reading and writing), is specific to the human being, but arguments have arisen about the degree to which human language differs from other animals' systems of communication. Several distinctions between animal and human communication are made by Hockett (1963). Some of the outstanding distinctions are the following:

1. Creativity—new sentences are generated freely and easily and unique sentences, never uttered before, are produced and understood due to the fact that
   a. Every language has a grammar containing meaningful elements (words and sentences) which are mapped into meaningless but message differentiating elements (phones or speech sounds);
   b. Every possible utterance is composed of a discrete repertory of the above elements;
   c. New or old elements can be assigned new semantic loads (meanings) by context or circumstance.
2. Use of language
   a. The relationship between the linguistic element and its denotation is arbitrary or independent of any physical or geometrical resemblance between the two.
   b. The signal has no direct biological consequences but may trigger some action and stands for something rather than is the thing it denotes.
3. Displacement—language is used to refer to things which may be remote in time or space or both from the cite of communication and, therefore, in human language we can
   a. Report on the past and future;
   b. Communicate about communication;
   c. Form hypotheses and lie.
4. Language learning
   a. A speaker of one human language can learn any other.
   b. A speaker can be a listener and vice versa.

Hockett states that although other animals' communication systems contain some of the above elements, there is no other system of communication outside of human language which contains all of them. In addition to the distinctions noted above, there are obviously factors which shape human language and its acquisition which are related to the human organism's innate capacities. There are restrictions imposed by the physiology of the human and his milieu just as there are restrictions on the nature and structure of other animals' communication due to these restrictions. The following are some of these capacities and restrictions.

1. Man's memory is finite.
   a. The auditory-vocal channel results in rapid fading of messages; therefore the import of a rapidly fading message must be stored in some manner.
   b. Language must consist of a discrete repertoire of elements which are used in the grammatical patternings of sentences since an infinite memory would be needed if each word or sentence differed holistically from all others.

2. Use of auditory-vocal channel:
   a. The repertoire which composes the meaningless segments (the phones) must have features which can be both articulated and heard by the human organism;
   b. The repertoire which composes the possible manipulation of meaningful elements must have features or patterns which can be stored, produced and understood by the human organism.

Since there is no one to one relationship between what is heard (the phones) and what is understood (the meaning of the message), it has been hypothesized that in acquiring a language the child "has" as part of his biological structure (1) the mechanisms and procedures for acquiring knowledge in general and deriving the grammar of his language in particular (Slobin, 1966), or (2) hypotheses about grammatical relations in language in general and the capacity to discover how classes and relations operate in his own language in particular (McNeill, 1966).

It should be noted that the observations that have been made concerning the structure and neurophysiological functioning of the organism that acquires a language have been very limited. Therefore, it is difficult to define what is meant by "part of his biological structure." If it is accepted as fact that human language and animal communication are different, the question that is of concern is: Are there structural and or functional differences in the brain of man and in his sensory-motor systems which can be correlated with the child's unique performance of acquiring a language? The research evidence that has been obtained concerning this question will be discussed in this chapter.

MAN'S BRAIN

Ajuriaguerra (1966) has put two pertinent questions. Are there areas of the brain which may be considered innate speech centers? If so, are these functional zones localized at an early age in a so-called dominant hemisphere? In his experimentation he notes that afferent and efferent nerve disorders, either sensory or motor, can disturb the organization of speech even in the absence of an anatomically localized cerebral lesion. In addition, cerebral dominance is much more labile in the child than in the adult. However, the child is communicating effectively before this dominance becomes stable. He concludes, therefore, that there are no pre-formed centers, but rather pre-formed mechanisms which take shape as the capacity to communicate develops.

Geschwind (1965), on the other hand, argues that man's brain is structurally unique and this uniqueness contributes to his capacity to acquire and use language in a particular way. He states, "The ability to acquire speech has as a prerequisite the ability to form cross-modal associations. ". . . it is only in man that associations between two non-limbic stimuli are readily formed and it is this ability which underlies the learning of names of objects" (Geschwind, 1965, p. 275).

Briefly, the structural difference is explained by Geschwind in the following manner. As one moves up the phylogenetic scale the primordial limbic and non-limbic centers for sensations of vision, audition, and somesthesis and motor cortex are increasingly separated by new areas of cortex. This separating cortex reaches its greatest extent in man where it occupies *most* of the surface of the cerebral hemispheres. This association cortex matures (or myelinates) later in the life of man than do other areas of the brain (at age 3 or 4 or later). In addition, the different parts of the association cortex are more like each other (structure-wise) than are the primordial zones, and there are no significant *direct* interconnections between the limbic regions, the motor cortex, and the auditory, visual, and somesthetic cortexes. Each primordial zone has a significant number of connections only to the immediately adjacent cortex. The association cortex itself, however, may have long connections to other regions, and there are connections of non-limbic sensory modalities. As an example, there is a connection from the primary visual cortex to the immediately adjacent association cortex which, then, has three sets of connections: one to the visual association cortex of the opposite side (via the *corpus callosum*), one to the association cortex anterior to the classical motor cortex, and one to the outer and inferior surface of the temporal lobe, which is the association cortex for the limbic structure. In the monkey there are connections between some of the visual and auditory association areas. There is evidence of fibers running from the auditory association cortex to the visual association cortex. However, there are none in the reverse direction. In addition, there are fewer association "fibers" in the monkey than in man.

Outside of the differences in connections between non-limbic association areas, other differences in the size and development of the brain in monkey and man have been cited. The gorilla brain, largest of the anthropoids, never reaches half the weight of an average adult human brain. At birth the human brain is at 40 percent of its final growth whereas in the monkey it is at 70 percent of its final growth. The greatest growth in man is in the inferior parietal region or the region placed between association cortexes of three nonlimbic modalities (association cortex of association cortexes). Development of cerebral dominance is related to greater development of this new parietal association area. Cerebral dominance is based on (or equivalent to) the ability of the hemisphere which is dominant to make cross-modal associations more readily than can the nondominant hemisphere.

What do these structural differences mean in terms of language acquisition?

The result of these structural differences in monkey and man noted by Geschwind is that the monkey can learn to form associations between the visual system and the limbic system (to gratify hunger, for example), but is unable to generalize from a visual stimulus to a tactile stimulus. That is, monkeys cannot form an association between two non-limbic modalities whereas man can easily do this (for example, associate between the picture of a cross and the feel of a cross). In summary, then, the argument is (1) there are structures in the brain of man which are absent or poorly developed in the brain of other primates and subprimates; (2) these structures allow man to make cross-modal associations; (3) the ability to make cross-modal associations allows man to name objects; and (4) object naming is the basic step in language acquisition. This argument about structural differences and their relationship to language acquisition has been discussed at some length since it is the only such argument in the current literature.

There are several questions that might be raised and have been raised concerning the foregoing hypotheses. Object naming does not seem to be simply a product of cross-modal associations but, rather, the product of a further ability to organize several types of incoming information under a supra-heading. Indeed, it has been stated that the ability to perform cross-modal associations is dependent on the ability to use language or to name, rather than vice versa. Brain (1961) suggests that naming involves *superimposing* upon the sensory-motor organization of speech (already being established) a physiological link between this organization and the physiological basis of recognition. Therefore, the formation of cross-modal associations may come about via the human organism's capacity to forge a link by naming. Further, at the stage at which single words are being used there does not seem to be a one-to-one correlation between the word uttered and a specific object in the environment (McNeill, 1968a). On the contrary, the single word used appears to imply a sentence rather than the name of an object. Therefore, it is difficult to conceive of object naming per se as a basic step in language acquisition. The relationship between cross-modal associations and object naming is questionable and the relationship between object naming and language acquisition is questionable. It seems, therefore, that the relationship between the structural differences in the brain of man that have been cited and language acquisition is also questionable or, at least, not clear.

Most of the current literature discusses man's unique capacity to acquire language in terms of *functioning* of the nervous system rather than in terms of structural differences. One observation that has been made about early (young childhood) brain damage is that there is flexibility in the use of structures in the nervous system. Some children who lose one complete hemisphere of the brain (hemispherectomies) are presumably able to acquire language normally, or normally but at a slower pace (Basser,

1962). In other instances where there is not total damage of a hemisphere but specific areas of damage, children may have great difficulty in acquiring language. Two things may be noted from these results. First, there is great plasticity in the use of available structures to acquire language at the early stages of development. Second, there may be a development of specificity in the functioning of structures. These seem to be contradictory statements. However, if one assumes that total loss requires the institution of new functions, whereas partial damage does not, since some type of activity can still occur, and that this activity is deviant because of specific damage in functioning, these results do not seem so contradictory. These findings indicate that man's capacity to acquire language lies in the functioning of his nervous system rather than in specific structures. However, this is an unsatisfying conclusion since one might then ask, "What is the basis of this unique functioning?"

Luria quotes Pavlov in stating the problem (Luria, 1965, p. 22). We can either attempt to "superimpose the non-spatial concepts of contemporary psychology on the spatial construction of the brain" or we can "identify . . . dynamic phenomena (taking place in the nervous system) with the finer details of brain structure." Luria defines these dynamic processes as functions which are the product of complex reflex activity, comprising a uniting of excited and inhibited areas of the nervous system into a "working mosaic," analyzing and integrating stimuli reaching the organism and forming a system of temporary connections. These functions are carried out by a network of complex dynamic structures of combination centers, consisting of mosaics of distant points of the nervous system, united in a common task. However, the apparatus for these tasks is the upper associative layers of the cerebral cortex, the vertical connections arising in the secondary associate nuclei of the thalamus, and the overlapping zones uniting different boundaries of cortical analyzers. Presumably this apparatus has attained its highest development in man as compared to other animals.

There is, thus, uniqueness of functioning based on differences in the degree of development of structures. Since, from Luria's point of view, speech is needed for memorizing, voluntary attention, and logical thinking —or, in other words, for the other higher mental functions—this unique functioning and the structural difference cited obviously account for man's unique capacity to acquire language. These comments imply innate specificity in the structure and functioning of the nervous system for the acquisition of language. However, since there is a great deal of controversy about the dependency of cognition on language, and the evidence obtained thus far has not clarified the issue, Luria's position must be viewed as hypothetical and certainly open to experimental question. It should also be noted that despite the arguments against Geschwind's position Luria's discussions imply that man's capacity to acquire language may lie both in unique structures in the nervous system and in unique functioning which may or may not be specific to language.

Lenneberg has stated,

> In general, it is not possible to assign any specific neuro-anatomic structure to the capacity for language. However, this capacity may be due to the structural innovations on a molecular level. Language is probably due to the peculiar way in which various parts of the brain work together or, in other words, to its peculiar function [Lenneberg, 1967, p. 72].

The fixed developmental scale of language usage (from cooing, to babbling, to words, to phrases, to sentences) is tied by Lenneberg to the longer period of brain maturation in man. Anatomical, histological, biochemical, and electrophysiological data is cited to indicate continuing maturation of the brain until the teens (Lenneberg, 1966). Thus man's unique capacity to acquire language is related to the peculiar functioning of his brain (or how the structures operate) and to the comparatively longer period of maturation.

The behavioral evidence cited for this process of slow maturation is the early, primitive beginnings in language performance that are observed, the regularities in the sequence of appearance of language behaviors observed in all linguistic environments, and the existence of a critical period for language development. One piece of evidence for the last observation is that a deficit (a lesion causing aphasia) can be overcome if it occurs early enough and is "confined to a single hemisphere" (Lenneberg, 1967, p. 146). This is due to the lack of cortical specialization or cerebral lateralization at an early age. Another piece of evidence is the fact that the mentally retarded child presumably shows a slow and modest beginning in language acquisition until the early teens. At this age the process is arrested since at puberty complete maturation has taken place. Thus, if the basic language skills are not acquired by the teens these skills will remain deficient regardless of the amount of training, presumably because the brain is set in its ways, and maturation has slowed down and reached asymptote. One more piece of evidence of a possible relationship between cerebral maturation and a critical period of development is what occurs in the case of acquired deafness. If the loss occurs after the second year of life, the child will respond better to speech training than if the loss is congenital. The response to training becomes increasingly better as the age of the child at the time of onset of deafness increases. Although what is meant by responding better to training is not clearly defined, these latter observations indicate that possibly the critical period for establishment of basic language skills may be much shorter than from birth to puberty (possibly the first three years of life). Altogether, the direct relationship between a long period of brain *maturation,* which is specific to man, and the acquisition of language, which is also specific to man, is not clear. Both aspects of development occur in man and not in other species but their causal relationships, except by inference, are not evident.

The connection between language acquisition and a long period of cerebral maturation is also inferred from the fact that environmental conditions do not seem to affect the sequence of development. Lenneberg (1967, pp. 135–39) cites the following experimental results: there are no differences in the sequence of appearance of language behaviors between the first and subsequent children, children of deaf and hearing parents, children of differing socioeconomic status, children whose mothers have varying degrees of ability to cope with them, and children who have or have not lost a parent. Institutionalized children may be slower than noninstitutionalized children in acquiring language but eventually they catch up.[1] Thus, the sequence or acquisition of *certain* speech and language capabilities is unaffected by an enormous variety of environmental conditions. The argument is that since language behavior emerges and changes before it has any immediate use (there is no need to babble or to use words or sentences because the child can fulfill his bodily requirements by crying), and since environmental factors do not affect the sequence of emergence of linguistic behaviors, language acquisition and development must be governed by the peculiar physiological development of the child—that is, the rate of cerebral maturation.

In addition, there are structural innovations in man which lead to peculiar functioning. Lenneberg states that there are probably alterations in *genetic material* (intra-cellular changes) which affect rates and directions of growth during ontogeny. There are also differences in functioning. There is "one peculiar mode of neural activity for aural-oral communication in man" that must run its own course like an automaton and can operate in just one essential way (Lenneberg, 1967, p. 221). This mode of neural activity is based on innate mechanisms such as the modulation of firing characteristics of nerve cells, the triggering of temporal patterns in neuronal chains, the modulation of oscillatory characteristics of endogenous activities, and the production of spreading of disturbances. Again, these descriptions are based on inference and logical conclusions rather than on hard evidence. ← A.H. tht!

In contradiction with the position that innate mechanisms are the basis for man's peculiar mode of neural activity in language processing is the position that modes of activity are affected by experience. At birth the child has his full quota of nerve cells. There is no further growth of nerve path-

---

[1] This question will be discussed in much greater detail in Chapters 7 and 8, "Deviant Language Behavior" and "Dialect Variations."

ways, but what occurs over time is that synapses are changed by activity. Repetition of a particular pattern results in changes in synaptic potency (Eccles, 1966). "Signals that are biologically important and effective seem to rely on multiple, perhaps fairly crude codings throughout the nervous system which have the advantage of being resistant to unavoidable environmental and internal 'noise' and interference from the other channels" (Rosenblith, 1965, p. 263). From these statements the conclusion that might be reached is that primitive language processing itself creates the peculiar mode of activity which then is developed, rather than that the peculiar mode of activity is the basis of language processing. However, we are still left with the question of how language processing is instituted.

The other factors cited in terms of structural specificity in man's brain raise many more questions than they resolve because the relationship of these factors to man's capacity to acquire language are, again, merely inferences. The weight of man's brain as compared to the weight of brains in other species is cited presumably to suggest more computing space, and its proportional weight to the weight of the body is cited perhaps to suggest its increasing genetic importance in man. There is nothing in these findings to suggest a specific language capacity. In addition to these differentiating factors, cerebral dominance in man has been cited.

The whole body of literature concerned with cerebral dominance, again, describes a circle. Is cerebral dominance the result of or concomitant with language acquisition and the acquisition of other perceptual and productive systems and developed as a *savings measure* for the kinds of operations that are needed for the usage of these systems, or is capacity for cerebral dominance innately given in the germ plasm and the acquisition of language preprogrammed by this means? The results of experiments concerned with cerebral dominance and the perception or recall of speech stimuli do not resolve this puzzle but have indicated, in essence, that the dominant hemisphere (most frequently the left) may be uniquely concerned in speech performance of a kind. Areas of the brain that are directly concerned with an aspect of language functioning such as Broca's motor speech area, are located in the dominant hemisphere. Figure 2–1 presents two simplified drawings of the dominant hemisphere. Drawing 2–1a indicates the behavioral results of stimulation of various parts of the dominant hemisphere and Drawing 2–1b indicates the localization of functions found in the examination of clinical cases. A detailed discussion of these functions can be found in Walsh (1964) and Penfield and Roberts (1959).

Experiments have been carried out which show the differential effects of presenting speech and nonspeech (digits and music) to the left and right ear (Kimura, 1961). Speech is more efficiently recalled when presented to the right ear and nonspeech when presented to the left. That is, speech is more efficiently processed when it reaches the dominant hemisphere first.

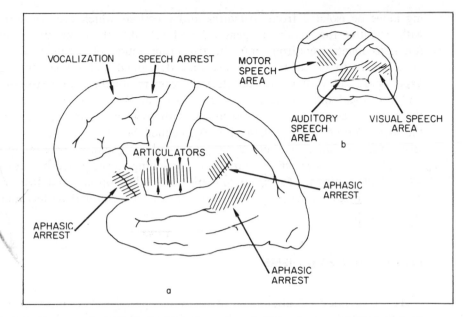

FIG. 2–1 Drawings of the dominant hemisphere of man's brain showing: (a) the behavioral results of stimulation of various parts of the hemisphere and (b) the localization of various speech functions in the hemisphere found by examination of clinical patients.

However, this does not tell the whole story. Differential processing of kinds of speech stimuli has also been found (Shankweiler and Studdert-Kennedy, 1966). Consonants are more correctly identified when presented at the right ear than when presented at the left. Vowel identification also shows a right ear superiority but this superiority is nonsignificant as compared to that obtained with consonants. This evidence plus other evidence obtained from the behavior of patients who suffer damage or disorder in various parts of the brain indicate that the dominant hemisphere may carry out some of the tasks of language processing but by no means carries out all of them. It has been concluded that both hemispheres are probably concerned with language although the labor divided between them may vary a great deal. Certainly during the language acquisition period there is great plasticity in the nervous system concerning the special language functioning of the dominant hemisphere, as has been indicated previously.

These views, observations, and experimental results concerning the structure and functioning of man's nervous system do not resolve questions about the infant's capacity to acquire language but merely point us in a direction. The unresolved questions are: (1) Is this capacity due to differences in the structure of the brain or functioning of the brain or both? (2) Can structures or functions which are concerned with language learning alone be isolated from structures and functions which are concerned with cognitive functioning in general? and (3) Are these structures and functions innate, requiring only the triggering action of language in the environment to set them off, or are they developed and shaped through experience? Certain tentative conclusions seem reasonable. Both structural and functional differences have been observed. We must postulate that these structures and functions are innate. Otherwise we cannot account for the *institution* of language behavior. We cannot, however, dissociate these structures and functions from those postulated for cognitive processing in general. Specialization in structure and functioning for language processing —cerebral dominance for example—appears to develop and stabilize only after the process of language acquisition has been instituted or has taken place.

PERIPHERAL MECHANISMS

The perception of utterances involves the peripheral auditory system and the central nervous system. The production of utterances involves the central nervous system and the peripheral vocal mechanisms. The most critical factors in the "normal" acquisition of language seem to be a sufficiently intact central nervous system [2] and intact auditory and vocal mechanisms. We can point to children whose central or peripheral system are obviously damaged or insufficient (deaf, cerebral palsied, mentally retarded children) to observe the gross effect on language perception and production of such damage and insufficiency. On the other hand, children with visual defects or those who have suffered crippling or loss of limbs do not manifest these effects. A description of the correlations between the functions of these systems and the acquisition of language might lead to a better understanding of the nature of the organism that acquires language and the processes of language acquisition. Such a description might, indeed, describe the human infant's specific capacity to acquire language whereas a description of the structure and functioning of the brain alone did not appear to do so.

Carmichael (1964) has stated that the recepter mechanisms and motor mechanisms of speech are functional at birth and even before birth. The question one might ask is: Can one observe in the structure of these mechanisms and/or the motor and receptive behavior of the neonate a particular readiness for speech?

---

[2] The definition of sufficiently intact appears to be dependent on the site and extent of lesions in the brain. One hemisphere, in the case of hemispherectomies, appears to be sufficient in early childhood.

The auditory mechanism

Studies of the comparative anatomy of the peripheral auditory mechanisms of man, monkey, and cat indicate that there are no significant differences between them. "Our measurements demonstrate that the auditory system of man and higher animals function in many respects as if they were governed by the same principles. Yet a more detailed quantitative study often brings out important differences in the functioning of certain parts of these systems" (Von Bèkesy and Rosenblith, 1951, p. 1075). Therefore, although no differences in structure have been noted, differences in functioning have, and these differences in functioning may be related to the child's unique capacity to acquire language.

Most of the studies which have dealt with infants' responses to auditory signals have not been particularly concerned with the characteristics of the signal. It is the characteristics of the signal, of course, and the infant's differential response to varying characteristics, which may lead to determining whether or not the auditory mechanism of the neonate treats speechlike and nonspeechlike sounds in different manners. This, in turn, may lead to a better understanding of the child's unique capacity to acquire language.

There have been some exceptions to this lack of interest in what specific signal is presented to the infant. Eisenberg, in a series of experiments, has examined the relationships between several parameters of the signal and infants' differing responses to these varying parameters. Some 700 babies have been examined. The specific response measures used in some experiments have been: motor movements, eye movements, and the behavior categorizations of arousal and orienting quiet (Eisenberg, 1964). In other experiments respiration rate and vocalizations have been measured (Eisenberg, 1966), and heart rate change as well (Eisenberg, 1967). The general response measures used are the proportion of responses to the number of stimulus presentations in the experiment, the pattern of response (the composition of response according to the response measures used; for example, motor plus eye movements), and the time characteristics of the response—that is, latency and duration of the response.

In all of the studies, responsivity (both specific and general response measures) was affected by the activity state of the infant,[3] and by *stimulus variables*. The latter variables were concerned with the structure of the signal. The intensity, range of frequency, and complexity of the auditory

---

[3] Activity state refers to the observable behavior of the infant, which may range from deep sleep to fully awake.

signals were varied, and the duration, repetition, rate, and intersignal interval were also varied for each type of signal presented (Eisenberg, 1965). The results of these studies have led the experimenter to the following conclusions, which appear to pertain to the question of whether neonates treat speechlike sounds in a unique manner:

1. The range of frequency of the signal has a significant effect. Signals in the range below 4000 Hz and those above produce highly dissimilar effects. Low frequencies evoke overt responses involving gross motor activity and are most effective during doze states. High frequencies evoke a high proportion of "freezing" behavior and are most effective during wakeful states. Lows are effective inhibitors of distress whereas highs tend to occasion distress. It should be noted that speech sounds fall within the frequency range of approximately 250 to 4000 Hz.

2. Constant or patterned signals [4] (band noises or modulated tones) have both common and differential effects. The differential effects of constant and patterned stimuli are that constant signals evoke nonspecific effects (defined as behavior that can just as easily be evoked by nonauditory stimuli), whereas patterned stimuli evoke effects which seem to be related to the kind and amount of variance within a patterned stimulus envelope.

The details of this differential response are quite interesting although the patterned signals used in the experimentation reported were limited to tonal sequences. Some of these sequences could be described as rising or falling in frequency. Grossly speaking, these are the intonation patterns in question (rising) and declarative (falling) sentences. Responses to constant stimuli were mostly gross body movements, cessation of such movements, or components of the startle reflex. Vocal activity was absent and visual behavior could be classified as a wide-awake look together with orienting quiet. Cardiac changes were correlated with motor responses (accelerative) or orienting quiet (decelerative), depending on the stimulus conditions. The cardiac rate change was state dependent and the magnitude of cardiac change showed a systematic relation to the pre-stimulus rate.

Patterned stimuli were effective under both sleeping and waking conditions. The forms of motor behavior elicited by patterned stimuli were quite different from those found with constant signals. When the infant was asleep the strongest movements were body stirring with arousal. The most usual forms of motor behavior were differentiated movements: facial

---

[4] Constant signals are defined by Eisenberg as being those signals of which acoustic parameters do not change during presentation. In this category are included pure tones, band noises (for example, drum beats with a frequency range of 500 to 900 Hz), or clicks. Patterned stimuli are those signals of which parameters may change during presentation. In this category are included signals which range from modulated tones which change their frequency characteristics during presentation (these were used in the Eisenberg experiment) to speech sounds.

grimacing, displacement of a single limb or digit, and even, in some few instances, a turning of the head together with visual searching. A large proportion of the responses was crying or the cessation of crying. It can be noted here that in another study (Simner, 1969) it has been shown that neonates respond to neonatal crying by crying significantly more frequently than they respond to bands of white noise by crying. These bands cover approximately the same frequency range as the cry and are presented at a high sound pressure level. In addition to the above results, found in the Eisenberg study, it was also found that the cardiac pattern in the presence of patterned signals was different from that observed with constant signals. Latencies were substantially longer, the response was biphasic, and there was some indication that rate change included both on and off effects plus differences reflecting the upward or downward nature of the tonal sequence. The magnitude of cardiac change showed no systematic relation with pre-stimulus rates.

These findings are highly tentative and the question of specific functioning of the auditory mechanism in response to the parameters of speechlike stimuli at birth is in need of further systematic exploration. However, these findings seem to indicate the possibility that the neonate is equipped with both peripheral and central mechanisms which cause him to differentiate between constant and patterned auditory signals and also cause him to differentiate between aspects of both constant and patterned signals. Some of these functions—such as particular types of responses to changes in frequency and intensity dimensions—presumably remain unaltered throughout life, and similar behavior can be found with other primates. The general or common responses to stimuli could be described as responses to novel stimuli in which the reticular system is engaged. In this case the stimuli may be nonspecific and the parameters changed in subsequent presentations may be nonspecific.

The neurophysiological model (Sokolov, 1960) proposed for the response of the organism to novel stimuli postulates a chain of cells in the cortex which preserves information about the intensity, quality, duration, and order of stimulus presentation. If a new stimulus does not coincide with the preserved model, excitatory discharges are sent to the reticular system, whereas a match sends inhibitory discharges to the system. Arousal evokes orienting or attention. The reticular formation acts as an amplifier and increases discriminatory powers. Brazier (1967) has termed this process a neurophysiological expression of communication from the environment to the organism in which a general rather than a particular message is received. However, the central neural mechanisms presumably concerned with language are vastly different and widely separated anatomically from the reticular formation. These mechanisms might be described as a neurophysiological expression of internal communication. The behavior of the neonate, as described in Eisenberg's studies, indicates that the general mechanisms needed for language, which may be precursors to the specific mechanisms needed, are present at birth. However, there is in addition some indication of possible specificity of functioning in the auditory mechanism. The neonates respond differently to sounds within the speech sound frequencies and sounds above these frequencies, and they respond differentially to patterned and constant stimuli. These differences can be summarized as the increased effectiveness of low range frequencies to evoke responses of motor activity and to inhibit distress, and of patterned stimuli to evoke fine motor movement, vocalization, and differential behavior related to the structure of the stimulus. These results indicate that the neonate may be differentially sensitive to aspects of the auditory signal which are of relevance in language. Although these findings are quite preliminary, they do indicate the importance of the structure of the stimulus in attempting to assess the response of the child to auditory signals.

There has been little research in this area of assessment of children's behavior during later infancy. The little research that has been done does not exhibit the careful control of the parameters of the signal shown in the work with neonates that has been described. However, the results are quite provocative and point to the fact that more detailed studies during this age range may elicit more and better information about the child's use of the auditory signal at various stages of development.

Kagan and Lewis (1965) have examined the infant's behavioral responses to varying auditory signals at 6 months and 13 months. At 6 months infants heard an intermittent tone, modern jazz music, and 3 human voices reading a prose paragraph in English. The human voices were those of an unfamiliar male, an unfamiliar female, and the mother's voice. The behavioral responses measured were cardiac rate changes, motor activity, and the occurrence of crying, fretting, or vocalization. It was found that there was more cardiac deceleration and less activity to the music or tone than to the human voices. In general, any auditory signal initially decreased vocalization. However, this effect was significantly elicited only in the cases of female voices. In general, there was more vocalization to the female voices than to the other signals. There was also an increase in vocalization during the rest period in response to the female voices. This sequence of response seemed to suggest a "speaking after listening" behavior. It was concluded that the response combination observed suggested that human speech had already acquired a psychological significance for infants of this age.

Indeed, this seems to be the case. In addition, if the results of this study are compared with the results of the studies of the neonate, it appears that the nonspeech stimuli produce effects similar to those observed in the presence of constant stimuli. Nonspecific stimuli produce nonspecific responses, which suggests that only the reticular system has been engaged in response to these stimuli. The model proposed for response to novel stimuli seems to fit these results. The speech stimuli produce a specific response: increased vocalization not associated with motor movements. Further, this response is particularly evoked by female voices, indicating that the frequency characteristics of the signal are being observed in a very sophisticated fashion. During the neonatal stage of development a different response repertoire was observed with signals which were in the speech sound frequency range and with signals which were above this range. At a later stage (6 months) of development the infant appears to be capable of performing a more complicated analysis of frequency than the gross dichotomization observed previously. Lewis has noted elsewhere (Lewis, Kagan, and Campbell, 1966) when examining infants' responses to a strange male's, a strange female's, and the mother's voice saying "hello" that there was a greater decrease in arm movement for mother's "hello" than for a strange male's or female's "hello." This is a speck of data and hardly conclusive, but it suggests that perhaps some rudimentary form of speaker recognition may have already been acquired at this age. Although it is well known that adults are able to recognize and identify speakers, the process by which we accomplish this task is not at all understood and probably involves a complex combination of acoustic and linguistic factors. Of course, it is perfectly possible that the differential responses to these signals observed at the age of 6 months could be observed at an *earlier* age as well.

The auditory stimuli presented to the children at 13 months were different from those presented at 6 months. A paragraph containing familiar words and another containing nonsense syllables which were syllabically matched to the words were read (the experimenters do not note the sex of the reader) either with normal intonation and stress or without. In the latter condition the words or nonsense syllables are essentially read as a list. Only the heart rate reactions are reported and, therefore, only the affect of the stimuli on attention, defined as heart rate deceleration, is presented. For the boys only the difference between the list of words, with which the greatest deceleration occurred, and the meaningless paragraph, with which the least deceleration occurred, was significant. For the girls there were no significant differences. The rank order of effectiveness of stimuli in producing deceleration for both boys and girls is as follows: the list of words, meaningful paragraph, list of nonsense syllables, and meaningless paragraph. We might conclude from these results (although the experimenters do not) that the infant pays greater attention, as defined previously, to meaningful speech than to meaningless and especially to word-length utterances. However, it is difficult to claim that heart rate deceleration implies language decoding, given the observations that were made at previous stages of development. This form of behavior appears to occur when nonspecific novel stimuli are presented. Indeed, those aspects of the acoustic signal which are most meaningful and useful to the infant in terms of language processing may evoke not heart rate change but other responses. Amount and timing of vocalization, as with 6-month-old infants, may be a more revealing measure for evaluation of infants' responses to various parameters of speech stimuli than heart rate deceleration. In addition, in these experiments so many parameters are being examined at once, because of the nature of the acoustic signals presented, that it is difficult to determine what is being responded to.

Friedlander (1967) studied the pattern of *selection* of varying auditory stimuli by infants aged 11 to 13 months over a period of 2 to 5 months. In the experiment infants could choose between pairs of auditory signals: mother speaking versus stranger speaking, speech with and without normal stress and intonation, speech containing familiar or unfamiliar vocabulary, dialogues or monologues, and speech with repetition of content at rates of 20, 40, 120, or 240 seconds. Among the findings were the following: (1) a consistent preference for mother's normal speech over stranger's normal speech; (2) an initial preference for stranger's normal speech over mother's speech without intonation and stress, followed by sharply increased preference for mother's speech; and (3) initial preference for mother's normal speech, then, mother's speech without intonation and stress. It should be remembered that speech delivered without intonation and stress becomes a list of isolated words and this factor may account for the infants' preference for mother's speech without prosodic features. Again, it is difficult to determine from this study what is meaningful or being used by the child, since there is such a huge number of possibilities, given both the nature of the signals and the fact that selection of a stimulus does not necessarily imply that that signal is more meaningful in terms of language processing than another. However, one might very tentatively conclude that mother's voice can be differentiated from that of a stranger, that initially signals containing prosodic features (intonation and stress) are preferable to those without, and that word-length utterances become preferable to continuous speech.

We are left with a great many hypotheses and questions concerning the specificity of functioning of the auditory mechanism in the presence of speechlike and nonspeechlike signals and the development of this functioning. This is obviously an area greatly in need of systematic and careful research. The results of the studies that have been cited, especially those undertaken with the neonate, indicate that such research would be most fruitful in determining the bases of the child's acquisition of language and the developmental course of this capacity.

The vocal mechanism

Unlike the case with the auditory mechanism, where no structural differences can be observed between man and other higher animals, Lieberman (1968) has described structural differences between the vocal mechanism of man and other primates as well as some forebears of man. He finds that, contrary to the oft-repeated statement that speech is a function which has been superimposed on the functions of eating and breathing, there is evidence which indicates that anatomically the human larynx is not optimal for the purposes of respiration and, as we have often noticed, the position of the larynx in man sometimes leads to difficulties when swallowing. One of the structural differences that have been noted between modern man and other animals is the position of the larynges. Other animals' larynges, in contrast to man's, are positioned quite high, almost in line with the roof of the palate. Man's tongue is thick and the root of the tongue forms a plastic anterior wall (the rear wall being the pharynx), while other animals' tongues are thin compared to man's and, thus, the many modifications which can be produced by man by changing the configuration of the upper vocal tract cannot be produced by other animals. It has been observed that there appear to be no manipulations of the tongue during monkey, chimpanzee, and gorilla vocalizations, and spectrograms of these vocalizations give some evidence of these structural restrictions on the output of the animal's vocal mechanism.

What of the infant? The infant's vocal tract is dissimilar to that of the adult and to that of the gorilla. There are some differences both in anatomical proportions and relative spatial arrangements of structures in the vocal tracts of infants and adults. Figure 2–2 indicates the location of the vocal fold in the gorilla's and modern man's vocal tract and the infant's vocal tract. As described by Lieberman (1968) and Bosma, Truby, and Lind (1965) both the infant and the gorilla, in contrast to the human adult, have larynges which are located high in the pharynx.

As the infant develops the pharynx walls become stabilized and the pharyngeal region enlarges differentially. This differential enlargement of the pharyngeal passageway is brought about by the supporting musculature of the pharynx, larynx, hyoid bone, and tongue, which adapt the pharyngeal contour and diameters to variations in the head, neck, and mandible position which occur during growth. Developmental changes occur in the proportions of the vocal mechanism until mature growth is reached. However, patterns of movement and of the mechanism and the use of respiration for vocalization, which are essentially similar to those of the adult, are very

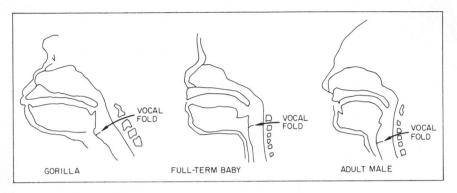

FIG. 2–2 Drawings of the outline of the gorilla's, full-term baby's and adult's vocal tract showing the approximate position of the vocal fold in each instance.

rapidly established, and some aspects of mature movement and use are present at birth.

The motions of neonatal cry have been described by Truby, Bosma, and Lind (1965). The act of crying is described as a remarkably precise and rapid motor achievement in which laryngeal coordinations are highly distinct. The pharynx diameters decrease progressively before and after onset of cry vocalization. They increase before expiratory vocalization ends. The *anticipatory* positioning of mechanisms for vocalizations described above is also found in speech sound articulation, and although obviously the *whole* act of articulation and of crying differs radically, nevertheless this anticipatory positioning is a prerequisite for sound making and is present at birth. The infant "gets ready" to cry just as he will at a later stage get ready to articulate. During the cry act, however, abrupt changes in frequency and volume occur and there is superimposed turbulence. The infant, in essence, may overblow his trumpet. These are patterns related to stress and are found only in infants' vocalizations. At this stage stability and accuracy of control of expiratory air flow and mature coordination to accomplish containment of air by laryngeal valve action and activation of the body wall are observed. However, in distress, the infant will sacrifice his tidal respiration schedule.

The maturation of the cry is related to the development of postural patterned stabilization and more discrete mobility of the tongue and soft palate in relation to this stabilization. Essentially these are the patterns of mature speech and the precursors of articulation. Upper pharyngeal and oral modulation is then superimposed on the already well developed vocal coordination. Abrupt shifts in the schedule of respiratory motions of larynx, pharynx, and trunk are no longer found at this stage. During the first weeks of life, no movement of the tongue is observed to modify vocal tract configuration, but by the sixth week of life there are changes in the configurations of the supra-laryngeal vocal tracts during vocalization.

As was stated earlier in the descriptions of the vocal mechanism and its operation that have been obtained thus far, there is evidence that mechanisms directly related to the production of speech are present at birth and that some other mechanisms develop within a very short period of time. In addition, there is some evidence that there are structural differences in the vocal mechanisms of man and other primates. The pre-programming of the vocal mechanism to acquire and use speech appears to be obvious but it is also obvious that this is an _insufficient_ condition. Otherwise deaf children would acquire speech.

The auditory and vocal mechanism

The systematic relationships between auditory and vocal mechanisms and how the infant is specifically structured to acquire language are matters of speculation. Lieberman (1968) has hypothesized that the two _necessary_ conditions for the presence of speech and language are an "output mechanism" and a "central mental ability." It is his contention that it would have been natural and economical for the constraints of speech production to be structured into the speech perception system if both these abilities in man developed at the same pace. We would then expect to find the speech recognition routines that involved a match with the constraints of speech production to be structured into a _speech perception center_ that would be specific rather than in the peripheral or central auditory systems, which are similar for man and other animals. In other words, the sounds that man was capable of making led to the development of a central nervous system center specifically designed to decode and identify the speech signals that man could produce. Of course we have no evidence of the existence of such a center at birth, but it is perfectly possible that such a center exists or that it exists potentially and develops during the acquisition period. This theory commands our attention not only because of its logical inferences but also because of experimental results with adults which indicate that speech perception is closely tied to speech production (Liberman, Cooper, Harris, and McNeilage, 1962).

A model of speech perception has been proposed in which the process of perception is considered to be an activity in which the listener to some degree regenerates the message internally, using the same routines as those used by the talker. This process has been termed "analysis by synthesis." This model presupposes that the auditory patterns heard by the listener are transformed into matching articulatory instructions since these are the patterns used by the talker to generate speech (Stevens and House, in press). Figure 2–3 indicates the general parameters of such a model and is a modified version of a model proposed by Stevens and House (in press).

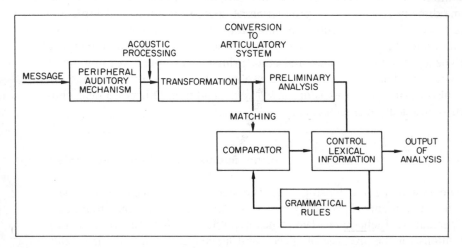

FIG. 2–3 A model of the process of analysis by synthesis.

Despite the fact that such a model or theory has logic and some experimental evidence to support it, the motor basis of speech perception is considered to be a learned process (Liberman, Cooper, Harris, and Mc-Neilage, 1962) achieving its greatest efficiency perhaps when cerebral dominance is established (approximately at age 4 to 5) or when the nervous system has achieved its full maturation and is "set in its ways" (approximately at puberty). It is evident that the language acquisition task has been accomplished to a great extent before age 4 or 5 and certainly before puberty. It is possible, then, given the slight evidence that has been obtained about the auditory processing which occurs during infancy, and given the fact that linguistic decoding and identification of the signal occur before such distinctions are made in production, that the development of such a speech perception center is a mature development of the nervous system, devised for purposes of economy, and that previous to this development, the organism makes use of auditory information in a special way. It is also possible that the language to be acquired contains types of categorizations that have to be dealt with by both auditory and vocal capacities in some kind of feedback arrangement and, thus, both capacities are involved in perception.

A pertinent question that might be asked is how closely are perceptual and productive mechanisms linked at various stages of development? It has been observed with adults that delayed auditory feedback of the subject's own speech results in (1) an increase in phonation time, (2) an increase in mean sound pressure level, and (3) repetitive and articulatory errors. The amount of time delay plays a critical role in the degree of disturbance. It has been postulated that since reference patterns corresponding to speech motor gestures (the movements involved in producing a speech sound sequence) permit matching of an auditory feedback and determination of degree of correspondence, and, thus, assurance that what was meant to be said has been said, a delay in auditory feedback can result in a disturbance of the planned articulatory behavior of the speaker (Chase, 1967). This phenomenon has been studied with delayed feedback of infant cry (Cullen, Fargo, Chase, and Baker, 1968) and delayed feedback of infant cry using several delay times (Cullen, Fargo, and Baker, 1968). It has also been studied with the speech of children aged approximately 2 to 3 years and approximately 4 to 13 years (Yeni-Komshian, Chase, Mobley, 1967). Measures of cry duration, pause time, and maximum sound pressure level were taken of the infants' cry in synchronous and delayed feedback situations in which the delay condition was always 200 milliseconds, and only measures of cry duration were taken in the experiment in which delay was varied (0, 100, 200, 400, 600, or 900 milliseconds). Measures of phonation time were taken, and mean sound pressure level and repetitive and articulatory errors were observed in the speech of children in synchronous and delayed feedback situations. The following results were obtained:

1. With cry feedback to neonates there were significant effects on duration and amplitude of the cry in the delay condition (200 milliseconds) but none on pause. However, amplitude did not consistently covary with the test conditions. Duration of the cry decreased rather than increased, which is directly opposite to what occurs to the length of utterances when delayed feedback is used with older children and adults. In the condition of varied delay times, no strict relationship between delay time and magnitude of reduction of cry duration was obtained and the earlier findings for 200 milliseconds were not replicated. There was a tendency, however, for subjects to decrease duration of cry for delay times in excess of 400 milliseconds. The average cry duration for subjects during the synchronous condition was 860 milliseconds.

2. At age 1 year, 9 months to 2 years, 2 months there were overall increases in phonation time but the increases were slight and none of the subjects showed marked behavioral disturbances.

3. At age 2 years, 4 months to 2 years, 11 months there was a significant increase in phonation time, syllable repetitions and articulation errors occurred, and there was an increase in sound pressure level.

4. At age 4 to 13 the results obtained were similar to those obtained with adults. There was a decrease in word rate and an increase in phona-

tion time. However, these results were significantly greater for 7 to 9 year olds, while 4 to 6 year olds showed no marked behavioral disturbances.

In still another study (MacKay, 1968), the effect of delayed feedback on the sentence repetition of children aged 4 to 6 years and 7 to 9 years and adults was examined. The effectiveness of delay in producing the classical symptoms was dependent on a particular delay time for each group. In a pilot study it was found that a delay of 524 milliseconds was most effective for younger children, a delay of 375 milliseconds was most effective for older children, and a delay of 200 milliseconds was most effective for adults. In the main study it was found in general that delay times of approximately 190, 300, and 380 milliseconds, respectively, produced the greatest frequency of errors, syllable durations, and stutters for the adults, older children, and younger children, respectively. The one notable exception is that a delay of 750 milliseconds produced the greatest amount of stuttering for the younger children. The experimenter concludes that the effectiveness of delay in producing disturbances is dependent on the rate of delay in conjunction with the rate of speaking. Since children presumably speak at a slower rate than adults, greater rates of delay are most effective.

The decrease in duration of infant cries may be merely the effect of listening or active auditory monitoring and, as the experimenters observe, might be the result of the infants' response to the auditory signal rather than to delay per se. Therefore, there is no evidence of closed-loop auditory feedback control in the infant even when delay rates are increased. There is also no evidence that this control is in operation at the beginning of the third year of life. However, as the age of the children increases from approximately 2½ years to 13 years, the effects of delayed auditory feedback becomes increasingly marked and increasingly similar to the effects observed with adults. Given the results of the study in which delay rates were varied, it is certainly possible that the gradual development observed is the result of the 200-millisecond delay becoming increasingly effective as the children's rates of speech increase. The relationship of this feedback loop to language acquisition at the phonological level can be obviously of great importance. Not only rate of speech but phonological content of utterances may play a role. This relationship has yet to be systematically explored.

SUMMARY

The study of children's distinct capacities to acquire language has been directed toward attempts to isolate either structural or functional differences in man's central and peripheral sensory-motor systems. It has been hypothesized that since man is the only organism to acquire and use language, these differences can be isolated and described.

Structural differences in the central nervous system have been observed, such as the marked development in man of non-limbic cross-modal association areas in the brain. However, most experimenters view man's unique capacity to acquire language to be the result of the *functioning* of his nervous system rather than the result of specific structures. This view must be further dichotomized in that some experimenters consider the functioning of man's nervous system as geared to learn the structure of a vast array of biologically important systems, one of which happens to be language, and other experimenters consider the functioning of the nervous system of man as being pre-programmed for the learning of language apart from learning other systems. The latter suggest that this must be so since men could survive without language. In addition, no other species uses language. Since we are unable to *observe* the functioning of the nervous system as the child acquires and develops language, conclusions have been drawn from what is known about the physiological structure of the neonate, the development of this structure during maturation, and the behavior that is observed during maturation.

Although there is no further nerve cell growth after birth, there presumably is biochemical and electrophysiological evidence of maturation of the brain until the teens. In relationship to this observation there is a fixed gross developmental schedule in language acquisition which is tied to this maturation. If language has not been acquired or if the developmental schedule has been retarded in the period before puberty, further development after puberty is extremely restricted. The behavioral effects of cerebral dominance are observed at approximately age 4. If damage to the dominant hemisphere occurs before dominance is well established, the nervous system adjusts and language develops normally or near normally, whereas damage after the establishment of dominance results in disturbances in language usage. On the other hand, if deafness occurs after some maturation of the system, children will respond well to language training, whereas if it occurs before some degree of maturation there will be great difficulty in training. Therefore it appears that there is a sufficient amount of plasticity in the system to overcome both peripheral and central damage of a certain kind. It is possible that the maturation of the system is pre-programmed for the acquisition of language and its acquisition in a certain sequence, but it is not clear that this programming is uniquely related to acquiring language. It may be simply uniquely related to the development of higher mental processes. All the observations about the schedule of development in language acquisition can and have been made about the development of cognition. There is also, presumably, a fixed developmental schedule in this process but, again, there appears to be plasticity in the system and it adapts to structural changes until maturation is reached. Further, some of the specializations in the system that have been observed—for example, cerebral dominance—may simply be the result of learning and not of pre-programming. If it is assumed that the complex system of connections needed in higher mental functions are developed on the basis of language, then the question is resolved. There is, however, great disagreement about this assumption.[5]

When we turn to the peripheral systems, vocal and auditory, and the question of the possible specific capacities of the infant to acquire language, the evidence is derived from the observable functions of these systems and, thus, is somewhat clearer. On the other hand, the data are extremely sparse. There is some evidence to indicate that the neonate, although his peripheral auditory mechanism can respond structurally to a wide range of frequencies in a general manner, responds differentially to those frequencies within and those without the speech sound range, and there is evidence that he responds differentially to constant and patterned stimuli. It is possible that there are species-determined sensitivity functions of the auditory mechanism which then cue specific eighth nerve responses and behavioral responses.[6]

There is evidence that the structure of the vocal mechanism of the infant as well as of the adult is quite different from that of other primates. Therefore the sounds that the infant and child can produce are potentially quite different from those that can be produced by other animals. In addition, because of the structure of the mechanism, functional differences develop, such as the use of the tongue and the pharyngeal wall to modify phonations.

If we couple both a unique perceptual and productive mechanism to a unique capacity to use the products of these mechanisms (the functioning of the central nervous system) we may have then described the unique capacity of the child to acquire language.[7] However, as has been pointed out, the relationship between productive and perceptual capacities, the relationship of these capacities to the developing capacities of the nervous system, and, finally, the relationship of all these to the acquisition of language have yet to be determined in any detail.

---

[5] The relationship of cognitive development and language development was discussed in somewhat greater detail in Chapter 1 under the heading Language and Thinking, and can be referred to.

[6] For a discussion of species determined responses, see Frishkopf and Goldstein, 1963.

[7] It should be noted here that a system of communication used by humans need not involve the auditory-vocal channel. The sign language developed by various cultures and by the deaf is an indication of this fact. However, the structure of sign language and its similarity to spoken language as a unique system of communication is a question that is now being explored. An example of such a study is Stokoe, 1960.

3

THE ACQUISITION
AND
DEVELOPMENT
OF PHONOLOGY

IN THE ACTUAL DECODING of an utterance both semantic and syntactic information is used. However, prosodic features (intonation, stress, and pause) are used as well to help identify word, phrase, and sentence boundaries as well as meaning. In deciding the differences in the meaning of two utterances which may have the same syntactic structure and prosodic features (for example, "He's walking" and "She's talking") differences must be perceived between segments that are smaller than word length. In the above example, perception of the differences between /h/ and /š/ and between /w/ and /t/ may be critical in accurately decoding the message. These types of differences must be identified and stored in memory by the child for use in the decoding and generation of utterances. In addition to segmental differences there is a set of rules in each language concerning permissable sequences of segments (consonant cluster rules for example) and a set of rules for marking number, tense, case, etc. Research in the course of development of these competences will be discussed in this chapter.

FROM BABBLING TO LANGUAGE

The role that pre-babbling and babbling plays in the development of "real" language is unknown. One of the primary problems in determining this role has been that no objective and, thus, accurate description of the performance of the infant during this period has as yet been obtained. Since listeners to either the baby or to tape recordings of his utterances are native speakers of a language, there is the possibility that the sounds produced by the infant are interpreted according to the categorization system of the listener rather than in terms of the actual acoustic signal that has been produced. In addition, most of the data that have been collected thus far have been on the infant's production of utterances. Very little has been collected on his perception of speech sound differences and prosodic feature differences. Although, at some stage of development, the infant's productions may be labeled (for example /p/, /b/ and /m/), we do not know if he can perceive differences between these speech sounds. During this period and the later period of sentence production which follows, the speech sounds the infant distinguishes (can he distinguish between /p/ and /b/, etc.) and the order of distinction (can he distinguish between /b/ and /m/ first, then /p/ and /b/ etc.) have not been determined.

Another problem in obtaining an accurate description of this period of language acquisition and determining its role in later development has been the difficulty in clearly defining the transition from babbling to "real" language. Until the infant begins to produce utterances which are clearly understood by the adults in his environment to refer to specific objects or situations he is said to be babbling, and until he responds in some clearly defined way, perhaps by pointing or turning to an object that has been named, he is said not to comprehend language. However, these are arbitrary decisions, and probably underestimate in some instances and perhaps overestimate in others the child's linguistic competence.

A third problem in determining a relationship between this period and later development has been that no accurate description of the role of interaction, both verbal and nonverbal, between the speaker (the baby) and the listener (the caretaker) has been obtained. Interpretation on the part of the listener may not produce an accurate record of the baby's utterances but may play a role in his acquisition of the language. Although there are many hypotheses about this interaction, there are few facts.

Because of the lack of basic information several hypotheses have been presented to describe the function of this period and the content of the utterances produced at this stage. It has been proposed that what occurs during this period is a gradual transition from babbling to word approximation to words (Murai, 1963/64), and that the purposes of babbling are to explore the possibilities of the vocal mechanism, to gain pleasure in vocal performances, and to learn to control the output of the mechanism, and thus to repeat certain sequences (Lewis, 1963, pp. 13–26). In addition it has also been proposed that there is a leap from babbling to word or sentence production, well defined by a period of silence (Jakobson, 1962, pp. 317, 328–402), rather than a gradual transition.

Following from these proposals, several claims have been made about the content of the utterances produced during this stage of development. The first is that since the infant is exploring all possibilities in vocal production, all the possible sounds of all languages are produced during this period. No regular or valid sequence in sound making can be observed until the sentence production or morpheme construction period. The second claim is that, far from producing all possible linguistic sounds throughout this stage, the set produced is restricted by the infant's perceptual and productive capacities and, therefore, a regular and valid sequence can be observed. Both these claims imply that the performance of children from all linguistic environments is the same. Their performance during this stage is unaffected by the particular language they hear. A third claim is that the sounds produced are shaped by the infant's specific linguistic environment and, thus, at an early stage of babbling attempts are made to imitate or reproduce the sounds heard. The results of these attempts become more and more accurate as the infant's ability to reproduce accurately increases. The process is one of gradual shaping toward the well articulated speech sounds of the language in the child's environment. Lack of accurate information has led to this wide variety of opinions about the function and content of babbling. We will reexamine these claims in the light of current research on the structure and content of the utterances produced and to some extent understood at this early stage of development.

Supra-segmental features

In Chapter 1 the structure of sentences was discussed. Sentences are made up of phrases, phrases are made up of syntactic classes, and each syntactic class represented in the sentence has certain properties. In addition, the underlying structure of the sentence contains markers (Neg., Imp., Q, Emph., etc.) which indicate the transformations that apply. In like fashion the utterances produced at this stage are made up of syllables, the syllables are made up of consonants and vowels, and each consonant and vowel has certain features. In addition, these utterances are marked by the prosodic features of intonation and stress. The features of each consonant and vowel in the utterance are called segmental features, and these will be discussed later. The other aspects of the utterance are called supra-segmental features, and it is these aspects which will be discussed now.

Several developmental changes occur in the supra-segmental features of babbled utterances. The length of the typical utterance changes, the consonant-vowel composition of utterances changes and the intonation and stress patterns of utterances change.

The first utterances of infants are cries. It has been claimed by those experienced in listening to baby cries that the cries can be differentiated into two categories at least: hunger and pain. It has also been claimed that cries can identify the "speaker." Mothers presumably can identify *their* baby in the hospital nursery. These claims, however, have not been validated by adequate experimentation. Spectrographic analysis of cries produced by neonates indicate that (1) the acoustic characteristics of the cry of a given neonate are his and his alone, and (2) since a general physiological or motor condition produces certain acoustic results, there are patterns that can be observed from infant to infant (Lind, Truby, and Bosma, 1965). This evidence appears to lend some substantiation to the claims that have been made about individual speaker identification and cry identification. The cries produced by infants have been roughly categorized as (*a*) basic cry, having a simple source of sound production; (*b*) turbulence, having a complex source (sounds rough, hard, raucous); (*c*) shift, having a constrained source (sounds extremely high pitched); or (*d*) a combination of the described phonations (*a* + *b* + *c*) (Lind, Truby, and Bosma, 1965, pp. 30–33). Although crying, in procuring relief of discomfort for the infant, serves a useful purpose, it is not directed toward obtaining this relief at the early stages but is only the product of a physiological state.

Nakazima (1962) notes that, from 2 to 5 months of life, one phonation is much longer than one normal respiration, so that phonation at this point is presumably superimposed on the normal respiratory cycle, and there are changes in pitch in one utterance. The central tendency and variability of fundamental frequency, amplitude, and duration within and between utterances produced by two infants from birth to 5 months and sampled periodically was measured (Sheppard and Lane, 1968). Vocalizations were sampled every fourth day and three 95-second samples obtained. The acoustic signal was sampled every 25 milliseconds and the acoustic parameters noted above extracted by analog devices, converted to digital information, and processed by an on-line digital computer. Thus, the linguistic prejudices of the listener or the viewer, in the case of spectrographic analysis, were bypassed. The following results were obtained: (1) fundamental frequency of vocalizations at birth decreased initially then rose and stabilized at a somewhat higher frequency than at birth; (2) there was neither more nor less fluctuation in the fundamental frequency within a sample as the infants matured; (3) the average duration of an utterance within a sample became more uniform as a function of age (an utterance is defined as a 100 millisecond sample); (4) the variability in amplitude within utterances was greater than the variability in fundamental frequency; and (5) longer utterances had greater amplitude and shorter utterances had lesser amplitude. It was found that although many responses were of short duration, a number of long ones were produced. However, the utterances could not be categorized.

The authors observe that the changes in fundamental frequency may be due to developmental changes in the dimensions of the vocal cords and maturation in control of the respiratory mechanism; or they may be due to developmental changes in the nature of the crying, which is first "unconditioned reflex" crying which decreases with the appearance of "motivated crying." Of course it is perfectly clear that later crying which is labeled "motivated" cannot appear unless there is increased control of the vocal mechanism regardless of its supposed motivation. The increasing uniformity in the duration of utterances is probably also the result of increasing control of the vocal mechanism. Interestingly, it has been observed that at approximately 2 months the average duration of an utterance is 400 milliseconds (Murai, 1960), and this is roughly the length of a CVC (consonant-vowel-consonant) syllable. Although the technique for handling data in this study avoids the prejudice and perhaps error of listening and looking, the results of the study do not provide us with much information about the changing structure of utterances as infants mature. The data indicate central tendencies and variations within samples and arbitrarily defined utterances, but do not provide any information about the patterns of changes in duration, amplitude, and fundamental frequency or about their interaction over a breath group and between breath groups. It is just these patterns which provide a description of the prosodic features of utterances. The data collected do indicate maturational changes in the control of the vocal mechanism.

Lieberman (1967, Chapter 3), in his discussion of intonation in infant speech, states that the infant cry is marked by a rising and then falling fundamental frequency contour with the fall gradual until the end, where it typically falls at a faster rate due to the fact that the cry is protracted until the last possible moment. In a babbled utterance there is not as sharp a fall in pitch at the end of phonation, but there is a fall. Spectrograms of infant cries indicate that there is not as much change—that is, not as much rise—in fundamental frequency over the neontal cry as can be found in the 5-month-old's cry.

The infant cry might then be a precursor of the typical fundamental frequency contours observed in a babbled utterance (rise then fall) and in a declarative statement (ends with a falling fundamental frequency contour). Lieberman has termed this contour of fundamental frequency which falls at the end the "unmarked breath group." It is "what comes naturally" as the infant runs out of breath. In contrast to this is the marked breath group or the typical fundamental frequency contour associated with questions, where there is a concluding rise in fundamental frequency. The infant must then impose some control on the natural out-flow of air. The concluding rise in fundamental frequency in babbling is observed long after the concluding fall in fundamental frequency is observed. Thus the sequence of development of intonational patterns appears to be from the unmarked pattern to the marked. It is this same sequence of development that is suggested for the acquisition of segmental features. In addition to these two patterns, however, another has been observed which appears to be an alternation on the unmarked breath group. This is the emphatic or stressed utterance. Sheppard and Lane (1968) noted that longer utterances have greater amplitude or, in simpler terms, that louder utterances are longer. An increase in subglottal pressure, a technique used to stress utterances (Lieberman, 1967), can lead to comparatively greater amplitude in the acoustic output and to increases in the length of utterance. It may also lead to greater changes in the fundamental frequency contour of the utterance (a sharper rise) over the breath group. There are indications from spectrograms that this pattern occurs abruptly in neonatal cry and more smoothly in later cry. There has been no evidence obtained as yet of this pattern in babbled utterances in this country.

It is at 6 to 8 months of life that Nakazima (1962) notes repetitive babbling and imitation of intonation. Immediately following this period changes in the rhythm of a single utterance are noted. This may be an indication of contrastive stress. One long babbling is segmented into pieces consisting of several syllables, changes in pitch and stress are observed, and rising intonation patterns as if asking a question are observed. It is immediately after this period that words begin to appear, along with repetitive babblings, that are marked by differing intonational patterns.

The fundamental frequency characteristics and intensity changes in the vocalizations of infants during the first two years of life were sampled and analyzed and compared with the intonational patterns of adults (Tonkova-Yampol'skaya, 1969). The experimenter states that patterns of intonation are developed and mastered (that is, they match adult patterns) much earlier than conceptual words and individual sounds. Intonational patterns similar to those found with adults appear at various ages. "Narration" and "assertion" utterances which rise gradually and then fall in fundamental frequency appear during the second month. "Commands" which have fundamental frequency contours which rise sharply, then fall, appear in the tenth month and "questions" which rise sharply at the end of the utterance appear at the beginning of the second year. All these types of utterances presumably display the distinctive characteristics of fundamental frequency contour and changes in intensity that are found in like types of adult utterances. These data substantiate a theory of increasing markedness on the breath group to differentiate meaning. However, although these data are interesting and provocative, the question of mastery needs to be corroborated by observations of the context in which these types of utterances are produced, the consistency with which they are produced and the consistency of adults' responses to these utterances.

The perception of prosodic feature differences by infants aged four months and eight months was examined (Kaplan, 1969). Sentences ("See the cat.") were read in a steadily rising and steadily falling tone of voice and read as declaratives and questions. These sentences were recorded and presented to infants and their heart rate and motor behavior was measured. The four-month-old infants did not indicate by their behavior that they differentiated between steadily rising and steadily falling sentences or between declarative and question sentences. The eight-month-old infants did not differentiate between steadily rising and steadily falling sentences but, both in heart rate changes and in motor behavior, they did indicate that they differentiated between question and declarative sentences. Again, some intriguing data have been obtained but it is not clear from this study whether the categorizations of question and declarative sentence were being differentiated or whether some single acoustic characteristic of the signal, such as changes in the intensity of the final word in question sentences, was causing the infants to pay attention to these sentences. One needs to establish whether the acoustic characteristics as a whole of declarative versus question sentences are causing the differentiation or if some aspect not necessarily related or only partially related to this linguistic difference is causing differentiation. This is far from a simple task to carry out. As can be seen, the amount of research that has been carried out to examine the development of prosodic features during the babbling period has been quite limited thus far.

The use of prosodic features at the stage of development which succeeds babbling has not been examined in detail either. This is the period in which the child is said to produce sentencelike strings or holophrastic utterances (McCarthy, 1954). These utterances are called sentencelike because the child appears to be uttering a sentence rather than simply naming an object. These utterances are presumably marked by stress and rising or falling intonational patterns and are presumably interpreted or responded to in varying ways because of intonation and stress. For example, distorted utterances such as "baw" for *ball* may be marked with (*a*) emphatic stress —"baw!" (*b*) interrogative intonational contour—"baw?" and (*c*) declarative intonational contour. Presumably (*a*) is interpreted as "I want the ball" or "Get the ball"; (*b*) is interpreted as "Is it a ball?" or "Where is the ball?" and (*c*) as "That's a ball." *Context* plays a role in interpretation as well as stress and intonational contour since (*a*) and (*b*), in the above examples, may be interpreted differentially due to the presence or absence of the ball. Lewis (1963, Chapter 1) states that because these patterns become functionally effective—that is, they have a manipulative and declarative effect—they become stabilized.

The above comments are interpretations of observations. Some alternative speculations have been offered. One such speculation is that all the words produced at this stage of development are names of objects. The first step in language acquisition is to learn that there are verbal labels for the things and events that can be observed, and that, therefore, the function of these first words is to tell us "That's a (or it's a) thing." In this case all first words would have the basic intonational pattern of a declarative statement. Alternatively, if variations on the basic patterns are observed, these can be accounted for by the fact that infants imitate adults' utterances and these utterances are always marked with varying stress and intonational patterns. If one takes these two speculations and puts them together, a third speculation can be and has been derived. These utterances are first acquired as imitations of adults' utterances. Utterances marked with the basic or varied patterns of intonation are produced by adults in certain situations and in the presence of certain objects and events. Infants imitate the names of these objects and events and, as parts of the name (i.e., as part of the phonological structure of the utterance that names), they also memorize a particular intonational pattern. For example, they learn the sequence "su?" Therefore, even when they are spontaneously generating this utterance they never produce "su!" or "su." but only "su?"

A study was undertaken to examine these various hypotheses (Menyuk and Bernholtz, 1969). The recorded utterances of a child at the stage at which she was primarily producing one-word utterances were examined and a series of utterances which were repetitions of the same word was isolated and re-recorded. These series contained words which would traditionally be classified as nouns, verbs, and prepositions. None of these utterances were repetitions of the mother's utterances but, rather, were introduced by the child into the conversation. Two listeners attempted to classify the isolated utterances as declaratives, questions, and emphatics, and found that each series contained exemplars of the three classifications except the proper name series which contained no emphatics. There was 81 percent agreement between the two listeners. All the disagreements were concerned with emphatics and whether or not these were tense or worried statements or true emphatics. Spectrograms were made of the utterances and it was observed that, although there was some variation within a category in terms of specific numbers, a general characteristic of each type of utterance could be found. Declarative utterances terminated with a falling fundamental frequency contour, questions terminated with a rising fundamental frequency contour, and emphatics had a sharp rise and then fall in fundamental frequency contour during the utterance. Figure 3–1 presents a plot of the measurements taken of the utterance "door" as a statement, a question, and an emphatic.

These results indicate that first one-word utterances are not simply the names of things and events. It is illogical to suppose that "door!" and

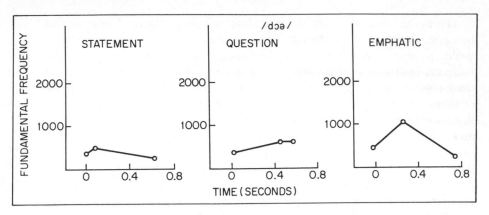

FIG. 3–1 Measurement of fundamental frequency at beginning, peak and end of the utterance /dɔə/ as a statement, question and emphatic.

"door?" as well as "door" are all being used simply to state that "That's a door." Further, these utterances are produced spontaneously and not in imitation of adult utterances. Finally, all three intonational patterns are applied to a whole range of lexical items rather than being found only with specific lexical items. One could ask if the child intends to make a statement, ask a question, or be emphatic, or if the productions of these patterns are simply accidents. Although these data cannot provide conclusive answers to these questions, they nevertheless indicate that the child probably did intend to produce these different sentence types since specific purposeful effort is needed to generate question and emphatic utterances.

Although the data are very limited and the experimentation preliminary, there are indications that the child's single-word utterances are not simply names of objects and events and that the child uses prosodic features generatively to produce various sentence types rather than merely imitates or memorizes prosodic features in association with the phonological structure of words.

One of the first patterns that can be observed in infants' vocalizations which are consistent with adults' patterns and, therefore, possibly with a *shared semantic interpretation* are the intonational contours and stress patterns in these vocalizations. The unmarked pattern and its alternation (unstressed and stressed) appear in the first utterances (cry) and become more stable over the first few months of life. The marked pattern appears somewhat later, presumably around 7 to 9 months. These same patterns can be observed in the first words produced by infants.

Murai (1963/64) states that during the babbling stage there is an increase in the frequency and variety of resembling utterances (i.e., utterances resembling those of the adult). In essence, the utterances produced by infants sound increasingly like adult utterances as the infant matures. One reason for this increased resemblance, outside of the changes in the production of speech sounds per se, may be a change in the consonant-vowel patterns in the babbling.

Irwin (1946) examined the mean ratio of consonant frequencies to vowel frequencies in the utterances of infants over an age range of 1 to 30 months. There is an overall increase in the frequency of usage of consonants in utterances until the period of 29–30 months when the ratio is .98. This indicates an increasing usage of CV patterns rather than simply V patterns. There are some assymetries in the developmental progression. At 11–12 months there is a sharp increase in the ratio followed by a small decrease at 13–14 months. There is also a small decrease at 17–18 months. At 21–22 months there is a sudden sharp increase in the ratio. Factors such as increasing control of the mechanism in the early months and additions to the lexicon in later months may account for the sharp increases observed, and the small decreases may perhaps be accounted for by a period of stabilization of acquisitions. However, this is merely speculative since none of the corroborating simultaneous developmental data on these infants is available and one can merely make logical guesses. An asymmetry is also noted in the consonant type-vowel type ratio. A temporary plateau is reached during the 13 to 18 month period. This is the period during which one-word or two-word sentences are beginning to be used and the asymmetries observed in frequency and type ratios before, during, and after this period may indicate a recycling of the developmental process now geared to mapping phonological information into syntactic and semantic structures. This "shifting" of gears can be observed periodically during the entire period of language acquisition. It may be represented by a plateau or even a slight regression in the development of the linguistic system at all levels—phonological, syntactic, or semantic—and reflect the beginning of a new kind of development in the system because previous acquisitions have led to new strategies.

The frequency of occurrence of certain CV patterns changes over the 13–18 month period (Winitz and Irwin, 1958). The most frequently used patterns during the 13–14 month period are CVC (V) (for example, *mommy, baby*), CV (for example, *me, ma*) and CVCV (for example, *mamma*), in that order. At 15–16 months the most frequently used patterns are CV, CV(C) (for example, *boat, top*), and CVC(V), in that order. At 17–18 months there is, again, a shift, and the most frequently used patterns are CV, CVC(V), and CV(C), in that order. At this stage (17–18 months) when a lexicon is being acquired, we may be observing the influence of that lexicon on the frequency of consonant-vowel patterns. It should be noted that the repetitious pattern of CVCV drops in frequency after the

13–14 month period. From the previous data on consonant-vowel ratio it is clear that the infant has begun to produce the basic linguistic unit, the syllable, early in the developmental period and long before words appear. At 13–14 months he is consistently producing utterances composed of these units.

Segmental features

Throughout this discussion the cautionary statements made in the introduction concerning the accuracy of the observations that have been made about the content of segments in infants' utterances should be kept in mind. The task of measuring and categorizing the supra-segmental features of these utterances, although not an easy one, is simple compared to the task of measuring and categorizing segmental features.

As has been noted, the mechanisms necessary for the production of noncrying utterances are ready at birth. However, maturational changes in the proportions, posture, and control of the vocal mechanism occur over the first month of life. At about one to two months of life the infant is producing noncrying utterances. These utterances, in their turn, also seem to be brought about by the physiological state of the infant. Lewis has categorized the noncry utterances into discomfort and comfort sounds (Lewis, 1963, pp. 13–26). Initially, discomfort sounds are narrow-nasalized sounds and comfort sounds are back-open sounds. The articulation of the noncrying comfort utterance seems to be governed by chance since in the comfort state the infant is relaxed with his mouth slackly open, so that a phonation simply appears at the end of an expiration. These phonations have been labeled as being, usually, the midvowel /ə/ or back of the throat sounds such as /x/.

The course of development of the phonetic content of infants' utterances has been described in the following manner: back vowels are produced first and then front to back vowels are produced, *or* middle and middle to front vowels are produced first and then middle to back vowels; back consonants are produced, *or* front to back consonants are produced. This apparent controversy about the order of production of speech sounds during the babbling period, in terms of place of articulation, probably stems from the particular labeling that experimenters give to physiological sounds related to bodily states. Some experimenters consider the *back sounds* produced during the early stages of development to be outside the category of speech sound production because they are the accidental products of a physiological state, while other experimenters include these sounds.

Despite the arguments, it is clear that the articulated sound repertoire of the infant increases over the babbling period. This increase in the sound repertoire of the infant seems to be directly related to physiological maturation and the increasing control of the vocal mechanism which is the result of this maturation. The direction that speech sound production takes, the specific sequence of the various sounds produced, seems to be a function of physiological maturation. It becomes evident, when a comparison is made of the speech sound development of infants in two differing linguistic environments, that changes in the repertoire produced cannot be a function of the specific linguistic environment. In a study of the utterances produced by Japanese and American children, which included a spectrographic analysis of these utterances, Nakazima (1962) found that there were no differences in the speech sound repertoires of the two groups of children even through the stage when words and phrases were beginning to appear. The first words of both groups of children were very similar in phonetic composition. Lewis (1963, pp. 33–43) has also noted that an infant's first words are often composed of those sound combinations frequently found in infant babbling (*mamma, nana, papa, baba,* etc.).

Some other experimental results reinforce the position that the development of speech sound production is a function of the infant's changing perceptual and productive capacities rather than of the specific linguistic environment. The acquisition of a particular aspect of production, voicing onset time (Preston and Yeni-Komshian, 1967), was examined. It was found that although infants were exposed to different languages (Hungarian, English, and Arabic) in which the pattern of voicing onset times for stop consonants differs, their productions did not reflect these specific language differences even at approximately one year of age. The voicing onset time patterns were quite similar for all children and tended toward the *middle range* of voicing onset time. This pattern is considered the neutral or *unmarked* voicing distinction. This is an important finding and studies of other specific aspects of vocal production, if undertaken, may yield similar results.

If indeed speech sound usage is prescribed by physiological state in the early stages and by maturation of both perceptual and productive capacities in the later stages, then those productive and/or acoustic features of speech sounds which cause early or late usage can be isolated and found in the babblings of infants of differing linguistic environments. However, the speech sound labels (for example, /p/, /b/, /m/, etc.) applied to these utterances may be inaccurate. A linguistic description of the speech sounds of languages postulates that they are not indivisible entities (that is, sound /t/, /d/, etc.) but, rather, a bundle of distinctive features whose parameters can be observed in the articulatory gesture and the acoustic signal (Jakobson, Fant, and Halle, 1963). These features may be more or less prominent in the production of utterances throughout the babbling period, and this should be true of infants from differing linguistic environments.

Irwin's data (Irwin, 1947) measuring the proportion of usage of consonants at various ages was analyzed observing the proportion of usage of the features +grave (produced with closure at the peripheries of the oral cavity both front and back), +diffuse (produced with closure at the mid portion of the oral cavity), +strident (turbulence at the point of articulation), +nasal, +continuant, +voice over the age range of 3 to 30 months (Menyuk, 1965). The percentage of departure of certain features from the expected percentage of usage, given the number and type of speech sounds in the language containing this feature, was calculated for the various age levels. For example, since only 3 nasal consonants exist in the language and there are 26 consonants in all, there should be 12 percent usage of the feature +nasal throughout the age range if all consonants were used equally frequently during this age span. Figure 3–2 indicates

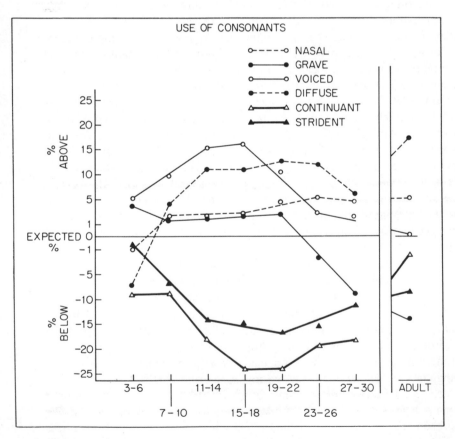

FIG. 3–2 Percentage of departure from expected percentage of usage of consonantal features at various ages during infancy.

how much each feature's usage departed from the expected percentage.

In the Irwin data consonants with the features +grave, +nasal, and +voice are used proportionately more than expected from the 3–6 months period until the 19–22 months period, and then usage only of +grave drops below the expected percentage. Production of diffuse consonants rises markedly during the 7–10 months period and remains high throughout the age range. During the 27 to 30 months period the rank order of proportionate usage of consonants containing various features is similar to that of adults, except that the percentage of usage of consonants that are +strident and, particularly, +continuant is disproportionately low. Proportionate frequency of usage of features in adults' speech is still not reflected in frequency of usage in infants' speech at 30 months, although this is the period when most children are producing sentences.

During the early vocalization period (3 to approximately 6 months) both Japanese and American children first produce and proportionately use with much greater frequency sounds which are +voice, +grave, and +nasal. The Japanese data are taken from Nakazima (1962). The rank order of dominance for feature usage, at this stage, for both groups is: +voice, +grave, +nasal, +diffuse, +strident, +continuant.

Later, during the morpheme formation period, approximately the same ordering in usage of features for productions considered to be *correct* articulations can be observed with both Japanese and American children (Menyuk, 1968b). Several hypotheses are suggested from this analysis of the data. The first is that the proportion of usage of certain speech sounds and shifts in this proportion of usage over the babbling period is dependent on the distinctive feature composition of these sounds. This would imply that it is at least not the case that infants produce all possible speech sounds proportionately equally during this period. Nakazima (1962) states that the /s/, /z/, /ž/, voiced and unvoiced *th* (/θ/ and /ð/), /f/, and /r/ are articulations which do not appear consistently in the babblings of infants 9–12 months old. All these speech sounds are +continuant and many of them are +strident. Some of the vocalizations that have been observed in infant babblings, as has been noted, may be the result of accidental usage of the articulators, whereas others appear to be the result of purposeful movements. Nakazima notes instances in which sounds *like* /l/ and /r/ are produced with a unique usage of the articulators (with tip of tongue and upper lip and tip of tongue and upper teeth, respectively).

The second hypothesis is that the hierarchy of feature usage is largely determined by the perceptual and productive capacities of the infant, rather than by his linguistic environment. This does not merely imply the simple notion that the sounds in all languages are governed by the human organism's limitations. Obviously they are. We do not produce speech sounds above a certain frequency because our vocal mechanism cannot produce them and our ears could not hear them. Beyond these gross limitations, it appears to be likely that as the infant develops there may be certain perceptual and productive distinctions that he can make before others. This differential ability is related to developing central nervous system capacities for decoding, storage and encoding, as well as peripheral capacities. This may account for the fact that the same pattern of development in proportional speech sound usage can be observed in infants from two differing linguistic environments. To explore this hypothesis, data must be collected from a sufficient number of differing linguistic environments, and these data should be collected by some standardized procedures. In addition, a much clearer understanding of the developing vocal-motor capacities of the infant and an understanding of the speech sound discrimination capacities of the infant and young child must be obtained.

It is possible that the rank ordering of features in terms of ease of discrimination matches the rank ordering of features in terms of proportionate usage and mastery in production. Research examining the speech sound discrimination of infants is presently under way (McCaffrey, 1967). Cardiac rate change after habituation to a vowel or CV syllable when a new vowel or new CV syllable is introduced is now being examined to explore the child's perception of distinctive feature differences. A recent study (Moffit, 1969) examined the cardiac rate response of infants aged 20–24 weeks to a change in the consonantal segment after habituation. One group of infants listened to /ba/ over six trials and then /ga/ on the seventh and eighth trials, another group listened to /ga/ and then /ba/ on the eighth trial, and a third group listened only to /ba/. Each stimulus was presented 10 times at one-second intervals during a trial and there was a 40-second interval between trials. It was found that there was a significant cardiac deceleration for group 2 between trials seven and eight, a cardiac deceleration but nonsignificant between trials six and seven for group 1, and essentially no change over these latter trials for group 3. One acoustic difference between /ba/ and /ga/ is a quite subtle difference in the frequency of the second formant in relation to the vowel. The experimenter concludes that these results indicate that the infant might be particularly sensitive to a fairly subtle difference because it is essentially this difference which distinguishes two speech sounds. However, there are also intensity differences between these sounds, so that it is possible that infants were responding to a difference which is not necessarily associated with speech sound differentiation.

Although the research is quite preliminary, the questions being explored are important in terms of understanding the infant's phonological development. Determining the order of discrimination between speech sound sets (nasal and nonnasal, voiced and unvoiced, etc.) and between members of the sets (/m/ and /n/, for example) and the relationship of this discrimination to particular feature differences among and within sets can lead to an explanation of this development. It is possible that out of this kind of research the particular parameters of speech sound sensitivity at various stages can be isolated and tested both with speech and nonspeech stimuli.

A third hypothesis that might be derived from the data collected thus far is that the babbling period is indeed a time for both identification of speech sound feature differences and overt practice of the production of these differences. During the morpheme formation period (approximately 2 to 6 years) the order of mastery of articulation of consonants containing certain features is almost exactly that found in the proportionate usage of sounds containing certain features observed during the babbling period. Thus, speech sounds containing certain features are successfully mapped into morphemes in approximately the same order of their proportional usage during the babbling period, and this is true of two differing linguistic environments (Menyuk, 1968b). The babbling period, then, not only appears to be a time in language development for vocalizing to obtain pleasure or to "tune in" on the communication process, but also serves a useful linguistic purpose and is probably necessary for later development. This correlation between order of acquisition and use in babbling and order of acquisition and use in later phonological development in terms of distinctive features should be examined in many linguistic environments to substantiate this hypothesis.

DEVELOPMENT OF PHONOLOGY

It is obvious that when a child uses the morpheme "hosh" in the presence of a large dog at the early stages of the use of meaningful words, he is not substituting the phonetic sequence "hosh" for the phonetic sequence "dog." Rather, he is noting the similarities in appearance between horses and large dogs and labeling this similarity. However, it has been observed that substitutions of segments do occur in the early words of children, and these substitutions continue for a long period of time. As indicated in the discussion of babbling, there appear to be certain features of speech sounds which the child selects before others for reproduction into articulatory gestures. In addition to the substitution of segments, other types of behavior have been observed from the beginning of the morpheme formation period until articulation mastery has been achieved.

Some experimenters have noted that throughout this period the child produces approximations to completely well formed morphemes and that these approximations in some instances appear to be random. That is, sometimes a particular speech sound may be produced accurately and at other times omitted, substituted, or distorted. It is possible that the observed behavior is not truly random in nature but that differences in speech sound production are dependent on the particular context in which the speech sound is produced. The child must acquire both segmental features which distinguish the speech sounds of his language and the sequential rules of his language for appropriate word formation.

Segmental features

Since speech is continuous in actual utterances it is difficult to determine where one sound ends and another begins within a word, and sometimes where one word ends and another begins within a sentence. Figure 3–3

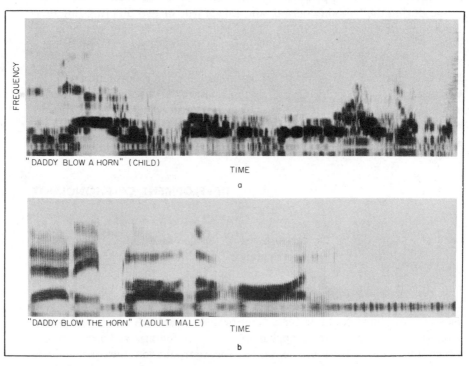

FREQUENCY

"DADDY BLOW A HORN" (CHILD)   TIME

a

"DADDY BLOW THE HORN" (ADULT MALE)   TIME

b

FIG. 3–3 Spectrograms of (a) a child aged 24 months saying "daddy blow a horn" and (b) an adult male saying "daddy blow the horn."

contains spectrograms of (a) a child (aged 24 months) saying "daddy blow a horn" and (b) an adult male saying "daddy blow the horn." As can be seen, a word is a continuous stream of sound and, especially in the case of the child, the complete utterance may be a continuous stream of sound. To segment the stream of speech is, then, a difficult task. To further complicate the task of the child, individual utterances of the same word may vary. Therefore, the acoustic products of segments may vary from speaker to speaker. Figure 3–4 contains spectrograms of (*a*) an adult fe-

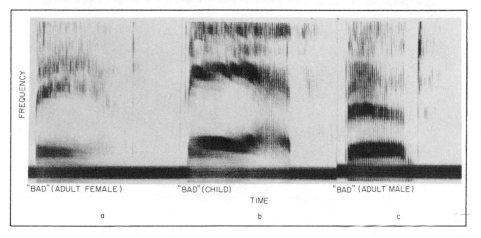

FIG. 3–4 Spectrograms of (a) an adult female saying "bad," (b) a 4-year-old girl saying "bad" and (c) an adult male saying "bad."

male saying "bad", (*b*) a 4-year-old girl saying "bad"; and (*c*) an adult male saying "bad."

There is an additional complication. In the acoustic output of VCV syllables, for example, it was found that the terminal frequencies of the vowels in these syllables are affected not only by the consonant in the syllable but also by the entire vowel context (Öhman, 1966). Therefore, the acoustic output of the production of speech sounds of the language may vary not only from speaker to speaker but also from one word to another. Yet, by the end of the phonological acquisition period, the child determines the parameters or bundles of distinctive features which differentiate the speech sounds in the language from one another, and determines how these bundles of features should be used in particular environments.

By the time the child reaches the morpheme formation stage he is producing the linguistic sequences CV, CVCV, CVC, and VCV. It is possible that instead of differentiating between members of the set of each of these sequences on the basis of their segments (each C and V), he differentiates between them on the basis of the properties of the whole sequence or on the basis of the properties of the syllables in a sequence. There is some evidence which indicates that pre-school children have difficulty in dividing word sequences which commonly appear together in a phrase (Hutten-locher, 1964) and that children with a mental age of 5 or 6 cannot report what is left of a word after the deletion of one of its speech sounds (Bruce, 1964). However, when children in 1st and 3rd grade are asked to resynthesize segmented CVC syllables, they do fairly well if the segments make up a meaningful word and if the interval between segments is not too long (Shriner, Daniloff, and Nemec, 1969). It appears then that although children have difficulty in segmenting a meaningful whole, they can convert segments into a whole as long as the reference is meaningful.

Ervin-Tripp (1966) reports from Velten's data that a child at the end of the second year of life used a particular phonetic sequence for an array of morphemes which labeled widely differing objects and actions. The example given is use of the sequence /pat/ for "black," "bark," "block," "bought," "button," "bite," "pat," "spot," and "pocket," and the phonetic sequence /nu/ for "new," "knee," "near," "nail," and "no." It is obvious in these instances that the child is not perceiving the distinguishing properties of, for example, "knee" and "nail," as being similar in nature, and so labels both these objects as being the same (/nu/). From some limited evidence (Berko and Brown, 1960) it appears that there is a period during which the child comprehends differences between phonological sequences but cannot replicate these differences in his own utterances. From the instance of behavior given above, it appears that when this child listens to the phonetic sequences composing such words as button and block, he does not hear them as the same words, but, rather, translates the auditory signal into particular articulatory gestures.

One can observe that the set of words reproduced as /pat/ are composed of the sequence, labial stop + back vowel + nonlabial stop, or of this sequence in the first syllable, as in "button"; and that the set of words reproduced as /nu/ are composed of the sequence, dental nasal + high vowel. Possible translations of these sequences are (1) /pat/ and (2) /nu/. These kinds of data, although quite limited at the moment, do indicate that at the earliest stages of mapping speech sound components into words, the child is able to observe segmental features and translate segmental features into gestures.

The above translation of the phonetic sequences described is only one possible translation. To fit the given descriptions the child could produce /bæk/ or /bæd/, etc. as well as /pat/, and /ni/ or /ne/ etc. as well as /nu/. The questions are Why does the child select one sequence and not another? and What is the basis of this selection? It has been hypothesized by Jakobson and Halle (1956) and other linguists that the content of the speech sound approximations observed throughout the morpheme formation period can be explained by a hierarchy of feature distinctions. Certain distinctions appear before others, and later distinctions cannot be made unless previous distinctions appear.

The first distinction the child observes is that between vowels and consonants (vocal tract unconstricted, vocal tract constricted), and then he proceeds by observing further differentiations between members of these sets. Given that the structure of the first sequences used are usually CV, the optimal consonant would be the one with the most closure and the optimal vowel would be the most open. This is the phonological sequence labial + /a/, or /pa/, /ba/, or /ma/. Since replication of CV often occurs, the child produces "mamma" and "pappa" but not "mapa." When these speech sounds are deliberately repeated in particular contexts the child is said to be in the morpheme formation period. Jakobson (1962a) claims that these facts about the features of the speech sounds /p/, /m/ (maximal closure), and /a/ (maximal openess) account for their early and frequent use in all linguistic environments. As was discussed previously, these speech sounds, appear early and are used proportionately more than other sounds during the early babbling stage. These same sounds are selected and used early and frequently in meaningful morphemes.

Further differentiation of this optimal set of CV presumably takes place in an orderly sequential fashion which is determined by the features which distinguish these speech sounds. Figure 3–5 is a schematization of hierarchical ordering in the differentiation of features which distinguish a set of vowels and consonants as proposed by Jakobson and Halle (1956). The features high in the tree structure are differentiated before those lower in the tree.

In examining the hierarchy of distinction in Figure 3–5, the performance of the child who translated one set of words composed of labial stop + back vowel + nonlabial stop into /pat/ and another set of words composed of dental nasal + high vowel into /nu/ becomes somewhat clearer. What is implied in a hierarchical description of feature distinctions is that the child can recognize, distinguish, and identify speech sounds in terms of their features. The difficulty that children apparently have in segmenting phrases into words and words into their speech sound components may be due to the particular task requirements of the experiments, since pre-school children appear to be able to distinguish, identify, and reproduce minimal pairs of a certain kind ("pit" and "pat," "pit" and "mit," "pit" and "pick," for example). Indeed, Shvachkin (1948) found that he could teach very young children (age 11 months to 1 year, 11 months) to make all the vocalic and consonantal distinctions in Russian in minimal pair words, and the order in which they learned to make these distinctions was quite similar to that postulated by Jakobson and Halle (1956).

It is possible, however, that, at least in the production of utterances, constraints imposed by the particular contexts in which Cs and Vs occur —that is, syllabic constraints—may affect performance. This effect would be in addition to that of the distinctive features of the speech sound components. At the earliest stages of development there is very little, but in-

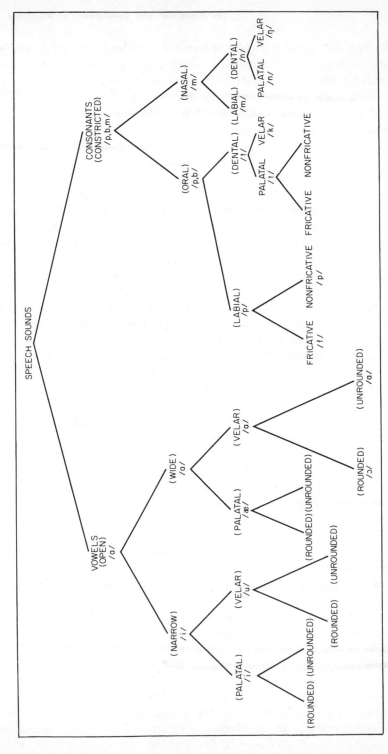

FIG. 3–5 Schematization of a possible order in the sequence of acquisition of speech sound distinctions with examples from English. Examples are given below features.

triguing, evidence that this may be the case. Jakobson (1962b) has noted, in his analysis of the observations made during this period by other linguists, that in early acquisition certain CV sequences occur and not others. The vowel /a/ appears after labials and dentals (/ba/ and /da/) but the vowel distinction /u/ and/i/ only after labials (/bu/ and /bi/) and the vowel distinction /i/ and /e/ only after dentals (/di/ and /de/). At a somewhat later stage of development a frequent occurrence in children's speech is that the glide /y/ may be omitted in a word (as in "esh" for "yes"), but is then used in substitution for /l/ (as in "yook" for "look") and the /l/ substituted for /y/ (as in "lellow" for "yellow"). Obviously, in these latter instances, the distinctive features which differentiate /l/ and /y/ are understood but are *applied* differently in certain contexts. These observations together with the results of Shvachkin's study (Shvachkin, 1948) on the comprehension of distinctive feature differences by very young children indicate that there are very real differences between the perception of the speech sound differences and their production at the very earliest stages of phonological development and that production of utterances may be governed by sequential rules which are different from those which affect perception.

Most of the data that have been collected on the use of either segmental features or sequential rules have been obtained from studies of the speech sound productions of children and very little from studies of their speech sound discrimination and identification. There are obvious problems associated with trying to describe the speech sound development of children from these data. Most of this evidence has been obtained from school age children, and, therefore, a great deal of the evidence is missing. The data have been obtained from either spontaneous speech samples or nonstandardized articulation tests, which may vary from each other to some degree in content, and therefore the results of these studies may vary somewhat in terms of the order of acquisition of speech sounds that is found. Further, it is possible that some of the test materials used influenced the results because of the particular phonological context in which the speech sound was sampled.

Snow (1963), in her study of articulation responses of first-grade children, found that, in general, responses were independent of the test word used (two for each sound), or the position of the sound in the word (initial, medial, or final). However, there were exceptions. The position of the speech sound for particular sounds affected the *number* of incorrect responses. For example /θ/ as in "thumb" was repeated with errors by 85 children, but in "birthday," with errors by 101 children, and in "mouth," with errors by 61 children. Further, /θ/ in "birthday" was most frequently repeated as /t/ ("birtday") but as /f/ in "toothbrush" ("toofbrush"). The /r/ was most frequently repeated as /w/ in the initial position but most frequently omitted in medial and final position. The /ŋ/ was frequently repeated as /n/ in a V + ing construction ("swimming") but repeated correctly in "swing." The articulation of these sounds is mastered fairly late in the developmental sequence. This same type of performance could possibly be observed with many other sounds if younger children were tested. It is obvious that context can affect the accuracy of production and, if this effect is multiplied by the number of *different* test items that are used in "normative" studies, the generality of the results obtained appears to be questionable. However, despite these factors there does appear to be a great deal of similarity in the results of studies examining the articulation performance of children in varying ways.

Irwin's data (Irwin, 1947) indicate that certain sounds are produced proportionately more often by children aged 29 to 30 months than by adults and other sounds are used proportionately less. In an examination of Wellman's data (Powers, 1957) it was found that some sounds were mastered in all three positions by 4 years of age and others were mastered after this age. Snow's data (Snow, 1963) show that certain sounds are incorrectly produced by substantially more first-grade children than are others. Table 3–1 presents the results of this examination of the available data.

There is great similarity in the rank ordering of speech sounds in each list. On the whole, sounds which are used with greater frequency are also

TABLE 3–1   RANK ORDERING OF USAGE OF SOUNDS, MASTERY OF SOUNDS, AND ACCURACY IN PRODUCTION

Irwin's Data		Wellman's Data		Snow's Data	
1	2	3	4	5	6
Greater than Adult Usage	Less than Adult Usage	Mastered by 4	Mastered after 4	From 1 to 91 Errors	From 100 to 1067 Errors
d	y	w	t	n	l
h	s	h	z	p	ŋ
b	ž	m	v	m	ǰ
m	š	n	s	b	č
k	θ	b	š	w	š
g	ŋ	f	ž	h	s
p	f	p	č	d	v
w	č	d	r	t	r
t	n	k	v	k	z
	z	g	ǰ	y	ð
	ð	l	ŋ	f	θ
	r	y	θ	g	ž
			ð		

mastered earlier and produced with fewer errors in a test situation, and sounds which are used less frequently are also mastered later and produced with a greater number of errors in a test situation. One should keep in mind that context must be playing a role in the types of performance that are observed with the various speech sounds. We have already noted this in Snow's data, but in Wellman's data as well the age of complete mastery of a particular sound is often delayed by the fact that it is not mastered in all three positions at the same age. For example, the medial /ŋ/ is mastered by 3 years but the sound in final position is not mastered until after 6; the final /r/ is mastered by 4 years but the sound in initial and medial position is not mastered until 5½; the initial /ǰ/ is mastered at 4 but the sound in medial and final position is not mastered until 6.

Two interrelated questions arise from these results. The first is: are there any correlations between the hierarchies of speech sound perception and speech sound production. The second is: what causes early or late mastery in the production of certain sounds? We will reexamine the sequence of mastery of sounds in terms of the distinctive features of these sounds and examine the few data that are available on speech sound perception.

All the sounds which appear in the odd-numbered columns of at least two of the lists in Table 3–1 are, with one exception (f), either stops (b, d, g, p, t, k), nasals (m, n), or glides (w, h, y). Within the set of stops the ± voicing distinction is usually observed by age 4 in all three positions, although /b/ is mastered before /p/ and /d/ before /t/. Both /k/ and /g/ are mastered by age 4. On the other hand, all the sounds which appear in the even-numbered columns of at least two of the lists in Table 3–1 are continuants (s, z, š, ž, v, θ, ð, l, r) or have gradual release (č, j). Stops and the voicing distinction among the stops, then, appear to be acquired before continuants are acquired.

In a study (Menyuk, 1968b) of the feature maintenance in the speech sound substitutions most frequently observed in normal development (for example, a substitution of /t/ for /k/ would mean a maintenance of all features except those of place), it was found that the rank order of feature maintenance in these frequent substitutions was Voicing, Nasality, Stridency, Continuancy, and Place. The speech sound discrimination of 3-year-old children was recently examined (Koenigsknecht and Lee, 1968). Every English consonant in initial and final position was compared to other consonants which differed in terms of a varying number of features from the key consonant. For example "man" was paired with "tan," "chan," "can," and "man." The children were asked to show the picture of the key word every time they heard it. The overall rank order of errors, in terms of confusion of features, from least to most errors was nasality, voicing, continuancy, and place. Children, aged 3 years to 5 years, 9 months were asked to repeat CV nonsense syllables (Bricker, 1967). The total frequency of errors decreased over the age range but the pattern of errors was maintained. The preservations of the features place, manner, and voicing in the repetition errors of the children was examined. It was found that voicing was best preserved, then manner, and finally place throughout the age range. In a recent study it was found that 3-year-old children categorize nonsense CV syllables which begin with varying voicing onset times either /t/ or /d/ approximately the way adults do (Preston, 1967).

All these data add substantiation to the hypothesis that there is a hierarchy in ease of discrimination of features. Although we have yet to determine the set of distinctive features which best describes the characteristics of the differences between the speech sounds of languages, the consistency of results from study to study indicates that features which seem to have absolute, or categorical, characteristics—such as nasality and voicing—rather than relative characteristics—such as continuant (continuant, gradual release, abrupt release) and place (closure at the lips or near the lips, etc.)—are easier to identify and produce. However, the above distinctions between speech sound *sets* (nasals, continuants, stridents, etc.) are not the only distinctions that are necessary in the acquisition of the phonological system of the language. Distinctions among the members of these sets must also be acquired.

The acoustic cues to differentiation between stop, nasal, and strident sounds are relatively clear, as is the distinction between voiced and voiceless sounds (for example, between /b/ and /m/ and between /f/ and /p/). To differentiate among members of these sets (for example, between /b/, /d/, and /g/) acoustic cues which extend over the CV or VC in syllables are necessary. That is, information about the frequency regions of the formant transitions from C to V or V to C are needed (Stevens and House, in press). The locus of the second formant transition for /b/, /m/, and /f/ is *low* compared to other members of their respective sets. This is also true of /w/ as compared to /l/ and /r/. The *particular* locus may alter dependent on the subsequent vowel. The types of acoustic differentiations found between sets as compared to those found between members of a set may, then, influence the sequence of mastery observed in the acquisition of speech sounds, and indeed the following sequence of mastery is observed:

> By age 3—/b/, /m/ and /n/, /f/, and /w/ and /h/
> By age 4—/p/, /d/, /g/ and /k/ and /y/ and /l/
> By age 5—/t/

Having acquired the paradigm member of a set, stop /b/, nasal /m/, strident /f/, glide /w/, the child then parcels out the characteristics of differing members of a set at differential rates. Thus, the ± voice characteristics of stops (/b/ versus /p/) and their labial/lingual (/b/ versus /d/), lingual/velar (/d/ versus /g/) characteristics are determined early as is the labial/lingual characteristic of nasals (/m/ versus /n/) and the labial/velar characteristics of glides (/w/ versus /y/). The same characteristics for continuants that are ± strident are parceled out and mastered later. The acoustic cues to the differentiation of the members of this set (/f/, /θ/, /s/, and /š/) and their voiced counterparts (/v/, /ð/, /z/ and /ž/) are relative amplitude (differentiating s, š from f, θ), the spectrum of the fricative noise (differentiating /s/ from /š/), and formant transitions of vowels (Flanagan, 1965). The following is the sequence of mastery of these sounds and other relatively continuant sounds.[1]

> By age 5—/v/, /s/ and /z/ and /š/ and /ž/
> By age 5½—/č/, /r/
> By age 6—/ǰ/
> By age 6+—/θ/ and /ð/

The acoustic cues which differentiate the members of the sets continuant, strident, and the liquids /l/ and /r/ are apparently not so clearly marked as those which differentiate members of the sets mastered by age 5, although there are some similarities in the distinctions that must be observed among the members of all sets. Observations of relative amplitude and spectrum noise may be more difficult to make than observations of loci of formant transitions, and some formant transition differences (second formant differences versus third formant differences) may be easier to observe than others.

An alternative hypothesis is that, indeed, certain acoustic cues are more obscure than others, but it is their translation into articulatory gestures which causes difficulty. Early differentiation of the members of the sets stop, nasal, glide, and liquid all seem to be between labial and lingual and lingual and velar forms in these sets, and only later are other feature differentiations acquired. In the production of labials there is complete or almost complete closure of the lips; of linguals, the tip of the tongue touching the alveolar ridge; of velars, almost complete or complete closure by the back of the blade of the tongue touching or approaching the palate.

There are, in other words, clearly marked anchor points in the vocal tract which produce the acoustic consequences which match those heard. Further differentiation of the continuant, ± strident sounds (/w/, /f/) which are mastered at an early age appears to involve articulatory gestures

---

[1] The sound /"eng"/ is mastered in the medial position at age 3 and not until age 6+ in the final position. It is possible that this observation is based on V+ing constructions in which /"eng"/ is substituted by /n/. Since this can also be considered a dialect variation, /"eng"/ is excluded from this discussion.

which are not so clearly marked. The sounds /l/ and /y/ which follow the pattern of labial/lingual differentiation and labial/velar differentiation are mastered comparatively early. But the /r/, /s/, /š/, and /θ/, which are not produced with these model articulatory gestures, are mastered late. The speech sound /č/ is produced with the tongue touching the alveolar ridge but with a degree of release lying between the stop /t/ and the continuant /s/; indeed, the most frequent substitution, in Snow's study (Snow, 1963), for /č/ is /ts/ and for /ǰ/ is /dz/.

One might ask if this pattern of productive distinctions among members of speech sound sets can also be observed in perceptual distinctions. Unfortunately, at this stage there have been very few studies examining how children categorize a range of acoustic signals which cross speech sound boundaries. It has been found that young children (age 3) categorize signals which vary from /i/ to /I/ to /E/ very much the way adults do although the frequency characteristics of their production are dissimilar from those of adults. It has also been found that children (age 4 to 5) categorize signals that range from /w/ to /r/, /w/ to /l/, and /r/ to /l/ very much the way adults do, but have greater difficulty than do adults in categorizing signals in these ranges when asked to make a three-choice identification (/w/, /r/, or /l/) (Menyuk and Anderson, 1969). This latter task is, of course, closer to what actually must be accomplished in distinguishing members of this set. Children do not reproduce the stimuli in these ranges as well as they identify them in both the two-choice and the three-choice situations. For the most part, the tendency is to reproduce the stimuli as /w/. These results indicate that children of this age can perceptually identify members of this set better than they can reproduce them. Before one can observe any pattern of development in perceptual distinctions of members of sets and the sequential relationship between perception and production, children's categorization of all speech sound sets needs to be examined.

The evidence from the data on production indicates that in mapping speech sounds into morphemes certain features are used to distinguish consonantal segments within speech sound sets. Later, an additional feature distinction is made, and additional consonantal segments are distinguished. Some frequent early substitutions and later mastery can be accounted for in this manner. Figure 3–6 shows some examples of the additional features which must be observed if distinctions are to be made between certain speech sounds. The speech sound /t/ is presumably often substituted for /k/ and /θ/ (a comparatively late acquisition), the speech sounds /t/ and /θ/ for /s/ (a comparatively late acquisition) and the speech sound /w/ for /y/ and for /l/ and /r/ (comparatively late acquisitions).

Does this process of refinement take place by closer and closer approxi-

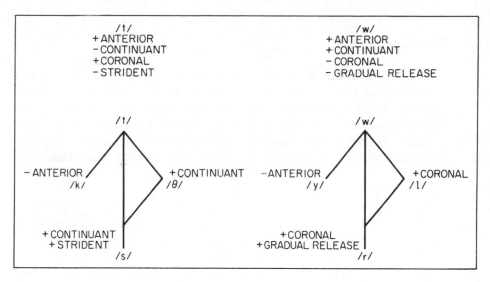

FIG. 3–6 A possible sequence of acquisition of distinctive features to further differentiate two sounds (/t/ and /w/) that are acquired early and are used in substitution for similar sounds that are acquired late. Some features of the two sounds are given at the top of the figure.

mation to adult productions? It has been hypothesized that the child acquires the speech sounds of his language by attempting to imitate adult models, matching his performance to that of adult models and correcting and modifying his performance to match these adult models until success has been achieved. An alternative hypothesis is that this process of refinement takes place, as previously described, in terms of further distinctions in the speech sound set that has been acquired, and that these distinctions follow an orderly sequence. In a study (Klein, 1969) of the acoustic properties of /r/ as produced by children, it was found that the /r/ which was identified as such by adults was no closer to an adult /r/ in terms of acoustic parameters than was an /r/ which was identified as /w/. It was the *relative position* of formant locations which distinguished between a /w/ and /r/ rather than *absolute nearness* to an adult model which made it acceptable. Therefore, the child's observation, in production, of an important distinction between two speech sounds, rather than a closer approximation to adult models, led to acceptability. The acoustic product of children's articulation of a set of sounds differs radically from that of adult models in terms of formant locations, but in differentiating between a set of vowels relative acoustic changes which are important in differentiating between them are preserved (Menyuk, 1967).

Phonological rules

In addition to omissions and substitutions of speech sounds, it has also been observed that at some stage of development a particular bundle of features comprising a speech sound may be used correctly in certain contexts at the same time that it is being omitted or substituted in other contexts. Taking as an example the development of the speech sound /ð/ in the phonological component of the grammar, the following stages may occur.

1. ð ⟶ zero in all contexts, as in " 'is" (this), " 'at" (that), "wi'." (/ð/ is not a part of the productive speech sound set, and, therefore, the child's set of rules for phonological performance is simpler than that of an adult.)
2. ð ⟶ zero or /d/ in all contexts except those of zero, as in " 'is," " 'at," "dem," and "wid." (There is some generalization of rules for phonological performance which still makes the set simpler than that of an adult.)
3. ð ⟶ zero, /d/, /v/, /ð/ in contexts a, b, c, d, as in " 'at," "dem," "bav," and "this." (Specific rules for substitution or replication of a matrix of features make the set of rules for phonological performance more complex than that of the adult).
4. ð ⟶ ð in all appropriate contexts. (The set of rules is simplified by reorganization of rules).

The above sequence of development from simpler to more complex to equal in terms of an adult model of grammar can be observed in all components of the grammar, and seems to be the developmental course taken to acquire the rules of the grammar which fit the language. These types of performance cannot be the result of imitations of adult models, but rather reflect stages in the development of the child's competence to abstract information from the data and reach tentative conclusions about the rules of the language which are then rejected in favor of those which more accurately fit the data. Results of some studies have indicated that both the position of a speech sound in a word and the syntactic structure of the word will affect whether or not a particular speech sound is omitted, substituted, or produced accurately. However, since most of these studies test production of speech sounds in a limited number of environments, the picture is far from complete. In addition, it is certainly possible that the role a particular morpheme plays in a sentence may also influence how particular sounds in these morphemes are produced. (Is it an article, a noun, etc.? Is it stressed or unstressed?) Since most of these studies test production in isolated words, our knowledge of this aspect of phonological development, the use of phonological rules, is very incomplete.

One of the contexts in which the child's knowledge of sequential rules has been observed is that of initial consonant clusters. It has been observed that at the beginning stages of consonant cluster formation the initial /s/ in an /s/ + C cluster ("spit") and the /r/ or /l/ in a C + (/r/ or /l/) cluster ("green," "glass") is frequently omitted. There is predictability in the rules found in clusters. If the sequence is C + C (as in /s/ + C clusters), then the initial segment must be /s/. If the sequence is C + −obstruant, the second segment must be /r/, /l/, or /w/. The fact that the predictable speech sound segment is omitted might be accounted for by the child's usual frequent omission at the early stages of development of grammatical aspects which are redundant. However, this would presume that the child has made some segmental analysis of morphemes beginning with initial clusters. It might also be the case that the child simply does not reproduce those segments (/s/, /r/, or /l/) which are difficult to produce accurately in the early stages of development.

There is some slight evidence that an analysis of segmental features in clusters may begin to take place at a very early age (18–24 months), long before initial clusters are adequately produced (Menyuk and Klatt, 1968). Some general principles concerning clusters versus singleton consonants are observed at the earliest stage when some segments are not being produced. The release of the consonant is lengthened ("jive" for "drive") or it is nonaspirated ("bane" for "plane"). In these instances the sequence characteristics rather than the characteristics of both segments are being observed at this stage. At a later stage segmental features of consonant sequences are observed and s + −obstruant clusters ("swim"), for example, are treated differently than s + +obstruant clusters ("stick"). The first is produced as "sim" and the second as "tick."

The sets of initial clusters in English contain certain sequences and omit others. For example, /pl/ and /kl/ are used but not /tl/. Both /sw/ and /sl/ are used but not /sr/. The sequences which are not used in English may be used in other languages. An interesting question, then, concerning the acquisition of sequential rules is how early does the child observe the phonological rules of his native language. Messer (1967) found that children aged 3 years, 3 months to 4 years, 3 months, when given pairs of syllables containing English and non-English initial and final clusters and asked to pick possible versus impossible words, showed a significant tendency to select as possible those syllables with English clusters. The "impossible" syllables were mispronounced more often than the possible, and the mispronunciations usually represented only one distinctive feature change. Messer gives as examples /ž a r j/ changed to /j a r j/, /š k ɪ b/ to /s k ɪ b/ and /ts l u f/ to /s l u f/.[2]

Morehead (1968) tested children's ability to immediately reproduce or to reproduce with some delay CCVC sequences varying in approximation to English cluster rules. Groups of children having mean ages of 4 years, 2 months; 5 years, 4 months; and 7 years and adults of about 20 years were tested. The number of exact repetitions, changes into real words, and phonetic changes which follow and which don't follow the rules were counted. The 7-year-olds most frequently produced changes which resulted in real words. The adults and children did not significantly differ in the number of phonetic changes they produced which resulted in English cluster sequences. These changes never differed from any segment in the original sequence in more than two distinctive features. Significantly more changes of syllables occurred as there was an increasing difference in the original syllable's approximation to English. These findings indicate that children who are 4 years of age have knowledge of the consonant cluster rules in their language. However, the 4-year-olds and the adults produced more phonetic changes in their reproduction of clusters which resulted in non-English sequences than did the other two groups. The experimenter attributes this last finding to lack of skill on the part of 4-year-olds and more skill on the part of adults. Although the experimenter does not state what direction these changes took, it would be interesting to know if the changes resulted in filling in gaps in English rules, such as /b w/, /f w/, /s r/, etc. Another conclusion that one might draw from these results is that the 4-year-old children had less knowledge of sequential rules in their specific language than did the other children and adults, and that the adults had more knowledge of sequencing possibilities in language in general.

Menyuk (1968a) found that children pre-school through second grade could learn possible and not possible phonological sequences equally well. There were no significant differences at any grade level between the percentage of children learning the two types of sets or in the percentage of correct responses. There was a shift in ease of learning of the two sets over the age range. Kindergarteners found the nongrammatical set easier to learn than the grammatical, while the inverse was true with second graders. There were, however, significant differences in the reproduction of the two types of sets. The task of reproducing nongrammatical sequences was much more difficult and there were significant differences between the sets at each grade level in the percentage of correct responses. The mean response time in both tasks was consistently longer for the nongrammatical sequences at each grade level. Both in grammatical and nongrammatical sets the most

---

[2] This last example of change can be considered to be more than one distinctive feature away from the original since in English phonology /ts/ is /t/ + /s/ and not a strident /t/.

frequent change was a phonetic change not a semantic change, but semantic changes occurred more frequently with grammatical than with nongrammatical sets. Most of the phonetic changes which occurred resulted in a grammatical phonological sequence.

It appears that children are aware of sequential rules in their language and of the fact that some sequences violate these rules. At what age the full set of exclusive rules has been acquired is an open question. It is certainly clear that children perform very differently when asked to reproduce possible than when asked to produce not possible sequences. It is also clear that this awareness is not limited to familiarity with sequential phonetic occurrences in words, since in reproduction the grammatical and non-grammatical sequences, which are *both* nonsense sequences, are nevertheless not treated alike. In addition, this knowledge appears to be stored as features of sounds rather than as sounds per se. In all the studies cited, modifications of both grammatical and nongrammatical sequences which occurred in the replication of these sequences by children usually resulted in a single distinctive feature change, indicating that children remembered aspects of the phonetic segments rather than the segment as a whole. There are interesting exceptions. In the Menyuk (1968a) and Messer (1967) studies all stop + strident clusters (/ts/, /gz/, etc.) were most often reproduced without the preceding stop (as /s/ or /z/, etc.). Obviously, omission of a segment cannot be equated with changing a feature. When decoding and storing an utterance in which sequential rules apply, the child perhaps determines one feature only of the initial segments (stop or strident) and then reproduces the initial cluster in accordance with these rules. Thus, in the case of reproducing stop + liquid, replacement of the liquid (/l/ for /r / or /r/ for /l/) occurs freely except in the instance where the initial segment is /d/. In this instance only /r/ follows /d/ in reproduction. In the instance where /s/ is followed by /r/, either the /s/ is replaced by a permissable strident /š/ or, much more frequently in the Menyuk study, by /st/ + /r/, and, as already noted, in the instances where a strident is preceded by a stop, the stop is omitted. These findings, plus the observations that have been made of the development of a child's production of initial clusters, indicate that perhaps information about initial clusters, at least, is stored in terms of sequential rules.

Another example of the use of sequential rules is that found in the use of morphological rules. The application of syntactic markers of person, number, tense, etc. requires the acquisition of syntactic rules.[3]

The final segment of a morpheme to which a plural marker or a past tense marker is added affects the way in which pluralization or tense is

---

[3] This aspect of development will be discussed in detail in Chapter 4, on the acquisition of syntax.

marked. Therefore, in addition to the acquisition of syntactic rules, the accurate use of these markers requires knowledge of phonological rules. Once these rules have been acquired, the rules for use of these markers are applied to the new instances as new lexical items are added to the dictionary. There is a subset of morphemes, labeled strong or irregular nouns and verbs, to which these rules do not apply. For example, the verb *be* is marked uniquely for person, number, and tense ("am," "are," "is," "was") and the plural of the noun "child" is marked uniquely in pluralization ("children"). Indeed, it is the case that verbs which are used very frequently are strong verbs. The following is a list of examples of the morphological rules for number and tense most frequently tested in experimental situations:

Plural of Nouns

1. boy, hand + plural $\longrightarrow$ boy, hand + z
2. mat, muff + plural $\longrightarrow$ mat, muff + s
3. place + plural $\longrightarrow$ place + ɪz

   but

4. wolf + plural $\longrightarrow$ wol + v + z
   house + plural $\longrightarrow$ hou + z + ɪz
5. child + plural $\longrightarrow$ children
   mouse + plural $\longrightarrow$ mice

Tense of Verbs

1. play + present participle $\longrightarrow$ play + ing
2. dance + past $\longrightarrow$ dance + t
   play + past $\longrightarrow$ play + d
3. paint + past $\longrightarrow$ paint + ɪd

   but

4. play + present, 3rd person sing. $\longrightarrow$ play + z [4]
   paint +   "   "   "   " $\longrightarrow$ paint + s
   dance +   "   "   "   " $\longrightarrow$ dance + ɪz
5. come + past $\longrightarrow$ came
   go + past $\longrightarrow$ went

Halle (1961) has described the rules for pluralization and indicates that rules for forms 1 through 3 increase in specificity. That is, the phonological

---

[4] It should be noted that the application of this tense marker follows the rules for pluralization of nouns.

context for application of the rule becomes more specific. In the spontaneous productions of children it has been observed that rules for pluralization are acquired in this order over an age range of 3 to 7 years. In the case of the specific subsets exemplified by forms 4 and 5, form 4 is acquired before 5 because the rules for form 4 apply to a number of lexical items although the number is limited whereas each item in form 5 is unique. Generalization of application of rules occurs for forms 4 and 5, and occurs in the phonologically correct form (Menyuk, 1969, Chapter 2). Thus the plural of "wolf" is produced as wolf + s (following the form used with "muff"), the plural of "house" is produced as house + ız (following the form used with "place"), and the plural of "child" is produced as child + z. In addition to this there is a period in which the irregular plural form is used plus the regular plural form (children + z as in "bins," mice + ız as in "places"), also following correct phonological rules. This latter type of performance *follows* the single addition of the general plural to the singular stem in the case of irregular nouns. Thus, forms such as child + z occur before forms such as children + z. However, this type of performance—that is, redundant use of markers—is also observed with a subset of regular nouns (wolves + ız) and on occasion with regular nouns (pencils + ız), and is still occurring during the 6 to 7 year period.

The acquisition of forms for marking tense generally follows the order indicated in the list of examples. Again, the most specific rules are acquired last, and again, generalizations and redundant use of markers occur with both irregular and regular verbs. Thus, forms such as "pushted" and "washted" (following the form used in "painted") as well as "camed" and "goed" (as in "planned" and "played") are produced.

In a recent study a comparison was made of children's ability to apply their knowledge of morphological rules to nonsense stems, using Berko's technique (Berko, 1958), and to meaningful stems (Newfield and Schlanger, 1968). Berko's technique was to ask children to complete nonsense stems by applying an appropriate marker when given a clue (for example, here is a "wug," here are two "wug-"). The children in this study, aged 5 years, 8 months to 8 years, 4 months (mean age 6.10 years), were asked to apply plural, tense, and possessive markers to real and nonsense stems. The rank order of correct responses to both real and nonsense stems, for pluralization and tense rules, generally followed the order observed in spontaneous productions. For example, the + z plural rule was more frequently correctly applied (99 percent of the instances) than the + ız plural rule (81 percent), and the +t and +d past markers were more frequently used correctly (100 percent and 100 percent) than the + ıd past marker (82 percent) and the third person, singular marker (87 percent). The children did better in applying rules to real than to nonsense stems, but the same order of difficulty was preserved with no marked differences except in the case of the + ɪz plural ending. For real stems there were 81 percent correct responses and for nonsense, 39 percent. The same order of difficulty in the application of plural rules found in this study was also found in another study with 6-year-old children in which the children were asked to pluralize nonsense names (Anisfeld and Tucker, 1967).

In spontaneous language production and experimental situations, rules which are the least restricted in terms of phonological context application are used first and most correctly, and rules which are the most restricted are used last and most incorrectly. We can observe children acquiring a set of phonological rules in a very orderly sequence reflecting the degree of complexity or number of selectional restrictions on the application of these rules. These selectional restrictions are based on a distinctive feature analysis of the context.

SUMMARY

The content and structure of infants' utterances change during the babbling period. The number of different speech sounds that are heard by the listening phonetician increases, and this change in the variety of speech sounds produced presumably has been validated in studies employing spectrographic analyses of the data. The first articulations appear to be accidents brought about by chance approximations of the articulators. Later articulations are brought about by purposeful manipulations of the articulators, by means of which the infant can replicate previous productions. The evidence that has been obtained thus far indicates that the auditory feedback mechanism may not be operative during the neonatal stage. However, the increasing number of repetitions of utterances during the babbling period may indicate increased monitoring of speech productions and the fact that the infant is testing possible productions. The proportion of usage of consonants containing certain distinctive features is greater at some stages of this developmental period than at others, and this sequence of proportional usage of consonantal sounds is similar for infants from differing linguistic environments up to and including the period in which the first meaningful utterances are produced.

Phonations which are at first only a part of the respiratory cycle—that is, they are produced at the end of an expiration—become longer than the normal expiration. The length of the utterance stabilizes, and the usual shape of the fundamental frequency contour is a terminal drop in fundamental frequency. An alternation to this pattern is a sharp rise during the utterance and then a fall at its termination. At a later stage utterances are produced with a concluding rise as well as a concluding fall in fundamental frequency. Similarly, the first meaningful structural patterns observed in the first words the infant produces are stress and intonational patterns. Thus, his early meaningful utterances appear to be not words but sentences, and their function is not to name objects but to make statements, declarative or emphatic, or to ask questions.

The sequence of events outlined here seems to stem directly from increasing control of the respiratory and articulatory mechanisms during phonation and of the auditory-feedback mechanism. This increasing control results in a capacity to detect and reproduce both segmental and structural aspects of the speech signal. The infant can and does produce many of the speech sounds, but not all, in CV, CVCV, and CVC sequences, and at the end of this period indicates that he can discriminate between some of the sequences he hears.

The number of facts that are not available to us about this early period of language development, from babbling to the first meaningful utterances, far exceed those that are available in terms of the parameters both of what is perceived and of what is produced. New approaches to the study of this period, such as examining the infant's discrimination of speech sound differences and tracing the acquisition of different parameters of the speech signal (such as voicing) in his productions, may provide these presently unavailable facts. We may then be able to describe the course of development during this period in detail, and to determine more exactly the relationship between what is acquired during this period and what is used at a later period of language acquisition.

Most of the data that have been collected in the phonological development of the child have been production data and not perception data. It is clear, however, that the child's production does not accurately reflect his perception of speech sound sequence differences or speech sound differences. From an analysis of children's productions, the process of development of the phonological system represents a hierarchy of feature distinctions beginning with the consonant vowel distinction, then distinctions between speech sound sets (between nasals, glides, stridents, and stops), and finally with distinctions among the members of these sets. Distinctions among members of certain sets (liquids, stridents, and continuants) are late acquisitions, whereas distinctions among members of other sets (nasals, stops, and glides) are early acquisitions. It has been hypothesized that this late acquisition of certain distinctions and early acquisition of others is due to the fact that the acoustic cues which differentiate the late speech sounds are much more subtle than those which differentiate the early speech sounds, and that it is much more difficult to translate these subtle cues into appropriate articulatory gestures. There is at present no evidence available to indicate whether or not the above sequence of development in production can also be found in the speech sound discrimination of children. It has been found only that certain features are more often preserved than others in the frequent speech sound substitutions of children who are in the process of acquiring the phonological system of their language; certain features are more often preserved than others in children's repetition of CV sequences; and certain features are more often preserved than others in determining which phonological sequence is the match of a model phonological sequence. In all of these situations the rank ordering of feature preservation is for the most part the same. Voicing and nasality are the features most frequently preserved and continuancy and place are the features least preserved.

In addition to acquiring the distinctive features which will distinguish the speech sounds in the language, children during the period of phonological acquisition also acquire the rules of their language which pertain to sequential segments. Both consonant cluster rules and morphological rules have been examined, and to a lesser extent the effect of position of the speech sound in the morpheme and the structure of the morpheme on the realization of the matrix of features of a speech sound segment. Although the data are limited, it has been found that these latter factors do affect the manner in which a speech sound segment is realized.

Consonant cluster rules begin to be acquired at an early age, and at age 3 children can distinguish between sequences that are permissible in their language and those that are not. However, it is not clear that they have acquired the complete set of exclusive rules at this age, since 4-year-old children more often produce phonetic changes which result in non-English sequences. It is clear that in *reproducing* initial consonant clusters English cluster rules are applied and non-English clusters are modified to conform with these rules. In most instances this results in one distinctive feature change in a segment of a cluster, indicating that segments are recalled in terms of their features rather than as speech sounds. However, there are other instances in which changes of more than one feature occur and, in fact, whole segments are deleted or added. These results indicate that clusters may be stored and recalled in terms of rules rather than as bundles of distinctive features for each segment of the cluster. In the use of morphological rules the pattern of development seems clear, and the same pattern is found in spontaneous speech and in test situations. The more *specific* the *context* in which the rule must be applied, the later the acquisition of the rule. In other terms, the greater the number of selectional restrictions for the application of the rule, the later the appearance of the appropriate rule. This same sequence can be observed in the acquisition and development of syntactic rules, as we shall see. Before more complicated rules are acquired and used in both the phonological and syntactic components of the grammar, rules that have already been acquired are *generalized* to other instances.

The study of the acquisition and development of the phonological system of the language is at its beginning stages. The use of techniques such as spectrographic analysis and the computer for analyzing and averaging data can be helpful in obtaining the details of this development, but only if interesting and pertinent questions are asked. These questions are concerned with the sequence of acquisition of distinctive feature differences both in perception and production and the sequence of acquisition of phonological rules within morphemes and within sentences.

4

THE ACQUISITION
OF
SYNTAX

WHAT WE SAY is interpreted by the form in which we say it, the lexical content of what we say, and the situational context in which it is said. A dictionary definition of language is as follows: the words, their pronunciation and methods of combining them, used and understood by a considerable community, to communicate ideas and feelings. In this chapter and the next we will be concerned primarily with the child's acquisition and development of methods of combining words together or, in other words, the development of syntactic rules. With these rules, which are finite in number, the child can generate an infinite number of different sentences conveying different meanings. We will also be concerned with his comprehension of these varying combinations of words.

One of the primary tasks of the child in acquiring his language is to determine how differing relationships are expressed in the sentences of his language. He must learn the syntactic forms used in his language to express subject-predicate relationships, modifier-topic relationships, affirmative-negative relationships, question-declarative relationships, etc. He must learn the syntactic forms used to express reference, tense, number, etc. Some questions that one might explore in studying the process of syntax acquisition are: (1) what forms does the child use to express various meanings at different stages of development? (2) what is the relationship between comprehension and production? and (3) why are some forms produced or understood before others?

Recent research in the child's acquisition of syntax has provided the following kinds of data: descriptions of the form of the utterances children produce from approximately 18 months to approximately 13 years and, to a much lesser extent, experimental data concerning the child's comprehension of various syntactic structures at certain ages. Much of the data on early syntactic development has been obtained in longitudinal studies of the utterances produced by a small group of children. In these studies language is sampled periodically over a number of months or years.

FIRST SENTENCES

The analysis of the syntactic structures used by children has usually begun at the point at which the child is, for the most part, producing two- or three-word utterances. However, as has been noted, there is a period before this in which the child seems to produce sentencelike words. He says "No!" or "No. No. No." and is telling us he can't have it or telling himself not to take it. He says "No?" and is asking us if he can have it.

There have been no detailed studies of the structure of the utterances produced by children at this stage of development. As has been discussed, there is some evidence that children do apply stress and intonational markers to single-word utterances in a generative manner—that is, applying these markers to the same word as in the examples given of the word *no*. However, very little data have been collected thus far. Until there is a careful analysis of the prosodic features of the utterances of more than one child in conjunction with an analysis of the situation, this is simply a hypothesis.

It may very well be that parents interpret these utterances in varying ways because of the situational context and logical possibilities as well as the structure of the utterance itself. For example, if the child points to a box of soap powder that he has been forbidden to touch and says "Mommy?" with an interrogative contour, it is not assumed that the child is confusing the box with his mother. A logical reply would be "No! Don't touch it," rather than "No! That's not mommy." Another aspect, then, of development during this period, which has yet to be detailed, is a description of these interactions and an examination of the role they play in syntax acquisition. Categories of interaction such as imitation, "expansion," and "modeling" have been examined at a somewhat later stage of development.

Several observations have been made about the structure of the utterances produced at this stage of development. The first is that these single-word utterances do not belong to any single grammatical class. They can be classified, according to dictionary classifications, as nouns, verbs, adjectives, and prepositions (Menyuk, 1969, Chapter 2). There may be a great similarity in the lexical items used by all children at this stage (the early use of words such as "momma," "pappa," "bye-bye," "bow-wow," "no," and onomatopoetic words such as "tick-tock") (Lewis, 1963, pp. 34–35), but there may also be great dissimilarity due to situational circumstances or the emphasis placed on particular lexical items in the environment. The second observation is that these single-word utterances are not functionally used to name objects. They may be used or interpreted as imperatives, declaratives, or interrogatives. The third observation is that these single-word utterances may be articulated in a standard manner or in a distorted manner, or they be inventions of the child. The fourth observation is that during this stage the child may be producing long babbled utterances containing no recognizable lexical items but marked by intonation and stress, as well as single, recognizable lexical items. Thus there may be an over-lapping usage of the structures observed at an earlier stage together with new structures. This overlapping or simultaneous use of structures used previously and new acquisitions can be found throughout all developmental stages.

In pursuance of the questions posed earlier: (1) the forms the child uses to express various meanings at this stage of development are single lexical items marked by intonation and emphasis; (2) the order of usage of these forms seems to be from the early imperative utterance of cry and declarative utterance of cooing to declarative, imperative, and question utterances in babbling, from babbled utterances to declarative, question, imperative, and negative single-word sentences. Comprehension of the meaning of lexical items, prosodic features, and, to some extent, the structure of the sentences in which they are produced seems to precede production of the lexical item by several months, but it is not clear that this is the case in all instances.[1]

Why is the form "lexical item plus sentence-type markers" used at this stage? There are some obvious answers to this question. First, the child may only have the capacity to store in memory the features and properties of a single lexical item and not a sequence of items for productive generation. Second, the very salient aspects of the structure of the utterances heard are their stress and intonation patterns. However, the particular choice of lexical items for use in children's generation of these utterances is not completely accounted for by these explanations. In other words, the question of the basis of selection of particular items has not been answered. Is it isolated bits heard, first bits, last bits, or stressed bits?

The child often hears the lexical item in a sentence, rather than as an isolated word outside of routines, such as "bye-bye." He seems to respond

---

[1] It has been noted that a child responds to the word "no" at 9 months of age, but uses the word "yes" at 20 months and does not respond to it until 21 months (Lewis, 1963, p. 43).

to the entire sentence and not simply the word. In the acquisition of a lexical item ("flower"), Lewis (1963, p. 59) notes that when asked "Where are the flowers?" or "Baby, where are the flowers?" the infant crawls to them or points to them, but when asked to "Smell the pretty flowers," he does not point to the flowers but smells them. His first spontaneous use of the word, however, is not in a sentence. He seems to select from the utterance the *topic* of the sentence. In the use of lexical items "light" and "on" by a child (Menyuk, 1969, Chapter 2), the following observations were made. The mother first used the item "light" in utterances such as "See the light," "Look at the light," when the light was on. The baby looked at the light or pointed to the light. The mother at some other time said, "Turn the light on," "Turn the light off," while she manipulated the switch. When producing the utterance "light," the child points to the light. When producing the utterance "on," the child points either to the light when it is on or to the switch when the light is off. At some later stage he climbs on a chair and manipulates the switch as he says "light on," "light off." His choice, then, of lexical items in the utterance he produces is dependent on what he is talking about and is used in conjunction with a particular action.

This *topic* may or may not be a naturally stressed item in the utterances the child hears. In these first sentences and in the first two- or three-word utterances produced by children, it has been observed that articles, copulas, and other so-called function words are omitted. It has been suggested that the reason for these omissions is the fact that these function words are not stressed in the utterances children hear (Brown and Bellugi, 1964). This factor might then account for the selection of items from utterances and, thus, the content of early sentences, but it is difficult to observe any grammatical classes that are consistently omitted. Quantifiers (such as "more"), prepositions (such as "on," "off"), and even instances of the use of the article are found in early two-word sentences.[2] It is possible, however, that grammatical classes which are normally unstressed will be stressed by parents in speaking to their children. No record of this information has as yet been obtained.

Shipley, Smith, and Gleitman (1965) compared the responses of children, aged 15 to 30 months, to varying types of utterances: N (horn), VN (blow horn), "telegraph" (Please, John blow horn), Imperative (blow on the horn), and utterances containing nonsense forms for the N, V, etc. Toy objects were present in the room and the noun of the utterance was always the name of a toy which the subjects could identify. The verbs used were either appropriate, such as "blow," or neutral such as "show" and "give." Relevant responses were categorized as touching (sometimes carry-

---

[2] For a sampling of such early utterances see: Braine, 1963; Brown and Fraser, 1964; Menyuk, 1969; Miller and Ervin, 1964.

ing out the task) or looking at the toy, a repetition of the utterance, or a reply to the command. The study population was divided into two groups: less advanced (primarily one-word spontaneous productions) and more advanced (primarily two-word spontaneous productions). Although the experimenters were not particularly concerned with the effect of varying stress on responses, some of their results are relevant to the question of the role of stress in the comprehension of utterances and selection of items for regeneration when children are primarily at the one-word utterance stage.

For the more advanced group, responses were made most often to the grammatical imperative sentence. With the less advanced children relevant responses were obtained most frequently with the word in isolation (necessarily the noun and necessarily stressed), and to the word-separated delivery of the telegraph utterance with each item distinctly stressed, in that order. However, the experimenters note that the presence of a known or familiar item was the primary factor in obtaining a relevant response with the less advanced group of children and that any sentence context at all appeared to make recognition of a known word more difficult. From the results of this study it seems that less advanced children seem to pay attention only to that item in the string with which they are most familiar, rather than to stress. In the "telegraph" utterance, although each item was equally stressed, the rule seems to be to ignore everything until you get to a recognizable morpheme. With the more advanced children it appears to be the structure of the utterance rather than the stressed word which cues a response. These are only partial answers. One would have to use stimulus material which is deviantly stressed to examine further the effect of stress on response to utterances, and this would necessarily eliminate the single-word utterance.

Blasdell and Jensen (1968) conducted a study with 2½- to 3-year old children to observe the effect of stress and *position* on recall of syllables. The material used was four nonsense syllables. The position of each syllable and the degree of stress on each syllable was varied at each presentation. Correct recall of a syllable was significantly affected by primary stress and position. Syllables heard last in a series of four were significantly more frequently correctly recalled. This study indicates that children of this age are sensitive to the acoustic cues of stress in the recall of a string of nonsense syllables and that the last syllable in this string of nonsense is more frequently correctly recalled. However, this study tells us very little about the role of these factors in recalling sentences or the role these factors play in the acquisition of structures. The question is, would the results have been the same if the nonsense syllables had been words in a sentence?

The data obtained in the Shipley, Smith, and Gleitman (1965) study also indicate that comprehension does not precede production with the less advanced group. Although the more linguistically mature group were still primarily producing utterances without articles or object pronouns, they responded most frequently to the completely well formed imperative sentences. On the other hand, the least linguistically mature children, who were primarily producing single-word utterances, also responded most frequently to single-word utterances. The gap between comprehension and production evidenced by the more linguistically mature children was not in evidence with the less advanced group. There may, then, be stages of development during which comprehension precedes production and others during which comprehension and production are closely matched. In acquiring new structures the child may be spending a period of time observing certain structures and how they are used, not producing them until some later time. He may then spend a period of time producing these structures and observing how well his production matches his observations before he again observes other structures. However, the experiment cited does not settle the issue of a possible gap between comprehension and production at the primarily one-word sentence stage. These findings may be very much confounded by the possibility of different strategies of response being used by the two groups, or what they thought the game was all about, or the role of intention (what the child intends to comprehend or produce), rather than marked differences in linguistic comprehension. Indeed, when we observe the number of responses which are most relevant—that is, following the command—we note that *some children* in the least mature group respond almost equally frequently to the completely well-formed imperative as to the isolated noun, and do so more frequently than do some children in the intermediate and most mature group.

Two possible ways of testing the width of the gap between comprehension and production at this stage are having the child repeat various structures which appear at a somewhat later stage of development in the utterances they produce, and having them repeat utterances which contain deviances ("horn blow," "the blow on horn," etc.). Although repetition was not given as a task in the Shipley, Smith, and Gleitman study, spontaneous repetition was observed. Repetition was the least frequent response in the total set of relevant responses measured, but the linguistically more mature group repeated to a greater extent than did the less mature group. A tentative conclusion that may be drawn from these results is that the likelihood and accuracy of repetition may be the result of the level of linguistic competence of the child—that is, of what he understands about the structure of the utterance. The technique of directly eliciting repetitions has not been used at this early stage of development, although it has been used with children who are somewhat older. In fact, the amount of experimentation and even the number of direct observations and comparisons of comprehension and production are severely limited at this stage of development.

DEVELOPMENT OF MODIFICATION

Two factors have been called upon to explain the changes in the structure of the utterances observed during this early period: that of maturation of capacities both peripheral and central, and the necessity of conveying more specific meaning in an expanding environment in some economical manner. As the child becomes more mobile and enters into situations with objects and people he has not encountered previously, his sentence-like utterances may not meet the requirements of the situation and, therefore, he expands his utterances. For example, "candy!" may become "want candy!" which may become "want more candy!" which may become "want more green candy!"

Several questions arise about "need for definition" and "economy" as explanations of further expansions. It is conceivable that by gesture and single-word utterances the child's needs would continue to be fulfilled even in new situations. In addition, although it is more economical to convey in a single utterance what is declared, demanded, and questioned rather than in several utterances and gestures, the child still has the task of determining the ways in which this economy is achieved. Economy appears to be the product rather than the motivation for further expansion. Finally, the structure of the expansion of utterances described above is not what actually takes place in the utterances produced. It is only at some later stage, the stage at which he is producing subject + predicate sentences, that the child puts together "want candy!" "more candy!" and "green candy," although words such as these may appear together in the utterances he hears.

Since sentences generally increase in length as children mature, and it is a fact that auditory memory span, at least for digits, as measured by standard intelligence tests, increases as children mature, it has been presumed that auditory memory span is a mechanism which has now developed and permits the production of longer utterances. It might also be presumed, although there have been no controlled tests of this function, that there are limitations on the vocal motor mechanisms of young children which restrict the length of typical utterances. It is possible that, if asked to repeat a syllable as many times as possible until he ran out of breath, a younger child would produce fewer syllables than an older child. It has been observed that children speak at slower rates than adults (Mac-Kay, 1968). Therefore, the utterances understood and produced should reflect these restrictions on memory span and productive span. However, although these explanations may account for the restrictions and expansions of the *length* of utterances, they do not account for the *content* and *structure* of these utterances even at an early stage of development.

Several things have been observed about these early sentences. First, classes which are traditionally conceived of as nonstressed (articles and prepositions) do appear in these utterances. Second, there seem to be restrictions imposed on the sequence of occurrence of morphemes in these utterances. For example, sequences such as "shoe my," "knee a," "baby it," "box that," and "shoe see" do not occur. Therefore, the selection of the morphemes produced and their arrangement appears to be nonrandom. Some of the utterances produced contain sequential combinations which children never hear. These children appear to be selecting certain morphemes from the utterances they hear and arranging their sequence in particular ways. What will be discussed now is the structure of these utterances and the functions they may serve in communication or the meanings that are expressed in these structures.

One manner of characterizing these utterances has been to classify them into pivot and open categories. A small group of morphemes in the pivot class occur with many morphemes in the open class. Thus we find utterances such as "see shoe," "see horsie," "see pencil," etc., with "see" belonging to the pivot class. The assumption being made in this description is that the child has categorized his lexicon into classes, and thus generates his utterances by selecting from the open class (O) in the case of single-word utterances or from either the open class twice (O, O) or the pivot and open class (P, O) in the case of longer utterances (McNeill, 1966). Sentences may be generated in the following manner: S ⟶ (P)O.

In Table 4–1 is a list of utterances taken from the language samples obtained by Braine (1963), Brown and Fraser (1964), Miller and Ervin

TABLE 4–1   EARLY TWO AND THREE WORD UTTERANCE

A		B		C
⌈big ⌉	boat	sweater	⌈off ⌉	a gas [here]
my	shoe	truck	⌊here?⌋	[there] bye-bye car
mommy	pencil	⌈it ⌉	horsie	[want] up
a	knee	⌊that⌋	box	[annuder one] shoes
the	dolly's	shoe	⌈fall⌉	[all gone] lettuce
want	baby	Rick	⌊go ⌋	paper kitchen table
have	it!	⌈where⌉	baby	
see	shoe?	⌊what ⌋	that	
no	a book			
no	truck			
⌊no ⌋	my			

(1964), and Menyuk (1969) at the stage at which two- or three-word utterances are being produced. As stated earlier, the language samples were obtained by periodically recording the utterances of a small group of children over a period of months or years beginning at the stage when two-word utterances were predominant. The bracketed words are those which have been classified as "pivot" in the literature and the unbracketed have been classified as "open" (Braine, 1963). The categorization of these utterances under the headings A, B, C will be discussed somewhat later.

The difficulty with this assumption that the child classifies his lexicon into the classes P and O is that it proposes that the child can classify before he has made any observations about the functional relationships expressed in utterances. This is contrary to logic. Morphemes in an utterance are classified according to the roles they play in these utterances. They are subjects (NPs), predicates (VPs), objects (NPs). They further define subjects (Determiners) or predicates (Prepositional phrases), etc. The Pivot-Open dichotomization seems to characterize the experimenter's classifications rather than the child's. There is, however, a similarity between the structure of the language that is being used by the children in all the studies cited and, as Slobin (In press) has found, the language of children about the same age in other linguistic environments. The question is how can one characterize this regularity or similarity. Slobin has described the functions of the pivot word in the utterances of English, German, and Russian children in the following manner. They are used to modify ("pretty," "my," "good," "all gone"), to locate and name ("there," "see," "it," "that"), to describe an act ("away," "on," "off," "walk"), to demand ("more," "give," "want," "please"), and to negate ("no," "don't," "not"). However, these are obviously not exclusive categorizations. For example, the word "more" is not only used to demand but also to modify, and the words "on" and "off" are used not only to describe an act but also to locate. These words have different functions which are dependent on the structure of the utterances and the context in which they are used.

It has been pointed out that the single-word utterances of children have an assertive function rather than being simply a labeling of objects in the environment. Something is being declared, questioned, demanded, or emphasized about something. In other terms, the *topic* of the sentence is now being modified. Gruber (1967a) has noted that although the "topic-comment" construction does not exist in English per se, it does exist in other languages. The subject-predicate construction found in English is a special case of the topic-comment construction. A possible linguistic description of the sentences that are generated at this stage may then be: S ⟶ (Modifier) Topic. From this description we observe that morphemes which have been classified as pivots because they occur with a number of other morphemes can either be topics or modifiers depending on the role they play in an utterance. Thus, under the heading *B* in Table 4–1 some pivot morphemes happen to serve as topics in the utterances ("it" and "that"), while others do not.

One other observation can be made about these utterances when the usual context in which they are produced is taken into account. They either appear to be predicate constructions as in set *A* or subject + predicate constructions as in set *B*. Sentences in set *A* may have underlying unexpressed subjects such as: "(That's a) big boat," "(That's) the dolly's," "(I) want baby," "(Do you) see shoe?" Sentences in set *B* all contain subjects and can be completed with the copula verb or some verb inflection such as "Sweater (is) off," "It (is a) horsie," "Shoe (did) fall." Subjects of sentences never appear alone, and predicate sentences appear before subject + predicate sentences.[3]

By observing the changes that occur in longer utterances that contain the same lexical items as do shorter utterances produced at an earlier stage, Braine (1965) also concludes that the earliest utterances are predicate phrases. An example of such a progression is that first the item "chair" may be produced, then "pussycat chair," then "pussycat on chair."

Gruber (1967b) has characterized some of these early utterances as performatives and somewhat later utterances as reportatives. The exemplars given seem to be predicate constructions in the case of performatives and subject + predicate constructions in the case of reportatives. The following are some of the examples given:

Performatives	*Reportatives*
me sock	Kathleen coming
no my	Teddy all gone
want beads?	Donnie out
see a pretty	Powder back

Performative sentences are those which do not attribute any characteristics to the topic of the sentences but, instead, are used to demand or indicate. These sentences are a verbalization of what one does by means of the utterance and at the time of the utterance (Ross, In press). Thus, "me sock" may have the meaning "I demand my sock" or "I say to you that that's my sock," and "see a pretty" may have the underlying meaning "I say to you that that's a pretty" or "I demand that you see a pretty" or "I ask do you see a pretty," depending on the stress and the intonational marker of the utterance. Gruber and others have noted that the child will

---

[3] For a fuller discussion of this development, see Menyuk, 1969, Chapter 2.

often be pointing to an object or holding out an object or be stretching out his hands in demanding an object or rejecting an object when producing these sentences. These utterances, therefore, serve an immediate function of labeling an overt act of declaring, demanding, negating, or questioning. Because of the actions accompanying these utterances and the prosodic features of these utterances, as well as their content, they convey basic meanings quite adequately if nonredundantly and can be classified under the following headings, despite the fact that they do not have the completely well-formed structure of these sentence types:

Declarative	Question	Imperative	Negative
big boat	want beads?	want baby!	no my
the dolly's	truck here?	more pencil!	no touch!
sweater off	where baby?	me sock!	no a book

Presumably stress and intonation are used not only in the manner described above, but also to indicate further differentiation of meaning within sentence types. Slobin (In press) cites such an example. "Christy room" with stress on the first word in the utterance indicates "Christy's room" or possession. "Christy roóm" with stress on the second word in the utterance indicates "Christy's in the room" or some prepositional phrase. Thus various meanings can be conveyed without employing the structural devices conventionally used by adults.

ACQUISITION OF STRUCTURES AND TRANSFORMATIONAL OPERATIONS

The universals of language—that is, those aspects which can be found in all languages—have been the subject of much study and discussion. The topic + modifier construction, the negation, question, and imperative constructions are considered universal aspects of language although different languages may realize these constructions in varying ways. They are probably universal aspects of language because of the communicative functions they serve. It has also been hypothesized that all languages have the same underlying base structure rules, although the order of elements in these base structure rules may vary from language to language. The first rule in the base component is described as follows: S $\longrightarrow$ (and/or) S. Thus, sentences can be generated by the conjunction of two or more sentences. The early sentences of children appear to be such conjunctions. If at some earlier stage of development the child's grammar consists of rules for the generation of one-word sentences, and memory span increases, the simplest procedure would be to add one sentence to another. However, in addition to joining one-word sentences together, it has been noted that restrictions are observed by the child on the conjunction of elements both in terms of the properties of these elements and of their order in the sentence. The child does conjoin elements but not freely.

In an analysis of the classes of the language which are found in sequence in the utterances of children, McNeill (1966) found that there were some sequences which were not used in these utterances. For example, sequences such as VVN ("go sit down," "come get your coat," etc.), which frequently appear in adult language, were not found. All sequences are described as being generated by rule (1) S $\longrightarrow$ NP + NP or rule (2) S $\longrightarrow$ Pred. P, Pred. P. $\longrightarrow$ V + NP. Thus, utterances such as "That my coat" are produced from rule (1) but not "my coat that," and utterances such as "want that coat" are produced from rule (2) but not "that coat want." Rule (1) and a conjunction of rules (1) and (2) (which may produce the sequence N V NP as in "me want that coat") result in the subject-predicate construction. The basic grammatical relationships in the language of subject ("that," "me")-predicate ("my coat," "want that coat"); verb ("want")-object ("that coat"); and determiner ("my")-noun ("coat") are realized in the sentences produced by these rules and are not violated in terms of ordering of segments. Inversions such as predicate-subject ("want that coat me"); object-verb ("that coat want"); and noun-determiner ("coat my") are not found in the language samples of children of this age. Ordering seems to be playing an important role in the structure of these utterances. However, this ordering is not a direct reflection of the ordering found in the language produced by adults, but rather an expression of universal grammatical relationships.[4]

Some other factors outside of the expression of a basic grammatical relation may be in operation as well. If we take the same *sequence* of *classes* but substitute among them, some utterances seem to be possible candidates for children's productions but others do not. If we exchange NPs produced by rule (1) ("my coat that"), or exchange NPs in a conjunction of rules (1) and (2) ("that coat want me"), or exchange the subject NP of rules (1) and (2) for the object NP of rule (2) ("want me"), utterances are produced which not only seem more peculiar than those actually produced but also never appear in the language samples that have been collected. Restrictions may be observed concerning the morphemes which can appear in particular grammatical relationships in utterances and, thus, one may observe some selectional restrictions based

---

[4] Slobin (In press) notes that although the typical order in Russian sentences is subject-object-verb, the sequence in the early sentences of Russian children is the same as that for American children—i.e., subject-verb-object.

on the syntactic properties of the particular lexical items used. Items that may be conjoined in early sentences are those that are syntactically identical ("that box"), have reference to each other ("big boat," "sweater off"), and indicate possession ("mommy pencil").[5]

There may also be selectional restrictions based on the semantic properties of lexical items. We observe utterances such as "mommy sit" and "me sit" but not "shoe sit" and rarely such utterances as "happy hair." Restrictions may be in operation between the constituents and within the constituents NP and VP, but the data are too sparse to come to any conclusions about the child's competence in this aspect of the grammar in early sentences. One way of approaching the study of this question is to test children's responses and the latency of responses to anomalous and nonanomalous constructions such as: "show me happy hair" and "show me long hair"; "blow the horn" and "blow the drum." The question that has yet to be answered in full is: What is the nature of the restrictions that the child uses to conjoin items in early sentences? The only comment that can be made at present is that some restrictions concerning conjunction of items can be observed in the utterances produced.

As was noted, the four sentence types, declarative, imperative, question, and negative, are being produced at this stage. All are being produced by the operation of conjunction of topics and modifiers, at the earliest stage, plus prosodic features. Thus, they are being produced without the specific structures and rules found in the language. The application of rules specific to the language is dependent on the development of structure.

At the earliest stage of development, sentences conveying the meaning of declaration, imperative, question, and negation have a typical form exemplified by the utterances under heading A in Table 4–2. Eventually they are completely well formed and may take several possible shapes, some of which are indicated under the heading C in Table 4–2. In the transitions between early productions and the completely well-formed productions, sentences are produced which show some development but are not yet completely well formed in certain specific ways, as indicated in the examples under heading B in Table 4–2.

Several changes are occurring in the development from A to C types of productions.[6] One change is the use of the subject-predicate structure in all sentences. Thus, for example, "big boat" becomes "that big boat" and "want shoe" becomes "me want shoe." "No play" becomes "I no play" and "see shoe?" becomes "Mommy see shoe?" Another development is expansion of the VP to now include auxiliary verbs, copula and the modals

---

[5] See a discussion of these restrictions in Gruber, 1967a.
[6] For a more detailed description of these transitions, see Gruber, 1967a; Klima and Bellugi, 1966; and Menyuk, 1969, Chapter 3.

TABLE 4–2   STAGES IN THE DEVELOPMENT OF DECLARATIVE, NEGATIVE,
QUESTION AND IMPERATIVE SENTENCES

	A Early	B In Between	C Later
Declarative	That box Big boat Rick go	That's box That big boat Rick going	That's a box That's a big boat Rick is going
Negative	No play No a book No fall down	I no play That not book (a) I not falling down (b) I'm not fall down	I won't play That's not a book I'm not falling down
Question	See shoe? Truck here? Where baby?	Mommy see shoe? Truck's here? (a) Where baby is? (b) Where's baby is?	Do you see the shoe? Is the truck here? Where's the baby?
Imperative	Want baby! No touch! Have it!		I want the baby or Give me the baby! Don't touch it! Give it to me!

(can, do, will) plus some inflections (present participle ending, as in "going"). For example, "that box" becomes "that's box" (or perhaps, "Thassa box"), "where baby?" becomes "where baby is?" and "no fall down" becomes "I'm not fall down" or "I not falling down." No transitional changes can be observed in the structure of imperative sentences, although one can postulate that an important development for this structure is the development of the *pronoun* class. In the early subject-predicate question ("mommy see shoe") the pronoun "you" is not used, but in the later question we find examples of its use ("Do you see the shoe?"). The final forms of this structure include subjects ("I want the baby!"), the modal *do* ("Don't touch it!"), and deletion of the subject "you" ("Give it to me!").

Other developments occur which are not structural acquisitions but, rather, operational changes or transformations on the structures that are now available. When the subject-predicate structure is being used, negative elements are found within the sentence and attached to the main verb ("I not fall down"). When auxiliary verbs and modals are being used, the negative element is attached to them ("I won't play"). When the VP is expanded in question utterances, the *wh* elements are found within the sentence ("Where's baby is?") and the verb or modal permuted ("Where's baby?").

The first development appears to be acquisition of structures, and the second, operations on these structures—and operations of a certain kind. There is sequential ordering in the kinds of operations used to generate these sentence types. The first kind of operation which can be observed is conjunction (S and S) to generate (modifier) topic sentences. The next is embedding of elements within a sentence, which is now composed of the subject + predicate structure. The final kind of operation involves permutation of elements. As will be seen, there is great similarity between the order of application of operations to generate these simple sentence types at this stage of development and the order of application of operations to generate more complex sentence types at a later stage of development when subject + predicate structures are combined with other subject + predicate structures. Possibly this may be due to the fact that sentences in which the NP and the VP of a sentence are not separated and appear in that order are more easily understood than those in which there are intrusions.[7] The order of the operations used to generate these sentence types may be dependent on the child's perceptual strategies—that is, on the way in which he goes about analyzing the structure of the sentences he hears regardless of their actual form.

It has been noted that a certain structure appears in some sentence types before it appears in others (Ervin-Tripp, 1963). The modal *do* appears in negative ("I don't play") and elliptic sentences ("I do") and, one might add, in negative imperative sentences ("Don't touch!") long before it appears in questions. It has been hypothesized, therefore, that the application of the *do-support* transformation is learned separately and independently for each sentence type. The case of the elliptic sentence may be accounted for by the fact that *do* in this instance is not a modal but in a special class of verbs which can appear with and without objects (for example, "I eat" and "I eat apples"). The other early occurrences of "do" with the negative might simply be the appearance of memorized forms rather than an application of rules, since both "can't" and "don't" are observed before these modals are used in declarative sentences. However, it is the case that when children are always producing completely well-formed aux/modal inversion questions ("Isn't that funny?" and "Do you remember me?"), they are also producing wh questions (what, where, when, how, why) with and without modal ("How you take it out?") and with or without permutation ("What you are writing?") (Menyuk, 1969,

---

[7] An example given by Fodor and Garrett, 1966, of a sentence in which there are intrusions between NPs and VPs is "The man the dog the girl owned bit died." Because of the permutation of subject and object in the passive construction this is much more difficult to understand than "The man who died was bitten by the dog that was owned by the girl." This latter sentence is more difficult to understand than "The dog that was owned by the girl bit the man who died."

Chapter 3). Wh questions appear early and long before aux/modal inversion questions since these latter questions are dependent on the expansion of the VP to include aux/modal, whereas the former can convey meaning without this development.

A possible explanation for the differences observed in the application of rules for the generation of these two types of question sentences may be in the differences in their structures. At earlier stages of development, questions take the form either of declarative sentence + intonational marker or of wh morpheme + sentence. The wh morpheme clearly marks the fact that a question is being asked, whereas the application of only an intonational marker may cause communicative confusion. The child may then be careful to indicate in such sentences the ways in which question is clearly marked before he performs similarly with wh questions. At this stage of development there may be structures and manipulative operations which are available to the child, but which he does not always use in the generation of utterances because they make no critical distinctions. Those aspects of utterances which the child searches for first and then uses to generate his own utterances may then be those which most clearly and effectively communicate intended meaning.

It has been observed that at the earliest stage of negative and question sentence usage the child does not appear to comprehend embedded negatives or the what-object questions (Klima and Bellugi, 1966). At the transitional stages of negative and question formation he does comprehend embedded negatives and responds appropriately to questions. In addition to the fact that these are simply observations, it also should be noted that at the transitional stages of negation formation the child is already embedding negatives ("I no play," "That not book"). At the transitional stages of wh questions the wh element is either a part of the sentence or embedded, and the child is just omitting auxiliary or modal verbs or not permuting. It is possible that at this transitional stage the child comprehends more about these structures than he produces. It is also possible that the child simply can pay no attention to the auxiliary and modal or their position in these utterances and still respond appropriately.

It is the case, then, at the transitional stage of development of these sentence types that certain structures—the auxiliary and modal verbs and the manipulative operation of permutation—do not appear in all sentence types at the same time. It may be the case that these structures and the manipulation of these structures are comprehended before they are produced. It may, however, be the case that comprehension of these structures is not necessary for the comprehension of these utterances. On the other hand, acquisition of the subject-predicate structure and sequential acquisition of the operations of conjunction and embedding appear in all sentence types simultaneously and these may, indeed, be the syntactic aspects which are basic for the comprehension of these sentence types.

EXPANSION OF BASE STRUCTURE RULES

Changes which occur in the structure of the sentences produced during this early stage of development are best characterized as expansion of base structure rules. Noun phrase is expanded into determiner + noun and noun + number. The verb phrase is expanded into verb + prepositional phrase and verb + particle. The auxiliary is expanded into tense, modal, and be + ing.

It has been observed in the utterances produced by Russian and German children that demonstratives are used rather than articles and particles rather than verbs in many instances, taking the place of these classes (Slobin, In press). The earlier sentences produced by American children also indicate the predominant use of particles instead of verbs in utterances. The demonstratives "this" and "that," on the other hand, are not used to modify NPs (as, for example, "This book here") but rather as NPs as in "This (is) here," "That (is) shoe" with the copula omitted. The same structure can be observed containing particles such as "That (is) off," "Shoe (is) on," and "Pencil (is) in." Notice that all these utterances can be described as subject + predicate sentences and that all these utterances described a *fixed state*. There are also instances of sentences composed of verb phrase such as "fix shoe" and "want bottle." Early development of VP, then, appears to be: VP $\longrightarrow$ (Part.) (V + NP). Another early acquisition in the development of VP is the use of the prepositional phrase. Utterances are not only composed of noun + particle ("Shoe on," etc.), but verb phrases are expanded in the following ways:

NP + VP + PP	"Dede fall uh floor"
NP + PP	"Bottle uh bed"
VP + PP	"Put on deks" (desk)

In the early use of particles, "in," "on," "off," of prepositional phrases, and of adverbs, "here," "there," "down," "up," the child clearly indicates that he first acquires those structures which describe states or desired states. These findings indicate that the child is not yet using language to communicate about activities removed from the time and place of communication.

In examining the utterances of three children, Cazden (1968a) found that tense markers were acquired before the use of the auxiliary and that the present progressive marker ("playing") was used before the present, third person singular marker ("plays"). Using the criterion of 90 percent accuracy in those instances in which the use of markers was clearly indicated, it was found that all the children were first using the present progressive marker up to criterion before all other markers. Then at a later stage two of the children were using the past marker up to criterion but only one was using the third person present marker up to criterion. At a still later stage, all the children were using the past marker up to criterion but only two were using the third person present marker up to criterion.

If we divide the time scale into past, present, and future, we observe that the progressive marker indicates ongoing action (for example, "He is playing the piano" [now]), the past marker indicates that action has already taken place (for example, "He played the piano" [before now]), but the third person present marker gives no indication of when the action is occurring or has occurred (for example, "He plays the piano" [all the time]). It may be because this latter marker does not clearly indicate time of action that it is acquired after the others. It should be noted that no one of these markers increases the word length of an utterance more than any other ("He plays," "He playing" [used without aux.], and "He played"). It should also be noted that plural noun markers are being used by all of the children up to criterion before third person present markers. Therefore, it is difficult to account for the sequence of development in terms of phonological complexity. These findings are consistent with the hypothesis that as new structures are acquired children first distinguish and store for generation those aspects of syntactic rules which clearly indicate the attributes, time, and place of the state of activity. The function of language use at this stage is primarily performative rather than reportative. Although this conclusion is speculative, given the number of children in the population, other sequences of acquisition lend some support to it.

The noun phrase develops into N + number at an early stage, although it is obvious that this aspect is no more clearly phonetically marked in the utterances heard than, for example, the be + ing construction. The final /z/ in "shoes on" is no more clearly marked than the final /z/ in "He's eating." A selection is being made of one aspect of syntax before another which cannot be accounted for by surface structure nor, very likely, by frequency of occurrence. At a stage at which the children in the population described above are using the plural marker up to criterion (90+ percent) and have been doing so for some months, one is using the auxiliary in only 18 percent of the appropriate instances, another in 23 percent of the instances, and the third in 79 percent of these instances. The state of activity is clearly marked by the *ing* ending and, therefore, the auxiliary is redundant, but number must be marked when determiners do not do so.

The development of NP into Det. + N has only been briefly examined, but a pattern seems to emerge which does indeed indicate that the child selects those determiners for early use which are definite rather than indefinite. It has been found (Menyuk, 1969, Chapter 2) that the earliest determiner is a pre-particle on the noun (for example, "Count uh buttons") which cannot be equated with the indefinite article *a*. The earliest determiners are demonstratives ("this" and "that") and definite quantifiers ("some," "more," "another"). At some later stage the articles ("a" and "the") and the indefinite quantifier ("any") are used. The pre-particle presumably is used both appropriately ("uh blue flower") and inappropriately ("uh my pencil") (Brown and Bellugi, 1964), although its appropriate use may be chance. To state "want that book" and, in addition, to point while producing the utterance is certainly more distinguishing than stating "want (the) or (a) book." In addition, the selection of the article may appear to be quite arbitrary to the child when the noun is singular in number ("I need the sponge" versus "I need a sponge"), and this arbitrariness is generalized to the selection of articles with plural nouns ("I see a trees") where the grammar of the language indicates that selection is nonarbitrary. The latter type of generalization continues for some time and might obviously create problems for children whose languages have rules not only for marking the number of the article but also for marking the gender (Slobin, In press).

The particular ages at which the various base structure and transformational rules appear in the utterances of children vary, but a similarity in the *sequence of acquisition* has been observed in all children whose language has been collected and described. This sequence of selection of structures that are used for the generation of sentences seems to be primarily dependent on the communicative function that language serves, and especially serves at this stage of development—that is, to describe the basic relationships of subject and predicate and to further define this basic relationship by aspects of the grammar which describe an ongoing state. As language usage in a reportative manner is expanded appropriate new structures are acquired.

Complexity of structure also plays its role in the acquisition of base structure rules, syntactic classes, and transformational rules. The term "complexity" is usually employed to denote number of rules needed to derive a structure. It takes fewer rules to generate the utterance (1) "No daddy go" than the utterance (2) "Daddy no go" and fewer to generate (3) "Daddy can go" than (4) "Can daddy go". It should be noted that the additional rules do not increase the length of the derived utterance. The following description indicates in a simplified manner the additional rules needed for sentences (2) and (4) as compared to sentences (1) and (3).

(1) NEG.	NP	VP		(2) NP	NEG.	VP
No	daddy	go + Neg. hopping rule		Daddy	no	go

(3) NP	MOD.	VP		(4) MOD.	NP	VP
Daddy	can	go + permutation rule		Can	daddy	go?

However, not only the numbers of rules required but also the types of rules seem to play a role in the sequence of production of structures. Adj. + N ("big chair"), possessive Adj. + N ("my chair") and possessive markers on the N ("baby's") appear quite early despite the fact that they are, according to linguistic descriptions, structurally quite complex. All of these structures are described as being derived from operations on two underlying sentences. To account for these early appearances, one can hypothesize that at some stage of development the structural descriptions in the child's grammar are somewhat different from those of the fully competent speaker of the language. There is ample evidence of this. Thus, the first utterances containing adjectives indicate that adjectives may be classified as NPs, as in the following utterances: "See pretty," "See hot," "See blue," "That green." Cazden (1968a) found that in the months preceding the use of the possessive marker ('s) up to criterion, the children in the sample population used the elliptic form of the possessive much more frequently than the possessive + N + N construction ("baby's" versus "baby's chair"). In this case, also, the possessive + N may be classified as NP rather than Adj. + N as in "I see mommy's" and "I want daddy's."

On the other hand, one could hypothesize on both logical and experimental grounds that the procedures used for comprehending utterances and for generating them need not be a regeneration of an utterance according to a linguistic structural description. There is ample evidence to indicate that ease of comprehension of an utterance by adult listeners or the time needed to decode an utterance is not simply dependent on the number of rules used to describe the derivation of the utterance (Fodor and Garrett, 1966).

Brown and Hanlon (1968) examined the emergence of negative (N), question (Q), and truncated (elliptic) (Tr) sentences and convolutions of these types (such as NQ, TrN, etc.) in the language of three children.[8] The prediction was that the simple-active-affirmative-declarative sentence type (SAAD), which requires tense marker placement rules, would emerge before those requiring tense marker placement rules plus the additional set of rules needed for the derivation of (N), (Q), and (Tr) sentences. These latter would emerge before sentence types which require, in number,

---

[8] These are the same children reported on in the study by Cazden (1968a).

two sets of rules plus additional restrictions on ordering, and so on. It was found that SAAD, the sentence type requiring the "least number of rules," emerged before all other sentence types and that, on the whole, TrNQ, the sentence type requiring the "most number of rules," emerged last. However, the sequence of emergence of the types of sentences that lie between these two points is not quite as orderly, and the underlying structure of the TrNQ sentences produced is not clear.

All TrNQ sentences produced by the children were tag NQ (for example, "We ate the cookies, didn't we"), which might be called a special instance of TrNQ. Further, in many instances in the language samples obtained, the statement of the tag is supplied by the mother and the child then produces the tag ending (mother says, "We can't do that" and the child says, "Can't we?"). On the other hand, with positive forms it was found that both TrQ ("Can you?") and tag Q ("You can do that"; "can you?") were produced equally often by the children. The status of TrNQ in the child's grammar is, therefore, questionable. In addition to the complication of tag versus truncation, truncations in general raise many questions. As was indicated earlier, there is a set of verbs, including auxiliaries and modals, which have the property of "object optional" (for example, "He can" and "He can sing"). The truncated sentences, therefore, may be examples of rules used with certain verbs rather than examples of the application of the additional transformational operation of deletion.

For all the children, it was found that N is used up to criterion before Q. For one child, N and TrN emerge at the same time, but before Tr; and for another Tr and TrN emerge at the same time, but the latter is used more frequently. Q emerges before TrQ in the language samples of all the children, but both TrN and TrQ emerge before NQ. If all Trs are eliminated as being questionable, the order of emergence is SAAD $\longrightarrow$ N $\longrightarrow$ Q $\longrightarrow$ NQ. With these results one can state that perhaps the number of rules needed to derive an utterance affects the order of emergence of sentence types, but the findings of this analysis clearly indicate that this is not the complete answer. Types of rules needed to derive an utterance (for example, observation of the properties of verbs in ellipses or permutation of the auxiliary or modal in the question) may affect order of emergence to a greater degree than number of rules.

The experimenters also indicate that semantic "complexity" cannot explain order of emergence, since negatives and questions as well as declaratives are being used (although not completely grammatically) at a much earlier age. Sentence length cannot explain order of emergence. SAAD sentences such as "We did go" are no shorter than Q sentences such as "Did we go?" and the latter is certainly shorter than N sentences such as "We didn't go," and yet the order of emergence is SAAD $\longrightarrow$ N $\longrightarrow$ Q.

FACTORS AFFECTING SEQUENCE
OF ACQUISITION

Children proceed from producing sentencelike words to producing two or more words in an utterance. It should be kept in mind that before and while producing single-word utterances, some children are also producing strings of utterances which contain sequences that are meaningless to the adult. Presumably these utterances are replicated or heard as replications in response to mother's "What?" or "Yes," and are reported as having the supra-segmental characteristics of sentences. However, no hard evidence of this performance has as yet been obtained. Such evidence would indicate that sequences which are longer than a single word can be produced by children when they are only producing one-word sentences.

Grossly speaking, utterance length (number of words per utterance) consistently increases as children mature. This result has been found in a number of studies. However, age alone is not the critical factor in determining mean or median length of utterance. Shipley, Smith, and Gleitman (1965) found that age and median length of utterance were not significantly correlated at 18 to 33 months of age. Length was significantly correlated with the use of the grammatical features that were measured in the spontaneous speech of the children, such as auxiliary verb, pronouns, verb inflections, and verb roots. O'Donnell, Griffin, and Norris (1967) found that the mean length of T-units [9] uttered increased at each age group level sampled from kindergarten to grade 7. However, the only significant increases in the mean length of these units were those which occurred between kindergarten and first grade and between fifth grade and seventh grade. Comparisons of the syntactic structures measured at the grade levels sampled indicated that the most remarkable changes in syntactic development also occurred between these grade levels.

In contradiction with these findings of a correlation between increasing length and increasing linguistic sophistication, Cazden (1967) found in a comparison of the acquisition of noun and verb inflections by two subjects that although one subject's mean length of utterance was smaller than the other subject's at a comparable stage, the subject with a smaller mean length of utterance had acquired more inflections than the subject with a longer mean length. This latter subject had, in the experimenter's terms, greater content in language. Furthermore, it should be noted that in the use of certain structures a more lengthy rendition of a sentence may

---

[9] T-units are defined (by O'Donnell, Griffin, and Norris, 1967, p. 33) as "a single independent predication together with any subordinate clauses that may be related to it." Conjoined sentences, such as S and S, are not included in this definition.

indicate less mature syntactic usage than the shorter rendition (for example, "The boy, who is lying on the ground, is hurt" versus "The boy lying on the ground is hurt").[10] Shriner (1967), in reviewing studies of the mean length of response, cites a study which indicates that mean length of response may be the result of the stimulus materials used, the particular experimenter, and/or the particular subject. Therefore, both the situation and the speaker's personal linguistic style may affect mean length of response,[11] and these factors may interact. To reinforce this notion that mean length of response is sensitive to factors other than degree of linguistic maturation, another study cited by Shriner indicates that individual children are not very consistent in mean length of response from day to day.

Mean or median length of utterance, therefore, appears to be merely a surface description of linguistic maturation in some instances. That is, as new structures are acquired, increasing utterance length may be the surface product of this maturation. In other instances, measures of mean length of utterance may be misleading or, at least, irrelevant to the study of linguistic maturation.

The Brown and Hanlon study (1968), examined the frequency of occurrence of the various sentence types in the language samples of the mothers of the three children in the periods preceding their emergence. SAAD sentences are used most frequently (139 utterances), Q and N are the next most frequent sentence types used (53 and 56 respectively), and Tr sentences are the next most frequent (12). There were two to four instances of the other sentence types. Although there is some relationship between the frequency of usage of sentence types and order of emergence, it is far from completely matching.

In an examination of the use of the prepositions "on," "in," "with," "of," "for," "to" by a mother and the correct usage of these prepositions by her child, it was found that the prepositions used most frequently by the mother ("on" and "in") were most frequently used correctly by the child. On the other hand, the preposition used least frequently by the mother ("to"), and used less frequently to a marked degree than "on" (157 to 31 instances), was third in the rank order of correct usage by the child. In like fashion, although appropriate responses to wh questions were most frequent when utterances began with "where," and although "where" was the wh question most frequently used by the mothers (228 sentences), appropriate responses to utterances which began with *when* were next most frequent, even though "when" is the least frequently heard wh morpheme (7 instances) (Brown, Cazden, and Bellugi, 1969).

---

[10] For a discussion of this aspect of grammatical development, see Menyuk, 1969, Chapter 3.
[11] The term "style" is used here to indicate that personality factors such as caution, timidity, impulsiveness, etc., may be reflected in the length of utterances habitually used.

Obviously, the frequency with which a sentence structure or a member of a syntactic class is heard is insufficient to account for the order of emergence. Further, frequency of usage by either mother or child may be confounded by factors such as optional choice of structures to express the same meaning. How we ordinarily express meanings can obviously affect frequency of usage of structures. A classic example is the active-passive construction. Given the option of stating (1) "John is hitting Jack" and (2) "Jack is being hit by John," the choice is obvious although there are instances when situation or properties of morphemes would make the passive preferred (for example, "The dog was fed" versus "The dog ate").

FACTORS AFFECTING
ACQUISITION OF RULES

In the transition from babbling to language the role of imitation has been examined. Once again, the possible effect of imitation on the linguistic maturation in these early sentences will be discussed. In addition, the possible effect of mothers' "expansions" of their children's utterances will be discussed.

In the Shipley, Smith, and Gleitman study (1965) the nature of the verbal response, as well as the physical response, to the verbal stimuli was noted. For the less linguistically advanced group, a repetition of an utterance immediately preceded the physical response. Therefore, the experimenters state, repetition was the *immediate stimulus* for the physical response. With the more advanced group, repetition was used for clarification. Some form of "did you say . . . ?" was part of the repetition. It might be concluded, then, that repetition for the less advanced group led directly to comprehension, whereas for the more advanced group the statement was comprehended and repetition was simply used to make sure that it was heard correctly. From the experimental results alone it is not clear that repetition or imitation is used to achieve comprehension, but merely that verbal behavior may trigger action and that the performative function of language is operative with the less advanced group.

By examining the data on the early sentences produced by children, it becomes clear that almost none of the utterances can be *direct* or mimicking imitations of what is heard in the environment. However, there are productions which may contain what appear to be memorized imitations of adult speech not used in a generative manner. Some of these imitations may be the use of the contracted form of the auxiliary verb or copula ("I'm," "you're," "he's"), the "don't" and "can't" in early negation, and past forms of strong verbs. Ervin-Tripp (1963) has noted that the correct past form of a strong verb may be used first, perhaps only in specific contexts. Later, a regular past form ending is used with the strong verb, and finally the correct past form appears again. Sequences such as "came," then "come" or "comed" and finally "came," or "did" then "do" or "doed" and finally "did" are observed. Having learned, and perhaps memorized, a form through imitation, the child then has the task of parceling out these forms so that he can use them productively: I + be, can + neg., come + past. In this sense exact repetition or imitation seems to be a hindrance rather than an aid.

Fraser, Bellugi, and Brown (1963) conducted a study in which 3-year-old children were asked (1) to repeat sentences containing various grammatical contrasts (subject-object, singular-plural, etc.); (2) to identify the pictures which exemplified the utterances produced by the experimenter; and (3) to give each of a set of two pictures a sentence name after the experimenter had given them names. Therefore the imitation task involved immediate recall and the production task involved recall with some delay. It was found, in terms of number of errors, that children could better repeat the utterances than identify the picture belonging to an utterance, and that they could better identify than give the pictures sentence names. These experimental results might indicate that the procedure in acquisition of structures is first the capacity to imitate and then the capacity to comprehend and finally the capacity to produce these structures, but several factors make this conclusion questionable.

One of the results of this experiment was that in some instances transformations of utterances produced by the experimenter occurred in the utterances produced by the children in naming a picture. These transformations preserve the meaning, but different forms are used (for example, substituting "The woman gives the teddy to the bunny" for "The woman gives the bunny the teddy"). However, these transformations do not occur in imitation. This indicated to the experimenters that imitation in this experimental situation is a perceptual-motor skill and that imitation is dissociated from comprehension and production. It may be, however, that the particular experimental situation led to these results. Sentence lengths were well within the immediate memory span of the subjects, and it is possible that most of the structures tested were within the competence of the children. Instances of comprehending and noncomprehending imitation may take place, depending on both the length of the utterance and the structure of the utterance. For example, in the repetition task, nontransformational changes took place in the indirect object sentence given above. Given the fact that transformations did occur in the production task, it is possible that the structure was understood in some other form, but that the necessity for immediate repetition conflicted with the way in which children might normally produce this structure. It is, therefore, possible that repetition is dependent on comprehension rather than the reverse, and certainly possible that imitation is not simply a perceptual-motor skill.[12]

Although there were significant correlations for the difficulty of problems from task to task there are some interesting reversals in rank ordering of correct response within each task for grammatical problems. For example, the singular/plural contrast in present progressive (is/are) is comparatively easy in the repetition and production task but among the five most difficult problems in comprehension, whereas the affirmative/negative contrast is the easiest task in both comprehension and production but among the five most difficult problems in repetition. The reasons for these contrasts are not readily evident, but they may involve the specific task requirements in the experiment.

Ervin-Tripp (1964) has analyzed language samples obtained from young children to compare the structure of their spontaneous imitations and nonimitative speech. The question posed was did the structure of these children's utterances differ when given a model from the structure of their spontaneously generated sentences? If the structure of their imitations was more complex than that found in spontaneous speech, then one might hypothesize that imitation was used as an initial step in acquiring new structures. Although in *some* instances *some* children imitated structures which they only spontaneously produced at some later time, the reverse situation also occurred. That is, they spontaneously produced structures which they only imitated at some later time. On the whole, there was no difference in the complexity of imitated and spontaneous utterances and children appeared only to imitate what they could spontaneously produce.

These experimental findings again indicate that imitation of utterances may be simply a perceptual-motor skill or it may be a process involving comprehension, depending both on the particular situation, experimental and natural, in which imitation is elicited, and on the structure and length of the utterance which is imitated. The child may imitate merely the phonetic string he has just heard or he may regenerate the sentence he has just heard by using the structures in his own grammatical system.

The important question is whether or not it is necessary for the child, in the acquisition of grammatical structures, first to go through the process of uncomprehending imitation of the phonetic strings or parts of them before he fully understands a structure. Must he essentially overtly play back what he has just heard before he comprehends? The language samples obtained indicate that aspects of the strings the child hears which exhibit their own unique syntactic regularities and order are produced in his early utterances much more often than are exact bits of what he has

---

[12] This aspect of development will be discussed further in Chapter 5.

heard. Although the end product of this period is, for the most part, the production of utterances which have the structure of the utterances heard, there are transitional periods in which this match is not observed, but in which there are systematic differences. The data obtained from experimental and naturalistic data do not indicate that imitation of a structure is necessary for its spontaneous use. Human beings can imitate a sentence in a language they do not know with varying degrees of accuracy, depending on their capacity to parrot the phonological sequences in the utterance and on the length of the utterance. The direct role that this capacity plays in the acquisition of language is questionable.

Slobin (1964) has discussed what he terms imitation of expansions and their possible role in language acquisition. Imitation of expansion is described as follows: mother says something and the child repeats part of it; mother then repeats her statement in its complete grammatical form and the child attempts to imitate what the mother has said; or the child simply says something, the mother repeats the child's statement in its complete grammatical form, and the child attempts to imitate what the mother has said.

An example of the process of expansion is as follows: (1) mother says, "There isn't any shoe," (2) child says, "no shoe," and (3) mother says, "There isn't any shoe." The sequence may be simply initiated by the child and consist only of parts 2 and 3. Imitation of expansion is considered to have taken place if the child repeats the mother's expansion by (a) repeating his original utterance ("no shoe"), or (b) reducing his original utterance ("no" or "shoe"), or (c) producing a new version of the utterance ("no not shoe").

Slobin examined these behaviors with two children. The mothers used this technique of expansion 30 percent of the time in which observations were made. The total amount of imitation by children was 10 percent of the time. About 15 percent of this 10 percent of the time, the children responded to the expansions by repeating their original utterance, reducing the original, or offering their own unique version of mother's expansion. This last was the most frequent response to mother's expansions (56 percent). This indicates that about 56 percent of 15 percent of 10 percent of the time (or about 1 percent of the time) the children responded to mother's expansions by some elaboration of their original utterance. These numbers place the hypothesis that imitation of expansions is an important factor in acquiring structures in a somewhat fragile state.

Nevertheless, there is the impressive fact that mothers expanded their children's utterances about 30 percent of the observed time. It is possible that it is not the imitation of expansions which is important but, rather, the expansions themselves. They may act as models from which the child can derive new structures or complete grammatical forms. However, unless one hypothesizes that children's utterances are merely reduced or "telegraphic" versions of adult utterances, and the language acquisition task merely one of filling in the gaps in these utterances, then obviously the child must be able to determine in what ways adult productions differ from his own. Theoretically, then, the child must understand or comprehend the nature of the structures and the use of rules in the generation of mother's utterances which he is not using in producing his own sentences. If mother's expansions of utterances are not used for exact matching purposes or imitation, and if they are not used for acquiring comprehension of structures or the use of rules, then the expansions appear not to play any role in the child's acquisition of language. However, again, expansions seem to occur frequently. An alternative role that expansions may play is that of clarifying what was said for the listener—that is, the mother. Expansions may be a technique used by mothers to recode the child's utterances into more familiar forms. This would, indeed, be an important factor in establishing communication between mother and child.

The mother's role need not be directly tutorial in the sense of providing completely well-formed models of structures by expansions. Brown (1968) has examined the possible effect of discourse between parent and child in establishing the underlying rules in wh questions. The following instructional patterns have been observed:

child says: "I want milk" mother says: "What?"   child says: milk
    "   "I want milk"   "   "You want what?"   "   milk
    "   "I want it"   "   "You want what?"   "   milk
mother says: "What do you want?" child says:————mother says:
                                                      "You want what?"

Utterances from mother such as "you want, what?" "you go, where?" "you go, when?" etc., can define the wh elements for the child by equating NP "it" or NP "milk" with a wh morpheme as in the sentences above. Obviously the child has still a great deal to accomplish in the derivation of wh questions, such as auxiliary development, permutation of auxiliary, and tense marker placement, but this type of discourse might establish important equivalences between NPs and wh elements. It was found that the two children (in a sample of three) whose mothers most frequently used questions of the type "you want, what?" more rapidly understood wh questions than did the child whose mother used this type of utterance comparatively less. In a sample of 7,000 utterances the mothers of the two children who comprehended these structures more rapidly used these questions 18 percent and 13 percent of the time, whereas the mother of the third child used this type in only 7 percent of the instances.

Of course, the necessity or even importance of the role of such types of discourse material in the comprehension of wh questions is not answered by this comparison between the children. An experiment observing the comprehension of wh questions and the emergence of wh questions in spontaneous speech by children who are not exposed to this type of discourse (children of deaf mute parents, for example) or who are over-exposed in experimental situations might supply information about its necessity and importance. Such an analysis also does not answer questions concerning the acquisition of other rules which are required for wh questions. Indeed, it may be that the primary purpose such discourse serves is to indicate the properties of wh morphemes, a semantic not a syntactic acquisition. However, this analysis does indicate possibilities for future analyses of naturalistic data and even experimentation.

To examine the effect of expansion on language development, Cazden (1965) conducted an experiment in which children were exposed to various types of language stimulation in a nursery school setting. The children's language was sampled at the beginning, middle, and end of a three-month experimental period. Various aspects of the language produced were measured: competence in sentence repetition, mean length of utterance, complexity of NP (noun + modifier), complexity of VP (tense marker, auxiliary verb, auxiliary verb + participle), and sentence index (proportion of utterances containing a subject and a verb). The children were divided into three groups. One group was simply left in the regular nursery school program. Each of the children in the second group was taken aside for play with one of the experimenters and, in the experimenter's terms, exposed to 30 minutes per day of modeling or well-formed sentences, with expansions deliberately excluded. The children in the third group were also taken aside, and each child in this group was given intensive and deliberate expansions of his utterances during a 40-minute period per day. During this third type of exposure, there were sentences spontaneously generated by the adults as well as expansions. A major finding of this experiment was that the second condition (exposure to increased verbal stimulation) was a significantly more effective treatment in encouraging language maturation than expansion of utterances.

McNeill (In press) has hypothesized that these results were obtained because of the experimental conditions. That is, the expansions given the children were probably inappropriate or incorrect expansions. When mothers expand, they are aware of extra-linguistic conditions as well as of what is actually said and, therefore, their expansions would more correctly match what the child intended to say. Of course, as was stated previously, if expansions provide the more complete form of what the child intended to say, then the child must be able to *recognize* what he intended to say in the expansions that he hears if they are to serve any purpose. However, a way of examining the validity of this hypothesis is to observe the language development of children in houses where varying amounts of expansion occur. In a study of the language produced by three children, Cazden (1968a) found that the child who received the fewest expansions was relatively the most advanced in the acquisition of noun and verb inflections. It is possible that expansions aid in the acquisition of structures other than those measured. However, this question can only be answered empirically.

SUMMARY

It has been hypothesized that the earliest structures used can be found in all languages and that they are the earliest structures used by children from different linguistic environments. The reason that they can be found in all languages and are the first types of structures used by children is that they serve basic communicative functions. Further developments in this period result in the child's increasing competence to expand basic structures, and finally his competence in determining how various sentence types are specifically realized in his own language.

Descriptions of early sentences indicate that the child at the beginning of this stage of development produces one-word utterances which have the structure S and then somewhat later have the structure S $\longrightarrow$ topic (modifier). This latter structure is generated by conjoining the elements of sentencelike words. By application of stress and intonational markers and the conjunction of elements, the child can create declarative, negative, imperative, and question sentences. As the subject + predicate construction begins to be used more frequently, the negative and question elements are embedded in this construction. At this stage the child may produce utterances which appear to contain the complete declarative and negative form such as "can't," "don't," "I'm," "he's," etc. However, it is only somewhat later that the verb phrase is expanded to include auxiliary and modal verbs. Thus, these early complete forms may be memorized items.

After the verb phrase is expanded, the child begins to permute elements within the sentence. First, the negative element follows the subject and later it is attached to the auxiliary verb or modal ("He not play" becomes "He can't play"). The auxiliary verb is attached to the question morpheme ("Where he can play?" becomes "Where can he play?") and the tense marker is attached to the auxiliary or modal "Where do he goes?" becomes "Where does he go?"). The child acquires structures and then applies certain operations to these structures. He first applies only those operations which do not disturb the subject + predicate construction of his sentences. It has been hypothesized that the order of use of syntactic operations is a reflection of the child's perceptual capacities or the way in which he understands grammatical relationships at various stages. In his generation of two or more word sentences, the child observes restrictions in the conjunction of elements in a string which are related to both the syntactic and semantic properties of these elements. (He says "That my coat" but not "That coat my" and he says "Daddy go car" but not "Daddy go shoe.")

At the end of this stage of development the child is for the most part producing completely well-formed declarative, imperative, question, and negative sentences as well as sentences containing conjunctions and embeddings of two sentences. He also simultaneously produces not completely well-formed instances of those types of sentences which are structurally similar to those produced at an earlier stage of development. (He produces both "How you do that?" and "How do you do that?")

These are some of the syntactic structures and operations that one can find in the early sentences produced by children, but many questions concerning which aspects of these syntactic structures and operations the child comprehends during this developmental period remain unanswered. Does the child's performance indicate his level of competence or does his competence exceed his performance? Are there either differences or lags between the child's comprehension grammar and his production grammar? There is contradicting evidence in the limited literature. There is some experimental evidence (Shipley, Smith, and Gleitman, 1965) that children will not respond to utterances that have some greater degree of complexity than those utterances which they produce. However, lack of typical response does not mean lack of comprehension. The age of the child and his total behavior repertoire may influence this type of response rather than simply the structure of the utterance. Some observations have indicated that at the earliest stages of development of negative and question sentences the child does not understand adult productions of these utterances which contain embedding and permutations (Klima and Bellugi, 1966). However, at the transitional stages of development of these sentence types he appears to understand operations and structures which he himself does not use. It has been suggested that understanding these utterances need not necessitate the comprehension of these structures and operations. To some degree there may be a difference between understanding a sentence for some practical purpose and understanding the detailed way in which it was put together.

Finally, it has been found that children approximately 3 years of age comprehend grammatical contrasts which they do not produce (Fraser, Bellugi, and Brown, 1963). This latter evidence may indicate a shift taking place, in time, in which there is an increasing lag between comprehension and production due to the fact that syntactic maturation is not accompanied by similar maturation of the productive mechanism. The children in this latter study were at least one year older than those in the other studies cited. Results obtained may be due to the nature of the experimental task as well as to the child's perceptual and productive competence. Answers to the questions, "Does the child produce only what he comprehends, or does he comprehend only what he produces?" will lead to a better understanding of the necessary and sufficient conditions for syntax acquisition and, perhaps, provide an explanation of the child's capacities and the techniques that he uses to acquire language.

There is little or no evidence that stress of words in the utterances the child hears, imitation of adults' utterances, expansion of children's utterances by adults, or imitations of adults' expansions by children *shapes* the structure of the utterances produced by children initially or the structural changes that occur during this period of development. There is evidence which indicates that limitations on memory span may account for *how many aspects* of an utterance a child can pay attention to and code, but these limitations do not account for *which aspects* he does pay attention to, as represented in the structure of the utterances he produces and the structure of those he responds to.

It is important to attempt to resolve questions about the role of imitation in the process of language acquisition, since statements about this role imply assumptions about the nature and functioning of perception, memory, and cognition in the child's acquisition of a verbal symbol system as well as about his linguistic behavior. If one assumes that imitation is a necessary step in learning language, and, in fact, must precede comprehension and production of all structures, then one also implies that overt mimicking and practice is the way in which the child learns to understand utterances and to produce them. If one assumes, in addition, that at some later stage the child can proceed from imitating utterances to understanding and generating utterances by some system of rules, then one also implies that by rehearsal of phonetic strings the child either can learn to categorize segments of the utterance into phonetic, morphemic, or syntactic bins and can memorize sequential rules or probabilities, or can derive a system of generalizations from the imitation of a limited number of utterances. The first assumption, memorization of imitations, implies that the child has an infinite memory capacity which operates at a very rapid pace. The second assumption implies that the child has a very large, perhaps also infinite memory capacity, since sequential ordering of a few phones, morphemes, and syntactic classes generate countless permutations and combinations. Both conditions imply that the child acquires a grammar consisting of surface structure rules of how speech sound segments are put together in the utterances heard.

The logical consequences of the various positions that have been taken on the role of imitation in the acquisition of syntax (or of the entire grammar) point up either their falseness or questionability. Memory capacity is not infinite, and there is no proof that imitation of utterances is necessary either to segment or to categorize aspects of the utterance, or to observe its abstract features. It seems clear that imitation of utterances, although it may occur, is certainly not a sufficient condition for acquiring language.

THE DEVELOPMENT
OF
SYNTAX

THE STRUCTURAL DESCRIPTIONS of the utterances produced by children, discussed in the previous chapter, indicated that early syntactic development takes the direction of establishing the basic relationships in the language—subject + predicate, modifier + noun in the NP, verb + object in the VP—and of developing rules for generating declarative, question, negative, and imperative sentences. In order to derive various sentence types, the shape of these rules changes over time from conjunction of elements to permutation of elements. Obviously, during this period, there has also been development of the syntactic classes described (modifier, noun, verb, object), and some development of grammatical markers such as tense, possessive, and pluralization. In addition to this, the transformational operations of addition of elements, deletion of elements, and permutation of elements are beginning to be applied to create even more varied sentence types. The child is thus observing syntactic, semantic, and phonological rules which are both universal in nature and specific to his language. Given the linguistic knowledge which the child exhibits in his production and comprehension of utterances, he can function very adequately in the communication situations he meets. Despite this, further development takes place and continues to do so for some time to come. An important reason for this change appears to be that the child expands his use of language to function in a reportative manner, to speak of things removed in time and space from the site of communication, and to hypothesize. To use language in this manner, structures conveying time, place, manner, dependent relationships, and conjunctive and disjunctive relationships are all needed.

Various aspects of the child's comprehension and production of syntactic rules have been examined: acquisition of context-sensitive base structure rules and members of a syntactic class, acquisition of transformational rules, and acquisition of morphological rules. We will begin with some linguistic descriptions of some classes, base structure rules, and transformational rules that have to be acquired. These are somewhat more detailed than the descriptions presented in the first chapter. We will then observe what the research findings have been concerning the sequence of acquisition of these rules in the sentences produced and understood by children, and conclude with some of the hypotheses that have been presented to account for the various sequences.

The appendix of a recent publication (Slobin, 1967) presents a summary of the techniques that have been experimentally used to examine children's comprehension of various structures or that are suggested for experimental use. The following are some of the techniques which have either been used or are suggested for use:

1. Repetition of sentences containing various structures.

2. Identification of a picture among a set of pictures which matches an orally presented model sentence containing a certain structure (for example, show the picture where "The boy is not sitting," for the negative structure).

3. Transformation of a sentence according to a model given of a certain structure (for example, "The boy hit the girl," "The girl was hit by the boy," "The mother baked a cake," ——————, for the passive structure).

4. Sentence completion given an example of the structure desired (for example, "The boy washed himself," "The girl washed ——————," for the reflexive structure).

5. Adding the correct inflection when given either real words or nonsense items.

6. Manipulating objects to portray the meaning of an utterance (for example, "Give the bunny the teddy," for the indirect object structure).

Most of the research in the literature is based on experimental designs (1), (2), and (5). A formidable problem is devising techniques which examine the child's linguistic competences rather than his ability or inclination to follow instructions. This is particularly true, of course, with very young children. Another problem is that in any test situation it is difficult to obtain an adequate assessment of the child's linguistic competence. His ability or lack of ability to comprehend or produce certain grammatical structures in these tasks may be due to the stimulus materials used, and his success or failure does not predict his competence with other related structures. Until such materials have been standardized and used with large numbers of children, and until our knowledge of the correlations between competences with various grammatical structures and operations is more complete, a safeguard that can and has been used in some instances is to observe the relationships between performance in these tasks and the child's spontaneous production of utterances.

LINGUISTIC RULES

The structures usually described in a list of base structure rules of English grammar can be found in Table 5–1. The rules given are not

TABLE 5–1   SOME BASE STRUCTURE RULES OF ENGLISH GRAMMAR

Symbol	Rewritten as
1. S	S and/or * S^n
2. S	NP + AUX + VP or Pre S + NP + AUX + VP or NP + AUX + VP + ADV or Pre S + NP + AUX + VP + Adv
3. Pre S	Q or Imp or Neg or Emp or any combination of the above except Q + Imp
4. NP	Det + N or NP (+S)*
5. VP	V + Part or V + NP or V + PP or V + NP (+S)* or be + Adj (+S)* or be + PP or be + NP (+S)*
6. Adv	PP
7. PP	P + NP
8. AUX	Tense or Mod or Perf or Prog or Pass
9. Perf	have + en (participle)
10. Prog	be + ing (participle)
11. Pass	be + en (participle)
12. Det	Art., Quantifier, Demonstrative
13. N	count, mass

* Structure derived from two or more underlying sentences.

complete but are representative of the rules which will be discussed in the text. Rule 1 indicates that any sentence can be composed of a sentence plus any number of additional sentences that are in a conjoined ("and") or appositive ("or") relationship. Rules 2 and 3 describe sentences that have the option of containing forms of the pre-sentence. Rule 4 describes the fact that the NP can dominate a sentence (for example, "The boy, who got sick, died."). Rule 5 describes the various possible expansions of the VP—for example, "take away," or "put away the book," or "go in the house," or "hit the boy (who ran away)," or "is fine (that you like him)," or "is in the house," or "is the man (who was elected)." The symbol "be" stands for the category of verbs that describes state ("seem," "appear," etc.). Rules 6, 7, and 8 describe possible expansions of Adv, PP, and AUX, respectively (for example, AUX can be expanded into "play" + present, or "will play" or "play" + perf, or "play" + prog). Rules, 9, 10, and 11 describe expansions of Perf ("has been"), Prog ("is walking"), and Pass ("was taken"). Rules 12 and 13 describe possible expansions of Det ("a," "some," "that") and possible expansions of N ("boy," "milk").

As one can observe in this simple description of base structure rules, both classes and structures are defined in terms of (1) underlying ordering, (2) segmentation, and (3) function (i.e., subject-predicate, modifier-noun, verb-modifier).

The application of transformational rules results in a variety of sentence types. However, the types of operations carried out by transformational rules are a limited set: addition, deletion, permutation, and substitution. Transformational rules which apply to two or more underlying sentences can be thought of as the application of these same operations *plus* the operations of conjunction and embedding now applied to structures which are dominated by the symbol S rather than to those dominated by sub-structures of S. An example of this difference is given in Figure 5–1. It should be noted that in permutation of PP the operation is dominated by Symbol VP in 5–1a, whereas the relative clause formation is dominated by the symbol S in 5–1b.

An example of the derivation of a structure in which the transformational operations of addition and permutation take place is the passive construction. Deletion is applied under certain conditions. The following is a structural description of (1) the underlying base structure of a passive sentence, then (2) the structural changes which occur by the addition and permutation of elements, and finally (3) deletion under certain conditions.

```
1. NP      AUX    (X PASS)   V           NP
   1        2                            3
   Jamie   Pres.   be + en    paint       the picture
2. 3        2                       by    1       addition (by)
   The picture  Pres.  be + en  paint by  Jamie   permutation (1⟷3)
3. NP             AUX (X PASS)  V   by NP          (some one/thing)
   3               2                 ∅  ∅          deletion (by, 1)
   3               2                    1
   The picture  Pres.  be + en   paint
```

An example of a substitution is in the relative clause construction where (1) the NP object of one sentence and the NP subject of another sentence are the same, and (2) a wh pronoun is substituted for the subject in the second sentence when it is embedded in the first sentence, as in the example

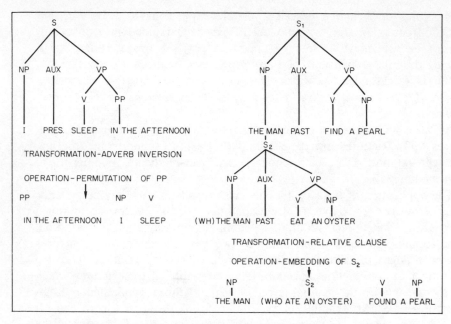

FIG. 5–1 Partial description of underlying structure of sentence in which operations occur on PP of S (S) and in which operations occur on S (S_1).

given below. The operations involved in this transformation may be deletion ("the boy"), substitution ("who" for "the boy"), and embedding.[1]

1. I know the boy.   The boy did that.   **3 = 4**
   1 2   3   4   5 6

2. I know the boy   who   did that.
   1 2   3   wh + 4   5 6

A final class of rules is concerned with the co-occurrence of items in a string. These rules are considered by some to be syntactic and by others to be semantic. There may be context-sensitive rules (local transformations) in the base structure rules which do not permit the co-occurrence of certain *members* of syntactic classes because of their properties.[2] It has also been suggested that syntactic rules allow the formation of any well-

---

[1] Descriptions of the various transformational rules used by a population of children aged 2 to 7 years can be found in Menyuk, 1969, Chapter 3.
[2] For a discussion of these rules, see Chomsky, 1965, Chapter 2.

formed string as defined by the base structure rules given in Table 5–1. Syntactic context-sensitive rules would, therefore, only apply in cases of agreement (for example, number of the verb or gender, number and case of pronouns). In addition to this, however, the lexical categorization of the verbs (their semantic properties and notations about which transformations can apply and which cannot) dominates the selection of possible subjects and objects. The following sentences are anomalous because restrictions of co-occurrence of NPs with Vs and restrictions on the occurrence of transformations with certain categorizations of Vs are not observed. In addition, restrictions on the co-occurrence of V + Adv (sentence 7) and Adj + N (sentence 8) are not observed.

Set A

1. Subject—Verb
   The ceiling is playing
2. Verb—Object
   He is shining us
3. Verb—Verb (as in complement)
   He gives to sing
4. Indirect Object
   He discovered John the book
5. Passive
   The truck was had by Francis
6. Prepositional Phrase
   He gave the book on the table
7. Adverb
   He thinks loudly
8. Adjective
   The happy table fell

There are other types of sentences which do not appear to be, for the most part, as deviant as those listed under the heading *Set A*. These not-so-anomalous sentences seem to be clearly the result of nonobservation of syntactic context-sensitive rules with some few exceptions (the exceptions are asterisked in the examples given in *Set B*). The sentence examples are categorized under the headings of NP and VP since they involve either these structures per se or modifications of these structures (Det + N, VP + PP).

Set B

NP
*1. (*a*) She takes   (*b*) He gave the book
*2. She is his father

3. She likes it the game
4. I see flower
5. I see a trees
6. I see some many soaps

VP

1. (*a*) He playing a game   (*b*) This a big house
*2. We used to make a club
3. He's will hit him
4. I go school every day
*5. He's sitting inside them
6. He lost it near to the table

Under the heading NP in sentences 1*a* and *b* the omission of direct and indirect objects may be considered either nonobservation of a context-sensitive semantic rule governed by the lexical categorization of the verbs "give" and "take" or nonobservation of a context-sensitive syntactic rule by nonexpansion of a symbol in the underlying string according to base structure rules. The other asterisked instances may possibly be instances of nonobservation of the semantic properties of the lexical items "she," "make," "inside," or nonobservation of syntactic rules of co-occurrence ("She-father," "make-a club," "inside-them"). Whether the deviance is due primarily to nonobservation of syntactic rules or nonobservation of semantic properties and rules in the asterisked instances is not clear. What is clear, however, is that although children produce utterances with the deviancies exemplified in *Set B*, they rarely, if ever,[3] produce utterances with the deviancies exemplified in *Set A*.

Other deviancies which occur in the sentences children produce are concerned with morphological and transformational rules and represent stages in the child's mastery of the syntactic rules of his language.[4] The following are some examples.

Morphological Rules

1. I have two shoe. He's a good children.
2. He play. Yesterday I play.
3. They plays. Now I played.

---

[3] The verb-adverb and adjective-noun deviancies in sentences 7 and 8 might be produced because the limited set of semantic properties that children have for lexical items might prevent the blocking of such utterances. This aspect of language development will be discussed in Chapter 6.

[4] More detailed descriptions of deviant transformational rules can be found in Menyuk, 1969, Chapter 3.

Transformational Rules

1. How he doing that.
2. I saw where is the hat.
3. I got the pencil what were there.
4. I didn't get nothing.
5. The boy went to the castle and she tells the king he wanted it.
6. I don't want they mess up my road.

Person, number, and tense rules of the context are obviously not being observed in the above examples of deviations from morphological rules. In the examples of deviations from transformational rules, the verb phrase is not expanded in sentence (1), the wh question is simply conjoined to another sentence to generate a relative clause in sentence (2), restrictions on both the wh substitution and the number of the verb in the relative clause are not being observed in sentence (3), the restrictions on negative placement (only once in one underlying string) is not being observed in sentence (4), both pronoun and tense restrictions in the conjunction of sentences are not being observed in sentence (5), and restrictions on compliment derivation (object form of the pronoun, *to* + V) are not being observed in sentence (6).

Taking as our starting point the syntactic development of a boy aged 2 years, 10 months,[5] we will examine what base structure and transformational and morphological rules he appears to have acquired, and then, working forward, describe the data that have been collected on children's production of structures up to the age of 13 years and on comprehension of these structures up to the age of 10 years.

Almost all the utterances collected from this child in a single sampling session (166 utterances) contain NP + VP. There are three exceptions and they appear to be a continuation of the nonproduced part of an utterance ("and a eyes, and mouf and tongue," "and some red sometimes," "and then fall down?"). Indeed, all of the base structure rules are used except for (1) S ⟶ S *or* S, (2) VP ⟶ be (+S), and (3) AUX ⟶ Perf.

All the syntactic classes are used, although only a limited number of the members of these classes have been acquired. For example, under the category NP ⟶ Det. + N we find the following: "I need *a* sponge," "I want *some more* milk," "I need *anudder* mouf now," "*This* one's riding." There are, however, no examples of *the* + N in the sample, and on occasion the Det is omitted, as in "I have pumpkin."

The use of the AUX in all aspects of tense and modal, except for the

---

[5] This boy was part of a nursery school population described in Menyuk, 1964c.

perfect, can be observed in the language sample. The following are some examples of the use of AUX in declarative, negative, and question sentences.

Declarative

Pres.	She belongs to another one
Past	I dropped some
Modal	You will carry it around
	It might fell down
	I can get it closer
	He did do it
Prog.	We're working so hard
Pass.	Mine is painted

Negative

You can't knock mine down
I didn't have any turns
You won't kick it down yet?
It's not getting dark either

Question

Isn't that funny mummy?
It's too heavy, isn't it?
Where did Billy go?
Can you do?
Who's crying?
Who will help me?

Verb phrase has been expanded into (1) V + NP, (2) V + PP, and (3) V + Adv:

1. I have some bubbles
2. Daddy's camera is at grammy Sage's
3. I went, boom bang, fast

This child produces, in addition to the transformations observed in single underlying sentences, utterances which involve conjunction and embedding, as in the following examples.

But I fall down and I got some blood
I got two pockets too but you don't
You can't knock it down cause it's gonna be big house for cars

I fell running fast, real fast
They're supposed to have this corner right here
I didn't see the book what the teacher reads
You will carry it around and it might break

DEVELOPMENT OF BASE STRUCTURE CONTEXT-SENSITIVE RULES

Despite the fact that the child, aged 2 years, 10 months, is using all the base structure rules described, this child and other children at this stage of development and for some time afterward do not always observe context-sensitive base structure rules in the utterances they produce. These deviations from completely well-formed sentences take a different shape depending on the degree of linguistic maturation of the children (Menyuk, 1969, Chapter 2).

At the earliest stage of development of base structure context-sensitive rules, when the child has recently acquired expansions of NP and VP (Det + N and V + NP, V + Adv), he *sometimes* does not expand these structures in contexts in which expansions are required. Some distinctions should be made between morphological rules and base structure selectional rules. There are instances in which the N should clearly be pluralized but is not, as in the following: "I have two book," "They're wagging their tail," "Billy's one of his friend." These deviations should not be confused with the selection of an appropriate determiner. There are obvious instances in which nouns, determiners, auxiliaries, modals, copulas, objects, particles, and prepositions are required. That is, the structure of the sentence makes their selection obligatory. There are other instances in which the context does not require inclusion of the class (for example, "I see crayons there" or "I want milk") or the nature of the omission is not clear (for example, "He do that," which can be "He does that" or "He can do that"). The following are some clear examples in which context dictates selection of an item in a class, but it is omitted in the child's utterance.

Noun Phrase

   That's the blue
   Did you get?

Verb Phrase

   He playing the piano
   He nice
   When you eat them?
   He not going

Determiner

I see book

Particle

He put the hat

Preposition

He goes work

When the child is *consistently* using the base structure rules S——→NP + AUX + VP and, further, the rules NP——→Det + N, VP——→V + NP, V + Adv, he still has the task of observing and applying the rules in his language which pertain to selectional restrictions concerning the co-occurrence of Det + N and the co-occurrence of V + NP, and V + Adv. He proceeds in a hierarchical fashion by acquiring first *expansions* of NP and VP and a minimal number of selectional rules and then additional rules which pertain to items in the frame. Of course, as class membership increases (N class, V class, etc.), further additional rules may be required. In terms of selectional rules, nouns have to be categorized into singular and plural and plural into mass and count nouns to select the appropriate determiner. Verbs have to be categorized into transitive and intransitive to determine whether or not an object is required and what modifiers are appropriate, and also categorized to determine what types of objects they take. Prepositional phrases have to be categorized to determine what prepositions are appropriate. The following are some examples of correct and incorrect categorizations which are typical of children's utterances from 3 to 7 years of age:

	Correct	*Incorrect*
Det + Count N	The boys were there	A boys were there
Det + Mass N	I want a lot of soap	I want many soap
V + NP	She makes dolls	She does dolls
V + comp.	I like going to the store	I want going to the store
V + Rel. Cl.	I know who he is	I think who he is
P.P. of time	He works in the night time	He works at the night time
P.P. of place	He flies in the sky	He flies on the sky

There is also a period of development during which each of these classes is being used redundantly. For example, "I want it the book," "He's will be nice," "Give me some many pencils," "He took off his hat off," "He'll take it in over there."

A developmental trend has been observed in the child's acquisition of selectional restrictions. Taking into account only those instances which are clearly marked, the development observed has been: first, the child primarily omits classes; next, he does not observe restrictions imposed by appropriate categorization and substitutes among the members of a class; finally, he uses the class redundantly. The first step is expansion of a structure (for example, NP ⟶ Det + N), the second is *free* use of members of a class, and the third is redundant use of classes to ensure appropriateness. Generally speaking, the utterances produced by young nursery school children (mean age 3 years), older nursery school children (mean age 3 years, 8 months), kindergarten children (mean age 5 years, 6 months) and first grade children (mean age 6 years, 5 months) indicate that nursery school children most frequently omit a class, kindergarten children most frequently substitute among members of a class, and first grade children most frequently use a class redundantly. The mean percentage of children in each population using omissions, substitutions, and redundancies with all the classes is shown in Figure 5–2. Variations occur *depending on the class* and on the stage of development of context-sensitive base structure rules concerning these classes. There is some overlapping of the types of nonobservation of rules that is found in each group but little overlapping for individual children. For example, prepositions are most frequently omitted and substituted in the young nursery school population, but in the other populations they are most frequently substituted and used redundantly.

As one can observe in Figure 5–2, the task of acquiring base structure context-sensitive rules has not, as yet, been accomplished in all instances by the first grade group. Even the children who fall into the last quarter of the age range (6 years, 2 months to 7 years) are still producing utterances without observation of context-sensitive rules. The degree to which context-sensitive rules are not observed is dependent on the class. However, a mean 9 percent of these children are still producing utterances with omissions of all classes, 15 percent with substitution of classes, and 26 percent with redundancies in classes, and these figures, of course, only include those instances in which deviations are obvious. It should be stressed that sentences with such deviations are only produced *sometimes,* not all the time.[6]

The task is complicated by changes that occur in the lexicon and by the acquisition of new structures. There is a period of time when generalizations occur between members of a class. For example, locative prepositions may be used in alternation with each other (both "I go at New York" and "I

---

[6] For measures of frequency of occurrence of deviant rules, see Menyuk, 1963a, 409–22.

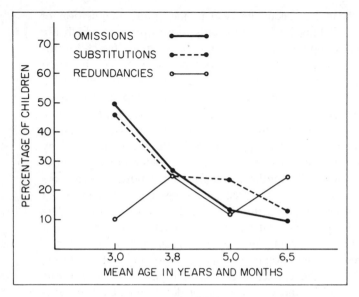

FIG. 5–2 Mean percentage of children at each age using omissions, substitutions and redundancies with all syntactic classes.

go to Maine" occur). Members of a class are used for those not yet acquired. For example, one preposition may be consistently substituted for another ("They went on Christmas," "Her birthday is on June," but never "in" + PP of time). As new members are acquired there may be a period of time during which rules which pertain to certain categorizations of classes are generalized to include these new members, but rules which pertain to further categorizations have not as yet been acquired. For example, a new manner preposition is acquired and its use is generalized ("She changes diapers with the baby," "We have to share with those"). At a still later stage there may be some ambivalence about the correct choice of a member in certain contexts and redundancies may occur. For example, a new locative preposition is acquired but its exact use is not understood ("They're in between of the houses," "They want to sit near beside him").

If the child has not, as yet, begun to use the members of a class within which further categorization is required, or to use structures which are permissable with these members, then clearly no instances which would indicate nonacquisition of a context-sensitive rule would appear. Since the lexicon continues to grow and class membership to increase for some time after the first grade period, it also seems reasonable to suppose that context-sensitive base structure rules are still being acquired for some time after the first grade period. However, such generalizations need not occur with new structures throughout the acquisition period. There may be a stage of development in which such generalizations no longer occur and new members are incorporated into the grammar completely categorized and ready for appropriate use. No study has, as yet, been undertaken to examine this question.

TRANSFORMATIONAL RULES

It should be kept in mind, throughout this discussion, that what has been described in various studies is children's production of structures. There may be certain structures which are produced by the child in everyday language (spoken or written) which are not fully comprehended or, at least, not comprehended in the manner described by the structural linguist. That is, the child may have acquired the form and may use it appropriately in everyday language but may not yet comprehend the underlying relationships expressed in the structure.[7] In this discussion, therefore, we will consider the acquisition of transformational structures by the child as being the task of determining what syntactic operations are required to generate various structures. We will then observe the sequence of development of these structures from this point of view. For example, it was noted previously that wh questions are produced first by *conjoining* the wh element with a sentence ("Where daddy?"). After the development of the subject-predicate relationship and the development of the AUX and Mod nodes, the wh element is *embedded* in the sentence ("Where daddy goe[s]?") Finally, *permutation* of AUX and tense markers appear ("Where did daddy go?"). The acquisition of transformational rules will be discussed in these terms.

As has been observed, the operations of addition, deletion, permutation, and substitution (if tense and number replacements and wh replacements for nouns and adverbs can be considered substitutions) are already being used in the child's production of declarative, imperative, question, and negative sentences, and these sentence types are early acquisitions. It is true that questions emerge at a somewhat later stage than negatives and imperatives, and the reason for this may be that permutation operations are required for questions. Operations which disturb the order of SV or SVO appear to be later acquisitions than those which do not.

The development of transformational rules from approximately 3 years to 7 years, as exhibited in the sentences produced by children, has been

---

[7] This aspect of development will be discussed in Chapter 6.

observed (Menyuk, 1964c). Structural descriptions of the utterances produced were obtained.[8] The structures in the utterances of children in kindergarten, first, second, third, fifth, and seventh grades have been categorized (O'Donnell, Griffin, and Norris, 1967).

In the first study cited (Menyuk, 1964c), it was found that the children produced both completely grammatical sentences and sentences which deviated from being well-formed in terms of transformational rules. It should be emphasized, however, that even children at the beginning of the age range of 3 to 7 years, for the most part, simultaneously produced sentences in which both completely well-formed and not completely well-formed structures could be observed. For example, the 2-year, 10-month-old child produced both "I don't want they mess up my road" and "I want him to do that" in generating the complement structure. However, over the age range observed, changes occurred in the number of children using the various transformational structures, and changes occurred in the *types of deviation* from the completely well-formed structures, just as differences could be observed over the age range in type of deviance from base structure context-sensitive rules.

By age 3 all of the base structure rules for the generation of sentences from single underlying strings are used by all of the children outside of context-sensitive rules. Not all of the transformational structures, however, are being used by all of the children at this age. In the young nursery school group (aged 2 years, 10 months to 3 years, 1 month) most of the transformational structures which involve operations on a single underlying string are used by all of the children. There are some exceptions. The following is a list of those structures with some examples:

1. Reflexive	He washed himself
2. Passive	Blackie got spanked
3. Adverb preposing	Now I want to color, here's the book
4. There insertion	There will be a lot of trouble
5. Particle movement	She took that rouge off, she put them on

Structures 2 through 5 all require permutation operations. Structure 1 (the reflexive) requires conditions of equality between subject and object, plus restrictions on verbs (we don't say "He danced himself") plus rules of formation ("myself," "yourself," but "himself"). There is an increase in the number of children using these structures from the nursery school period through the first grade period. However, even in the first grade group, the

---

[8] These descriptions can be found in Menyuk, 1969, Chapter 3.

Passive, There insertion, Particle movement, and Reflexive structures still cannot be found in the language samples of all the children. Permutation, then, is a transformational operation which is used by fewer of the younger children and more of the older children, but is still not used by all of the children at the end of the age range. The percentage of children (1) using the above listed structures and (2) using all other structures involving transformations on a single underlying string, at various grade levels, is presented in Figure 5–3. As can be seen, the percentage of children using structures other than those described above is far greater than the percentage using structures which involve permutations and the reflexive.

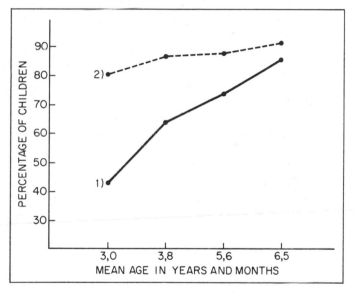

FIG. 5–3 Percentage of children at each age using (1) reflexive, passive, adverb preposing, there insertion and particle movement and (2) all other transformations involving a single underlying string.

Rules for the generation of sentences which involve operations on two or more underlying sentences obviously can require more rules, just as the generation of NQ in earlier sentences required more rules than either N or Q. If negative sentences are conjoined, the rules used for generating one negative must be applied to two sentences ("He doesn't sing and he doesn't dance") plus additional restrictions observed about the conjoining of sentences (such as tense and pronoun restrictions). If a declarative sentence is embedded in a question sentence ("Who took the pencil that was on the table?"), rules for the question generation plus relative clause generation plus additional restrictions (on tense and wh pronoun substitution) must be observed. Although the number of children using various structures which involve operations on a single underlying sentence does not increase markedly over this age range (from 81 percent at the beginning to 85 percent at the end of the age range), the number of children using structures which involve operations on two or more underlying strings does (from 47 percent at the beginning to 77 percent at the end of the age range). This cannot be accounted for simply by the increasing ability to produce sentences of greater and greater length since, as we noted previously, some of the structures which are used by greater numbers of children at a later age reduce sentence length. For example, conjunction deletion is used with greater frequency at older ages than is conjunction ("I want the pencil and crayon" versus "I want the pencil and I want the crayon").

The power and limitations of the *number* of rules to derive a structure in explaining the sequence of early acquisition of structures has already been discussed. In addition to the number of rules required for their derivation, several other aspects of the structures to be acquired seem to play a role in the sequence of increasing usage observed over this age range. The first are the functional relationships expressed by these structures. Modifiers of noun phrases, such as adjectives and possessives, and modifiers of verb phrases, such as complements, are early acquisitions. This is true, despite their described complexity (they involve two underlying strings), probably because of their functional usefulness. It is true, as has been discussed, that the strategies used to understand and produce these structures need not involve parceling out the rules used to describe these structures in linguistic descriptions. On the other hand, the rules that are used at the beginning stages of structural acquisition are applied to only a limited set of lexical items which, in turn, require a limited set of context-sensitive rules. For example, early complements consist of utterances such as "I wanna do that," "I gotta go home," "I like to eat spaghetti." Therefore, the *total* number of rules required for the generation of these sentences may not be any greater than those required for some sentences which involve operations on a single underlying string. These structures (adjective, possessive, and complement) are used by many three-year old and some two-year old children.

Outside of the structures already discussed, the first sentence type which involves operations on two or more underlying sentences that is used by a great many of the children in the nursery school population is conjunction with "and." The sentence types used by none of the youngest nursery school children and by only 47 percent of the first grade children are (1) participial complement ("I don't like practicing the piano"); (2) nominalizations

("Stuffing yourself makes you sick"); and (3) iteration ("You have to drive a long time to get to Canada"). All of these sentence types involve embedding one sentence into another plus deletions and may also require permutations, as in (2) nominalizations.

O'Donnell, Griffin, and Norris (1967) observed the frequency of occurrence per 100 T-units [9] of various structures in the spoken and written stories of kindergarten, first, second, third, fifth, and seventh grade children. It should be kept in mind that frequency of occurrence of a particular sentence type may be determined by many factors other than linguistic competence or even facility in using the structure. These are factors such as the topic, the situation, the particular participants in the situation (for example, mother and child, teacher and child, peer and child, etc.). Indeed, fluctuations occur in the frequency of usage throughout the age range sampled in this study, and in many instances there is no steady increase in frequency of usage of structures from kindergarten to first grade. However, some interesting trends can be observed which give us some insight into the sequence of development.

First, all the structures listed by the experimenters could be found in the language sample of the kindergarten children, and few of them were used significantly more frequently at older grade levels. It was found that conjunctions with "and" occurred with great frequency throughout the age range in the spoken language samples obtained (from 51 percent usage in kindergarten to 70 percent in the seventh grade). On the other hand, structures which involve embedding, such as relative clause, relative clause reduction, participial complements, etc., are used much less frequently. Even at the seventh grade level these structures are used in less than 10 percent of the instances and, in many cases, in less than 5 percent of the instances. Further, in some instances structures are used much more frequently at the beginning of the age range than at the end. There is some indication that these structures may be replaced by more widespread use of other structures at later stages. An example of this is relative clause reduction, where sentences such as "I saw a man who was wearing a red coat" are reduced to "I saw a man wearing a red coat." Another example is that participial complements replace infinitival complements. Sentences such as "That's to bake bread" are replaced by sentences such as "That's for baking bread." The relative clause structure is used more frequently by kindergarten than by seventh grade children, whereas the inverse is true of the participial complement.

Conjoining sentences, then, is the operation employed by children before embedding. This seems reasonable since conjunction preserves the lexical

---

[9] T-unit is defined as one main clause plus all the subordinate clauses attached to it.

items in the underlying sentences and their order, whereas embedding involves deletions, substitutions, and possibly permutations. The developmental trend seems to be first the acquisition of structures which maintain or add to underlying sentences, and then the acquisition of structures which involve deletions, substitutions, and permutation of items in underlying sentences.

Sudden shifts occur in the usage of structures. There seem to be some developmental periods in which more new structures are rapidly acquired and others during which there is not much change. The latter may be periods during which previously acquired structures are tested and perfected. During these periods there is a decrease in the number of children not observing the complete set of rules for the derivation of structures which have been acquired. The nursery school and first grade periods were found to be times during which rapid changes occur in syntactic competence, and the kindergarten period a time when little change occurs. There is also a simultaneous decrease during the kindergarten period in the number of children using deviant versions of both base structure rules and transformational rules, whereas there are rises in the use of deviant structures during the old nursery school and first grade period (Menyuk, 1964c). The first and seventh grades were found to be periods of rapid change in the O'Donnell, Griffin, and Norris (1967) study.

One other factor should be kept in mind in observing the sequence of usage of transformational operations. Although conjunctions with "and" occurred very frequently in the language sample obtained from kindergarten through seventh grade children, conjunctions with "but," "so," and "or" occurred significantly less frequently (O'Donnell, Griffin, and Norris, 1967). It was also found in the study of the transformational development of nursery school through first grade children (Menyuk, 1964c) that although many of the nursery school children and all of the kindergarten children were using conjunctions with "and," conjunctions with "if" and "so" were being used by significantly fewer of the children. Only 19 percent of the young nursery school children were using the latter types of conjunction, whereas 88 percent of these children were using "and" conjunction. Only 61 percent of the first grade children were using the latter types of conjunction, whereas 100 percent of these children were using "and" conjunction. It has been hypothesized that although all these conjunctions appear to be similar in terms of the syntactic operations involved in their generation, they are very dissimilar in terms of the semantic relationships expressed by the connectives and, therefore, are dissimilar in terms of the restrictions imposed on the content of the sentences to be conjoined under these conditions.[10]

---

[10] For a further discussion of this aspect, see Menyuk, 1969, Chapter 3.

Another aspect of structures which seems to affect sequence of development over the age range observed is not only complexity in terms of the *number* of rules, *types* of operations required to derive structures, and semantic relationships expressed in structures which require the observation of additional *restrictions,* but also complexity in terms of the *context* in which rules apply. Rules which apply over phrase boundaries and sentence boundaries are acquired later than those which apply within phrases and within sentences. Cazden (1968a) noted that at the stage at which three children were applying appropriate plural markers within the NP ("many toys") in 89, 77, and 83 percent of the necessary instances, they were not applying these markers outside the NP ("These are my cups") with the same frequency. In this latter case, appropriate markers were applied in 30, 43, and 54 percent of the necessary instances. There are, as has been observed, context-sensitive rules of co-occurrence which apply to a single underlying string and context-sensitive rules which apply in the generation of sentences from two or more underlying strings. Number agreement between N and V is required within a single sentence ("He plays" versus "He play") and also in conjoined sentences ("He plays and sings"), as is tense agreement ("He played and sang"). Pronominalization rules concerning number, case, and gender must be observed within the sentence ("It's a big table" versus "He's a big table") and between sentences when one is embedded in another ("It's the big table that's broken" versus "It's the big table who's broken").

Most of the nonobservations of restrictions on the generation of single underlying strings involve structures which have permutation as one of the operations in their derivation. These are also structures which are acquired comparatively late. The following is a list of the structures in which restrictions are not observed from 3 to 7 years and examples of these nonobservations.

Question	Where's the mother and father going
Adverb preposing	Here's the houses
There insertion	It isn't any more story
	There's a lot of things I see
Particle movement	He took off it

It can be observed from these examples that in the Q structure, the AUX and Mod sometimes do not agree in number with the subject, that in the Adverb preposing and There insertion structures, the verb number restriction is sometimes not observed, that in There insertion a pronominalization rule is sometimes not observed, and that in the Particle movement structure the restriction that pronoun objects must separate V + Part is sometimes not observed. The emphasis is on the word *sometimes* since, at this stage of development, restrictions on the generation of structures involving single underlying sentences are for the most part observed, with nonobservations occurring infrequently and in alternation with completely well-formed structures (Menyuk, 1964a).

In addition to the above deviant formations, children, at the earliest stage of this period of development, sometimes (1) do not expand the AUX-be node ("I playing a game"), and at later stages frequently (2) do not expand the AUX-have node "I been going there for a long time." They infrequently produce double negatives ("He doesn't get into no trouble") and invert the object ("His paw he has to get up"). They frequently do not observe restrictions on the third person reflexive ("He's washing hisself" and "They don't like to wash theirselves").

In the generation of structures involving two or more underlying sentences, restrictions are also not observed. Since the simplest operation to perform in generating sentences from two or more underlying sentences is conjunction without observation of any restrictions, in the earliest conjunctions the connective "and" merely joins sentences but does not impose any restrictions. Therefore, sentences are produced which indicate no observation of either the syntactic or semantic relatedness of the conjoined sentences. Early relative clause constructions and early elaborated complements also exhibit nonobservation of restrictions on the embedding of sentences and appear to be merely conjunctions. In the following examples it can be seen that S_2 is conjoined to S_1 to create relative clauses and complement without further operations or restrictions: "I can't know what is it"; "I like he jumps very high"; "He's thinking about he had a new sister."

During this period of development from 3 to 7 years, conjunction and embedding operations change from simply adding one sentence to another to increasing observation of restrictions imposed by operations, although more primitive forms may appear as additional verbs, allowing different types of structures are added to the lexicon. For example, sentences such as "He *seems* like he's in a dream" are produced by first graders. For the most part, however, pronominalization restrictions and tense restrictions in conjoined and embedded sentences are observed after the young nursery school period, rather than simply a process of adding one sentence to another as in the following examples.

Conjunction

Wendy and he wanted them to be a mother
My brother doesn't play with me but she hits me
Don't take that out or you would get in trouble

Relative Clause

  I hear what's crying
  He see a dog what's white

Just as in the development of base structure rules, the frames of the structures for transformation types are developed and then context-sensitive restrictions are observed. In general, nonobservation of restrictions declines over the age range of 3 to 7 years. There are periods during which greater numbers of children are using certain transformational structures than at previous periods. It is, naturally, at these periods that peaks in nonobservation of restrictions concerning these structures occur. As with base structure rules, omissions of rules and generalizations about transformational rules based on previous acquisitions occur during the time when a structure is being incorporated into the grammar (Menyuk, 1969).

An example of the general decrease in nonobservation of restrictions is the percentage of children during the young nursery school, nursery school, kindergarten, and first grade period who are not observing the restrictions on certain structures based on a single underlying sentence (adverb preposing, Wh Q, Particle movement, and *there* insertion). An example of the rise in nonobservation of restrictions due to the acquisition of new structures is the percentage of children not observing pronoun and tense restrictions with transformational structures based on two or more underlying sentences. Since a great many of the older nursery school children are already using the transformational structures involving a single underlying sentence and very little change in their use occurs over the age range, a peak in nonobservation of restrictions concerning these structures should occur during the nursery school period, followed by a decline at later stages. Since the number of children using transformational structures involving two or more underlying sentences rises steadily over the age range, a peak in nonobservation of restrictions concerning these structures should occur later in the age range, and then a less sharp decline should occur. These developmental trends do indeed occur, as can be seen in Figure 5–4.

SYNTACTIC COMPETENCE

As was stated before, attempts to assess the child's syntactic competence, without reference to the utterances produced, have been limited. This is particularly true with children under the age of 3 years because of the problems involved in devising suitable tasks—that is, tasks which test the child's syntactic competence rather than his understanding of the task.

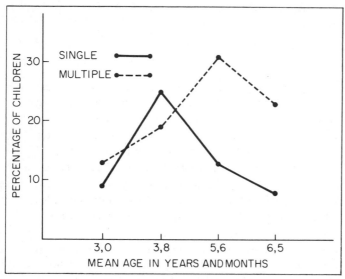

FIG. 5–4 Mean percentage of children not observing restrictions on transformational operations involving single and multiple underlying sentences at various ages.

Evaluation of syntactic competence, in recent research, has been limited primarily to two techniques: picture identification and repetition of sentences.

In the previous chapter a study using both techniques was cited (Fraser, Bellugi and Brown, 1963). However, the use of picture stimuli obviously limits the set of structures to be assessed to those that are picturable. In the next chapter, a number of studies will be discussed which test the child's ability to relate a picture to a sentence, to evaluate its truth, and to carry out a task so that the situation will match a sentence. Again, it will be noted that the structures tested are limited. Therefore, in recent studies, the technique of repetition has been used. This technique allows for the testing of a range of syntactic structures. In addition, other factors, such as length and lexical content, as well as the syntactic structures in the sentences, can be varied, controlled, and measured.

The accuracy of immediate recall of sentences could be affected by the length of the utterance, its lexical content, the semantic relationships expressed in the utterance, its syntactic structure, or its phonological structure (both segmental and supra-segmental). The sentences used in this task can be shaped to measure the relative effect of these factors—i.e., length, syntactic structure, semantic structure, and phonological structure. They can also be shaped to measure effects within each category—that is, the particular length, and particular syntactic, semantic, and phonological structures in the sentences presented for repetition.

Let us begin by stating that the results of all the studies to be cited indicate that repetition can be merely mimicry of the surface structure of the utterance or it can reflect the availability of matching structures in the subjects' grammars (or their linguistic competence), depending on the structure and length of the utterances presented for repetition. If an utterance is short enough to be within the immediate memory span of a subject, it can be mimicked despite its semantic and syntactic structure on the basis of the familiarity of its phonological structure or lexical content. Thus, utterances such as "gint ponta fip," "Flowers sing on a quick chair," "mother by spanked got he," and nonsense syllables read without intonation and stress patterns conjoining them (read as word lists) could be mimicked if the memory span of the subject is sufficient to deal with the length of the material. The hypothesis is that if the above types of utterances exceeded immediate memory span, only bits of them would be mimicked and the amount and items mimicked would depend on the length of the utterance and the position of the item. A further hypothesis is that utterances such as "Don't bother him," "Birds sing in our backyard," and "He got spanked by mother" would be more easily and accurately repeated and their repetition would not be as affected by length or word position as would the repetition of those utterances listed previously or word or nonsense syllable lists. Repetition of a well-formed utterance would be affected by the underlying structure of the utterance rather than by its surface structure.

In a recent study (Scholes, 1968) 43 children (aged 3 years, 4 months to 5 years, 10 months) and adults were asked to repeat utterances which were word lists. Each word in an utterance was produced separately with some pause between them and received equal stress (for example, "foód—iś— eáten—bý—thé—cát"). The words were recorded for presentation to subjects. The utterances varied in length from four to eight words and the structure of the sequence of isolated words was varied in the following manner: (1) "completely" grammatical (as in the above instance); (2) nongrammatical "semantically" ("cat is eaten by the food"); (3) nongrammatical "syntactically" by permutation of major constituents SVO ("by the cat is eaten food"); (4) nongrammatical "syntactically" by permutation of word order within constituents ("food eaten is cat the by"); and (5) nongrammatical "syntactically" by permutations within and without major constituents ("cat eaten food by is the"). Of course, in instances 2 through 5 both syntactic and semantic relationships are disrupted and only the semantic properties of isolated lexical morphemes are maintained since these items are not nonsense. It is also questionable to call instance 1 completely grammatical since it is produced without prosodic features.

It was found that the length of the utterance affected the *attempt* of children to repeat. Only four-word sequences were attempted by all the children and the median age of the 21 percent of the children who attempted seven-word sequences was 5 years. Therefore, age affected even the attempt to repeat. Adults repeated utterances of types 1 and 2 without errors, type 3 with two errors, type 4 with 15 errors, and type 5 with 21 errors. The results for the children are based only on four-word utterances. Unfortunately, the number of errors is not listed for each type in the case of children, so that, while it is clear that *degree of grammaticalness* affects adults' repetitions in an orderly manner, there are no data given concerning this question for children.

Percentage of errors for types 1 and 2 is compared to percentage of errors for types 4 and 5 at various median age levels. At the youngest age level (median age 3 years, 10 months) there is practically no difference in percentage of errors between the two groups (39.5 percent with types 1 and 2 versus 38.5 percent with types 4 and 5). The difference in errors between groups increases and the total percentage of errors decreases as age increases. At the oldest age level (median age 5 years) the percentage of errors is 8.0 percent with types 1 and 2 versus 16.5 percent with types 4 and 5. Errors were categorized as deletion, addition, substitution, or permutation of items in the utterances presented. For adults, deletion errors were related to length, serial position of item (first items were repeated most accurately), and type of utterance (occurring, of course, most frequently with types 4 and 5 since no errors occurred with types 1 and 2). For children, deletion errors were related to length but not to serial position of item or type of sequence. Addition and replacement errors were rare with adults but were common with children. These additions and replacements were unrelated to type of sequence and were often words heard in previously presented utterances. Permutation errors, on the other hand, were related to the type of utterance, and both children and adults most frequently permuted items in types 4 and 5.

The experimenter concludes that syntactic regularity is the most important prerequisite for regeneration of an utterance by adults (although the difference in errors between types 2 and 3 is not marked), and that supra-segmental features are unimportant. On the other hand, syntactic regularity seems to be unimportant to children until the second half of the fourth year. Although the experimenter does not do so, could it then be claimed that supra-segmental features are the most important and structuring aspect of utterances to children under 4½ years of age, since children under this age appear to do equally badly with all five types of utterances? It seems highly unlikely. What might be the case is that supra-segmental features take on great importance when the material is approached as meaningless material; indeed, it appears as if all the utterances presented for repetition were approached as meaningless material at least by the youngest group of children.

To determine the validity of such an assumption, a comparison would have to be made between children's repetition of naturally produced utterances varying in grammaticalness as well as word lists varying in the same manner. In a comparison of children's repetition of grammatical sentences presented naturally and those presented in reverse order but phrased and marked with intonation and stress (Menyuk, 1969, Chapter 4), it was found that children under 4 years of age imitated the stress and intonation patterns of the reversed word-order sentences when none or few of the lexical items in the utterance were reproduced (series of nonsense syllables with stress correctly marked and the intonation contour preserved were produced). Even children aged 3 and below were, however, correctly repeating grammatical sentences up to the length of nine words, depending on the structure of the utterance. It was also found that there was a significant correlation between the length of a reversed word-order utterance and the number of errors in repetition, although no such correlation was found with grammatical sentences, and that serial position of an item in a reversed word-order utterance affected the correct reproduction (first items were most correctly reproduced), although no such effect was found with grammatical sentences. These children treated grammatical and agrammatical utterances strikingly differently in repetition.

It is clear that the subject's approach to the repetition of utterances has an important effect on the results obtained in such experiments. Children, under the age of 4½ years at any rate, appear to approach all *word lists* as nonsentences, even if they are in the correct word order for sentences and, when put together, express correct syntactic and semantic relationships. Older children and adults appear to be able to detect the sentencelike aspects and resynthesize such lists into sentences, depending on the degree to which such lists deviate from the completely grammatical. However, even with older children, word length appears to be a critical factor which indicates that perhaps their first approach to the material is as if it were meaningless or simply a word list. The younger children may *first* analyze these sequences in terms of their prosodic features. If utterances do not match their structural descriptions in terms of these features, no further effort at analysis in terms of sentencehood is carried out.

Of particular interest to the student of syntax development is not only the question of which aspect of an utterance (i.e., length, or syntactic, semantic, or phonological structure) affects repetition success or failure most seriously at what ages, but more importantly, which particular structures are easy or difficult to repeat at particular stages of development, since in spontaneous speech, both heard and produced, all aspects of the grammar are obviously convoluted. Further, the student is interested in the correlations, if any, between production of structures and reproduction of structures.

Children aged approximately 3 to 6 years were asked to repeat sentences containing various syntactic structures found in their own spontaneous language production and sentences containing various deviations from complete grammaticalness which were also found in their language production (Menyuk, 1963b). Pre-school and kindergarten children, approximately 4 to 6 years of age, were asked to repeat the above types of utterances plus the same completely grammatical sentences presented in reversed word order. In addition, they were asked to correct the nongrammatical utterances (Menyuk, 1969, Chapter 4). As we noted previously, sentence length and accuracy of repetition were not significantly correlated for grammatical utterances but were significantly correlated for agrammatical sentences. This indicates that the approach to repetition of these two types of utterances differed. Some of the grammatical sentences were repeated with modifications. The youngest group of children and the middle-aged children in the group most frequently modified sentences which contained VP expansions, embedding, and conjunctions other than "and." The oldest children in the group most frequently modified VP expansions. Structures were most frequently modified by the youngest group of children. Most modifications were simplifications of the structure presented for repetition and, for the most part, meaning was preserved. For example, two sentences were substituted for conjunction, only one sentence of an embedded structure was repeated, the V form was simplified, etc. The following are some examples.

1. "He hurt me so I hurt him back" repeated as "He hurt me. I hurt him back" or "He hurt me and I hurt him back" or "I hurt him back."
2. "I've already been there" repeated as "I was there" or "I have been there."
3. "I like playing the piano" repeated as "I like to play the piano."
4. "Doing that is not nice" repeated as "He does that" or "He's doing that."

Another finding was that the youngest children in the group most frequently *spontaneously* corrected nongrammatical utterances, whereas the oldest children in the group most frequently corrected nongrammatical utterances when asked to do so. The youngest children least frequently corrected utterances when asked to do so and the oldest children least frequently spontaneously corrected nongrammatical utterances. The older children more faithfully followed the instruction, "You say what I say." Deviations from base structure rules were most frequently corrected, deviations from transformational rules were the next most frequently corrected, and morphological rules were the least frequently corrected by the total population. In other words, deep structure rules were most frequently corrected, whereas derived structure or surface structure rules were least frequently corrected.

There was a significant correlation between the structures found in an age group's spontaneous utterances and those successfully repeated. However, in some instances, structures not found in the spontaneous language of an age group were successfully repeated, and these were often structures that children who were *slightly older* were using in their spontaneous utterances. Given the memory aid of a model of a structure, these children could in particular instances exceed the syntactic competence displayed in their spontaneous productions.

These results indicate that children do not listen passively to sentences and then attempt to imitate the structure and content of sentences up to the limits of their memory span, although this characterizes their performance with nonsentences. Instead, they analyze sentences by attempting to match the structures in the sentence with those in the grammar and regenerate them in accordance with these structures. If a structure is not available, simplifications occur which, on the whole, preserve meaning. If a structure is nongrammatical and the well-formed rule is available, the deviant structure is corrected.

In another study (Slobin and Welsh, 1967), the structure of the utterances which could be repeated by a young child (studied from approximately 2 years, 3 months to approximately 2 years, 5 months) was examined. Copulas and auxiliary verbs were not repeated at age 2 years, 3 months, as in the following examples:

1. "The pencil is green" is repeated as "pencil green."
2. "The little boy is eating some pink ice cream" is repeated as "little boy eating some pink ice cream."

Note, also, in the above examples, that the article is omitted in both sentences but the quantifier ("some") and the adjective ("pink") are preserved. This correlates very well with what has been observed in spontaneous utterances.

In repeating conjoined and embedded sentences, the following kinds of repetition were observed:

1. Embedded sentences were omitted, as in "Mozart, who cried, came to my party" repeated as "Mozart came to party."
2. Embedded sentences were separated and conjoined, a simplification of embedding, as in "The owl who eats the candy runs fast" repeated as "owl eat a candy and he run fast."
3. Conjoined sentences are repeated or the meaning is preserved if there is some relationship between the conjoined sentences or some conjunction copying. "This one is the giant but this one is little" is repeated as "dis one little, annat one big," but "Mozart got burned and the big shoe is here" is repeated as "Mozart got burned and duh big shoe got burned."

4. Conjunction deletions are repeated, but only if the subjects match. "The blue shoes and blue pencils are here" is repeated as "blue pencils are here and blue shoes are here," but "The boy is eating and crying" is repeated as "boy eating uh crying."

The rules in this child's grammar obviously affect the repetition of utterances.

The experimenters found that when the child was asked to repeat immediately a fairly complex sentence which she had just produced (one containing structures not usually found in her spontaneous speech), she could successfully do so. However, when asked to repeat this utterance some time later, she could not. They conclude that when the *intention* to produce a structure is present, even though such a structure exceeds the child's usual performance, the child can reproduce it. Some time later when the child does not intend to produce this structure, she cannot reproduce it. Therefore, repetitions appear to be a conservative estimate of the child's syntactic competence. In the earlier study cited it was found that in particular instances children exceeded their spontaneous performance in their repetitions. That is, repetitions appeared to be a maximum estimate of their syntactic competence. This difference may be an indication of developmental stages in increasing syntactic competence. Certain structures may be used occasionally by the child before they have become part of the child's grammar. Since they are not part of the grammar they cannot be called upon at different times to repeat utterances. When they have become part of the child's grammar, although they are not usually used in spontaneous utterances, they can be recognized and can be called upon at any time for the repetition of sentences.

On the whole, however, the reproduction of sentences by this young child seems to reflect some of the developmental trends that have been observed in the spontaneous production of utterances: the auxiliary and copula are developed late and conjunction of sentences occurs long before embedding. Those structures which were beyond this child's competence were regenerated in terms of the structures in her grammar. In many instances these simplifications preserved the meaning of the whole or part of the utterance. This child could repeat sentences which contained violations of syntactic and semantic rules if the utterances were short enough. In these instances, the experimenters state, the phonological structure of the utterances was preserved.

In a study (Smith, 1966) of the repetition of sentences by 3 and 4 year old children, it was found, again, that the syntactic structure of the utterance affected the accuracy of its repetition, whereas the length of the sentence did not. The sentences presented for repetition were grammatical and nongrammatical. The grammatical sentences contained expansions of the NP into Det + N, expansions of the VP with AUX/Mod + V and conjunctions and embeddings. It was found that the grammatical sentences could be divided into two categories: easy to repeat and difficult to repeat accurately. Under the heading easy to repeat were the following:

Conjunction	John and Bill built their house or Bill ate the apple and orange
NP expansion	Two of the marbles rolled away
Complement	I want to play the piano

Under the heading difficult to repeat were the following structures:

Adjective	They played with long yellow blocks or
	The grey wolf ate the children
Relative clause	The lady who sneezes is sick
VP expansion	I may have missed the train
Conjunction inversion	Not John but Bill came along

The most frequent type of inaccurate response with grammatical sentences was omission of the complexity of the stimulus sentence so that it was repeated as a "simplex sentence." Thus, Adj + N was reproduced simply as N, and AUX + V was reproduced as V. Nongrammatical utterances were frequently spontaneously corrected, preserving the underlying structure of the utterance. For example, "Harry like to riding" was repeated as "Harry likes to ride." On the basis of modal utterance length, the children were divided into three groups: least mature, medially mature, and most mature. Accuracy of repetition of grammatical sentences and correction of nongrammatical utterances increased with the medially mature group. Accuracy of repetition increased with the most mature group but correction decreased.

These results, for the most part, seem to reflect what has been observed about the sequence of acquisition found in the structures used in spontaneous speech and the sequence observed in repetition accuracy. Nested relative clause constructions involve embedding and permutation (displacing the subject and verb of the sentence) and conjunction inversion involves permutation. Those structures which involve embedding and permutation, as has been noted, tend to appear in the sentences of children after those which involve addition or conjunction, deletion and substitution. Children's repetition of utterances indicates that they have less competence in analyzing sentences with embedded and permuted structures. However, VP expansion, involving further elaboration of the auxiliary node, but not requiring these operations, is a structure that is used comparatively late and is repeated inaccurately. As has been observed, the adjective and infinitival complement structures, which involve embedding, are used comparatively early. In this experiment the adjective structure caused difficulty in repetition but the complement did not. In other repetition studies cited, both structures were easy to repeat. It may be that a structure such as Adj + Adj + N causes difficulties but not Adj + N. The experimenter concludes that it is not the derivational history of the structure (or its complexity in terms of number of rules) which affects degree of difficulty in repetition but its surface structure or the amount of loading on the NP or VP nodes. Thus Adj + Adj + N constructions or N + relative clause constructions load the NP node and Mod + AUX + V loads the VP node. However, the same might be said of complement constructions, since on the surface they also load the VP node.

The results obtained in this study can be accounted for by (1) the types of operations which are easier or more difficult for children to acquire and use (for example, embedded constructions, as in the complement sentence, versus embedded and permuted constructions, as in the relative clause sentence), and (2) cyclical operations and how they function in children's grammar. It has been found (Menyuk, 1969, Chapter 3), for example, that although the infinitival complement construction is used at an early age, iteration (a double application of complement operation, as in "I need to get the crayons to draw the picture") begins to be used at a later age and is not used by all 7-year-old children. Adj + Adj + N constructions would involve a double application of the rules needed to derive the Adj construction, and VP expansion to include Mod + Aux + V involves two elaborations of the AUX node. Facility in *reapplication* of the same set of rules appears to be a comparatively late acquisition, although sentences which contain different constructions (for example, relative clause + complement, as in "I don't know what he wants to do in there") appear comparatively early. It is clear, from this last example, that length is not the factor which can account for this difference in usage.

The results of repetition experiments have corroborated general developmental trends that have been observed in children's spontanous productions. Those structures which are spontaneously used by increasing numbers of children as an increasingly older population is observed are also repeated by increasing numbers of children as the age of the population examined increases. Again, the type of operations needed for the derivation of a structure is an important distinguishing factor between structures that are easy or difficult to repeat. Structures which permute elements in the underlying sentence or sentences and separate subject and verb are those which seem most difficult to reproduce.

There is some indication that syntactic competence, as displayed in repetition, exceeds, in certain specific instances, what has been observed in spontaneous productions. However, in the types of structures examined thus far, the difference is limited. It may be that the distance between competence, as measured by the ability to regenerate structures, and the production of structures continuously increases as children mature. For example, although the nested (permuted) relative clause construction or have + be + verb may be rarely used after age 7, it may be easily regenerated. No answer to this speculation has been obtained, since repetition of utterances and comparison with spontaneous productions has not been examined after age 7. On the other hand, at an earlier stage of development (2 to 2½ years) a child was found to produce structures which she could not reproduce if repetition was asked for after some delay. This may be an indication that such structures are within the syntactic competence of this child, or it may simply be an indication that memorized structures which cannot be used generatively but only in specific instances are displaced by structures that are really in the child's grammar and used in a repetition task.

A technique other than repetition has been used to examine the syntactic competence of children aged 5 to 10 years (Chomsky, 1968). These children's comprehension of a set of specific structures was tested. There are constructions in English in which the surface structure of the sentence is misleading concerning the SVO relationship expressed in the underlying structure of the sentence. The passive construction is an example of this type where the *position* of the subject and the object is reversed ("The boy got spanked by his mother") or the subject is not expressed ("The boy got spanked"). There are other structures in which relationships are not clearly marked in surface structure. The following are some examples taken from the study cited.

1. John is easy to see	(John is the *object*)
2a. John told Bill to leave	(Bill is *subject* of to leave)
2b. John promised Bill to leave	(John is *subject* of to leave)
3a. The child asked the teacher what to do	(*child* is subject of what to do)
3b. The child asked the teacher to leave the room	(*child* or *teacher* is subject of to leave)
4a. When he was tired, John usually took a nap	(*he*=John, or *he*=somebody)
4b. He knew that John was going to win the race	(*he*=somebody)

In instance 1 the properties of the predicate adjective "easy" make "John" the object. In a sentence with another type of predicate adjective "John" would be subject (for example, "John is slow to get angry"). In instances 2 and 3 it is the properties of the verbs "tell," "promise," and "ask" plus the structures which they take (complement in 2*a*, 2*b*, and 3*b* and relative clause in 3*a*) which dictate the subject-object relationship in the sentences. It is the usual case that the indirect object in a complement is the subject of the complement ("He wanted him to go," "I told him what to do"). Notice also that in the usual cases the subject of the complement *immediately precedes* these constructions. With the verbs "promise" and "ask" this usual proximity is disturbed, as in 2*b* and 3*a,* and with the verb "ask" a conflict in interpretation can exist, as in 3*b*. In instance 4*b,* because of the structure of the sentence (it includes a relative clause or complement, as in "He wanted John to sing"), the pronoun must refer to someone outside the sentence.

The children were presented with toy objects and construction materials. After some initial questions and play to determine that the children understood the task, their comprehension of each structure was uniquely tested by asking them to answer questions, give instructions, and manipulate objects. For example, in testing structure 1, the children were presented with a blindfolded doll and asked, "Is this doll easy or hard to see?" In testing structure 2, the children were told, "Bozo (tells/promises) Donald Duck to hop up and down. Make him hop." In testing structure 3, two children acting as partners were told to (tell/ask) the partner ". . . what to feed the doll." In testing structure 4, the children were told "After he got the candy, Mickey Mouse left," and then asked "Who got the candy? Who left?" In addition, in testing structure 3, children were shown contrasting pictures and asked to show the picture, for example, of "The boy asks the girl which shoes to wear." Of the 15 subjects tested on both pictures and interviews, nine performed the same in both instances, five did better on the picture task, and one did worse.

One interesting finding of this study is that, unlike the case with the other types of syntactic structures that have been previously discussed, age was not a factor in the comprehension of structures 1, 2, and 3. Individual level of competence rather than age affected performance. Thus, children ranging in age from 5 to 10 years either comprehended or did not comprehend these structures, and, indeed the experimenter notes that in the ask/tell contrast some adults did not comprehend the structure. It was the case, however, that individual children displayed an orderly sequence of acquisition. For example, the comprehension of 3*a* was necessary for the comprehension of 3*b*. In contrast, comprehension of structure 4 was dependent on age, and beginning at age 5 years, 6 months, most responses were correct. The experimenter concludes that this difference is due to the fact that while the pronominalization principle applies to the *whole sentence,* the other structures apply to words (or verb categorizations). The acquisition of these latter structures appears to be dependent on the degree of language elaboration in the environment, intelligence, and rate of cognitive development.

Another interesting finding is that structures which cause separation of the subject from the verb are more difficult to comprehend than those which do not, and structures that potentially have two interpretations are more difficult to comprehend than those which do not. It has been observed previously that structures which do not disturb the proximity of subject and verb are acquired first, produced earlier and by greater numbers of children, and are repeated with less difficulty by young childen than are structures which do disturb this proximity.

SUMMARY

After the acquisition of base structure rules which define the subject-object relationships in sentences, and after the acquisition of the principle that various sentence types can be generated by the conjoining of elements (Neg. + S, Q + S, Emph + S), the child then goes about the task of determining the syntactic rules of his specific language. The course of development of such rules is affected by several factors: (1) the function of particular structures; (2) the number of rules needed to derive the structures; (3) the types of operations needed to derive these structures; and (4) the selectional restrictions which must be observed in the derivation of these structures.

Structures which presumably are derived from two underlying sentences are, nevertheless, acquired earlier than some structures which involve operations on a single underlying sentence. These are structures which add to the class of object (infinitival complement) and add to the class of determiners (adjectives and possessives). There is some question about whether or not these structures are analyzed in the same manner by the child and the linguist. The verbs used with complement are very limited, and possessives and adjectives often appear as nouns at the early stages of development, which may indicate a different analysis when these structures first begin to be used.

Structures which are derived by a combination of sets of rules on a single underlying string (for example, Negative Question) appear after structures which are derived by a single set of rules; and structures which are derived by a combination of sets of rules on two or more underlying strings (for example, various types of conjunction, relative clause) appear, with some exceptions, after structures derived from sets of rules on one underlying string. Therefore, number of rules appears to be one factor in the sequence of acquisition, but only one factor. Within each class of structures (those based on single and those based on multiple underlying sentences) the particular syntactic operations involved in the derivation of the structure markedly affect sequence of acquisition. Operations of permutation of items, as in the case of permuting the auxiliary in question and adverb preposing, or permutation of sentences, as in the cases of nesting one sentence into another, are acquired after operations which add, delete, or substitute items.

Finally, after structures are acquired and new items are added to the lexicon, more selectional restrictions must be observed. The deviations from completely well-formed structures that one observes at the beginning stages of further development are usually omissions at the base structure level and omission of a rule or operation at the transformational level. At the later stages of development generalizations based on previous rules occur. The specific restrictions on the use of modifiers with nouns and objects of verbs are not always observed. Substitutions, alternations in use, and finally redundancies occur before selectional restrictions are observed in base structure rules, and omissions and generalizations occur before the complete set of rules in transformations is used. This latter aspect of development continues long after basic rules have been acquired, and is complicated by additions to the lexicon which require further restrictions.

The results of repetition experiments give us some indication of how sentences are perceived by children and the changes that occur in this perception at various stages of development. It appears from the results obtained that utterances are first classified as sentences or nonsentences (within the grammar or outside the grammar). At an early stage of development this decision may first be made on the basis of the prosodic features of an utterance, and utterances without the stress and intonational patterns of "normal" sentences are perceived as word lists with items to be memorized. Number of words in an utterance should then affect accurate repetition for all such strings, whether or not there is correct word order for sentences, and it does.

When the child decides that an utterance is a possible sentence in the language, he then analyzes the sentence by attempting to match the structure of the utterance to structures in his grammar. The child appears to search for underlying strings consisting of subject and verb or subject, verb, and object; and to apply those operations which are within his grammar to match those in the sentence. Thus, at an early stage of development, embedded sentences are omitted or simply conjoined, and verb phrases are not expanded. When reproducing nongrammatical sentences, base structure rules are most frequently corrected. The consistent trend that has been observed in the modification of sentences, in the repetition task, is the simplification of utterances in terms of base structure rules and transformational operations when the rules and operations used for the derivation of the structures in the presented sentences are not available to the child.

It appears that adults do not analyze sentences by a resynthesis of their derivation, but by perceptual strategies based on determining the subject and verb and the types of structures that categories of verbs allow (Fodor, Garrett, and Bever, 1968). On the other hand, children in the process of acquiring transformational rules, achieving facility in their use, and applying them over sentence boundaries and for additional categories of nouns and verbs, appear to go through a partial process of synthesis to produce and analyze utterances. At some stage of development, probably the stage at which basic syntactic structures have been acquired, the process of sentence analysis seems to be quite similar to that of the adult. An utterance is heard, accepted or rejected for further grammatical analysis, analyzed in terms of the structures in the child's grammar, and regenerated according to these structures.

6

THE ACQUISITION
AND
DEVELOPMENT
OF
SEMANTICS

WHEN LISTENING to an utterance one derives the meaning of a word in that utterance from its relationship to the other words in the sentence. Because of the context and structure of the sentence we may interpret the word in various ways. Thus, when we hear (1) "The trunk is in the attic," (2) "Water squirted out of his trunk," and (3) "The trunk was six feet in circumference," the word "trunk" will be assigned a different meaning in each sentence because of the context. The word trunk in the instances given has the following three meanings: [1] (1) a box or chest for containing clothes or other goods; (2) a proboscis, especially of an elephant; and (3) the main stem, or body, of a tree. There are other meanings for the same word, "trunk," when it is used in other sentences.

Not only may a lexical item have different meanings in different contexts, but its syntactic role may differ as well. The following are some examples:

1. My mother likes *laughing*	N
2. My mother is *laughing*	V
3. The third grade gave a *play* yesterday	N
4. The third grade boys *play* football	V

---

[1] The definitions are taken from *Webster's Collegiate Dictionary*, 5th Edition. Cambridge, Mass.: G. C. Merriam and Co., 1942.

The structure of the sentences indicates the syntactic class to which "laughing" in sentences 1 and 2 and "play" in sentences 3 and 4 belong.

In other instances the structure of the sentence does not help in determining the meaning of a lexical item, and these sentences are, therefore, ambiguous. The following are some examples:

1. The trunk is large.
2. I saw a play that was wonderful.
3. The lion is ready for killing.
4. Shooting hunters can be fatal.

In sentence 1 we cannot determine from the structure of the sentence if the "trunk" is the elephant's, the tree's, or a box we put objects in. In sentence 2 we cannot determine whether "play" refers to a performance on a stage or a performance in a sporting event. In sentence 3 we do not know if the lion is about to kill us or if we are about to kill the lion. In sentence 4 we do not know if shooting hunters will cause our death or theirs. In these instances the conversational context and/or the situational context in which the utterance is produced will determine which meaning of a lexical item in sentences 1 and 2, and which syntactic relationship in sentences 3 and 4 should be assigned for a proper interpretation. Although context is used to disambiguate the ambiguous sentence, the listener must have available both syntactic information (subject-object relationships in structures) and semantic information (all the dictionary meanings of a lexical item and the logical relationships of these items) to carry out the required interpretation. If this information is not available, then regardless of context the sentence will not communicate the meaning intended by the speaker. In acquiring the semantic system of his language, then, the child must acquire knowledge both of dictionary meanings and of syntactic and logical relationships to understand utterances and to produce understandable utterances.

The number and references of lexical items that are acquired by a child are dependent on the child's linguistic community and his experiences. There are several very clear-cut examples of this first type of dependency. One example is that the number and reference of color terms a child will acquire is dependent on his native language. To divide the color range from purple to red, American English speaking children will acquire six terms (purple, blue, green, yellow, orange, and red) whereas Shona (a language of Rhodesia) speaking children will have four terms for this range, one of which, for example, includes orange and red, and Bassa (a language of Liberia) speaking children have two terms for this range, one of which, for example, includes yellow, orange, and red (Gleason, 1961).

As an example of the second type of dependency—the influence of environment on number and reference of lexical items—we can take the hypothetical case of a child who lives in a linguistic community in which there is no lexical item in the dictionary for the object "helicopter" simply because such an object has never been seen or imagined by the members of his community. If such an object should appear in his environment, the speakers of his language could invent a term for it, since "new" words are always being invented, and this term might then become part of this child's lexicon and part of the lexicon of future speakers of his language.

If it is indeed the case that the number and references of lexical items are largely dependent on the language acquired and the particular experiences of the child, it would be difficult to find any generalizations about the sequence of acquisition of types of lexical items or what children talk about at various stages of development that might hold not only between children from differing linguistic communities but also between individual children. However, certain general lexical categories have been found in many languages that linguists have examined.[2] If we take as a model these universal lexical categories, there may be some generalizations that hold between children from differing linguistic communities and children within the same community.

Considering the instance given previously as an example, although there was no one-to-one correspondence between the color names and their references in the different languages, each language had a lexical category which could be called "color." There are other such lexical categories. For example, each language will have structures and properties which indicate person, place, and time. Each language will have structures which indicate the attributes of objects, living things, and ideas. Each language will have structures which indicate sequential and logical relationships such as "and," "because," "then," "not," "but," etc. In other words, there are structures and properties of lexical items which can be found in all languages because all men find them necessary for effective communication.

Some questions that might concern the student of language development are: (1) Which properties of lexical items are understood and used by the child before others? For example, are properties which differentiate objects and living things (±human) determined before properties which differentiate size (±large)? Are these determined before properties which differentiate relationship (±mother)? (2) Why does this sequence of development occur? The research carried out on the semantic aspect of

---

[2] For several discussions of "semantic universals," see Greenberg, 1963.

language development does not provide us with answers to these questions, primarily because these are difficult questions to put either experimentally or in terms of naturalistic data. Cross-cultural studies of the sequence of acquisition of lexical items and structures may provide us with some answers to these questions.

Some developmental trends have been observed in the child's early vocalization, behavior and early use of lexical items, from which one may speculate about the processes of meaning and property acquisition. Most of the research to be reported has been concerned with stages in the acquisition and development of dictionary meanings and with the comprehension and use of structures which convey logical relationships. Research covering these aspects of semantic development will be discussed.

PROCESSES IN THE ACQUISITION OF THE MEANINGFULNESS OF THE SPEECH SIGNAL

In the course of development of comprehension of the meaningfulness of a speech signal, during the babbling period when this acquisition takes place, some gross behavioral changes in the responsiveness of the infant to the speech signal have been observed, and in some few instances data on specific responses to particular aspects of the signal have been recorded. Imitation has often been invoked as necessary to comprehension and as an indication of the infant's increasing comprehension of the speech signal.

As an example of the type of observations that have been made, Nakazima (1962) makes the following points. At 2 to 5 months, infants appear to be happy to listen to parents' imitations of the sounds the infants produce. By their behavior the infants can be categorized into two groups. The vocalization of one group is more "active" with parents than when alone. With the other group the reverse occurs. When the infant is looking at new objects, vocalization decreases until the object becomes familiar. At 6 to 8 months, parents' voices and other sounds cause repetitive babbling, and the infants stop activities in response to mother's "No!" At 9 months to 1 year, the infants' vocalizations show a marked increase when parents and dolls are present. There appears to be an increased understanding of the names of objects and situations. During the process of mastering other tasks, such as standing, vocalization decreases.

Before the age of 6 months, increase in vocalization seems to be dependent on parental vocalizations and presence for some infants but not for others. After this period both parents' vocalizations and other sounds, as well as human-like objects (dolls) increase vocalization. However, at 9 months there appears to be increased understanding of the names of objects and situations produced by the parents. Although it is difficult to determine which aspects of the situation the infant is responding to before 9 months (parents' or toys' presence or the speech signal or the meaning of the signal),[3] it appears, very grossly speaking, that comprehension of the meaning of adult utterances or aspects of adult utterances begins somewhat before 9 months. It is clear that no satisfactory evaluation of the infant's comprehension of the meaning of utterances during the babbling period has, as yet, been carried out, and in addition, the necessity of responding to parents' vocalizations by vocalization to establish comprehension of meaning has not been established.

Lewis (1963, Chapter 1) postulates that imitation is necessary for the comprehension of the speech signal. The process of imitation has three phases: first, a rudimentary vocal response to vocalization with no similarity to the stimulus; second, an abeyance of this rudimentary response during which the situation in which vocalizations occur is observed rather than the sounds themselves; third, specific responses to particular patterns. This third phase comes about because the child now has the capacity to produce a greater variety of vocal sounds and can recognize and manipulate the relationships between the speech signal and objects and situations in the environment. The stabilization of meaning occurs through the response of the environment. The mother states and the child imitates.

This speculation is somewhat confusing and certainly does not lead to an understanding of the process involved in the acquisition of the meaning of a speech signal. It is not clear from this description whether comprehension precedes imitation or imitation leads to comprehension. The only behavior which precedes the second phase, that of observation of the situation as well as socialization, is when the infant grossly responds to vocalization with vocalization. In both this description and in the description cited previously, imitation is equated with vocalization. The infants' so-called imitations are very poor matches of the model phonological and syntactic patterns presented to him, and will continue to be so for some time.

Murai (1963/64) discusses imitation and comprehension in his study of the development of words by Japanese children. He notes, first, no precedence of either imitation or comprehension in the acquisition of a word, since instances of either order are observed. Comprehension and production are considered by Murai to be independent since behavior which indicates comprehension occurs without actual production of an item. The first type of response, which indicates that the speech signal is

---

[3] Some question has been raised about the necessity of a speech signal in the environment to institute vocalization. Lenneberg, 1969, notes that hearing children of deaf parents who only use sign language vocalize in the same manner as children of hearing parents.

meaningful, is on a performance level. For example, the child stops his activity to the word "No!" or goes to the door when mother says, "We're going bye-bye" or "Daddy's here." When the child begins to produce symbols, he may use different symbols for the same object. For example, the child may indicate a ball as "bon, bon" in one instance and "dan, dan" in another. From this description and the experimenter's comments, it appears that there need be no strict sequence of imitation first and then comprehension to establish the meaningfulness of a signal for the infant. The infant need not attempt to imitate a word before he comprehends it. Comprehension, on the other hand, appears to precede production. Murai's data also indicate that use of the verbal symbol system, at the beginning stages of relating meanings to symbols, can be arbitrary. The child produces different strings when indicating the same object, and he produces words which have no resemblance to adult utterances.

This latter behavior has also been observed with infants in an American English linguistic environment (Winitz and Irwin, 1958). It was found that the first words of these children could be divided into three categories: standard words, word approximations, and self-language words. Word approximations were defined as utterances which contained at least one speech sound that could be found in the standard word. This seems to be a fairly generous description of a word approximation, and some of these utterances might be considered self-language words. In the 13th and 18th month age period examined with this population, the proportion of word approximations fell from 83 percent of the utterances at the beginning of this age period to 56 percent at its end. Standard words rose from 16 percent at the beginning of this age period to 38 percent. Self-language words rose (with a slight dip at the 15 to 16 month period) during this same period from 0.73 percent to 5.22 percent. Thus, for a fairly long period of time after children are comprehending the meaning of some utterances and are using utterances to communicate meaning, a large majority of the utterances they produce do not match or even roughly match adult utterances. It is difficult to label this performance imitation. The infant seems to have caught on to the principles of the communication game long before he can use the standard rules or models presented to him.

Bullowa, Jones, and Duckert (1964) have traced the acquisition of a word by a child. Because of the experimental design of this study (movie frames of the situation context, explanatory comments of an observer, as well as tape recordings), the experimenters could observe the situations in which the word was produced as well as note its phonetic composition at various stages. The following stages were observed in the acquisition of the word "shoe": (1) the mother pronounced the word in association with the objects; (2) some time later the infant attempted to imitate the word and the mother rejected the attempt; (3) some time later the child's attempt to imitate was accepted by the mother; (4) some time later the child used her word for "shoe" spontaneously, when the shoe was present, and was understood by the mother; (5) some time later the child used her word for "shoe" spontaneously when the shoe was not present; (6) some time later the child achieved adult pronunciation of the word. Phonetically, the child produced the word as /tu/, then /tu-tu/, then /tsu/, then /ču/, and finally /šu/.

The experimenters note that the child obeys commands about the shoe before she produces the standard form of the word. They do not know if the infant is responding to the word, the sentence heard, or the situation. They also note that although the infant does not produce a phonetic sequence which satisfies the mother, she continues to use this same phonetic string in situations with the shoe for a period of time, and that the phonetic string which the mother finally accepts is as different phonetically from "shoe" as the string she rejects.

The results of this analysis indicate that it would be a difficult task for the child to learn either to associate a symbol with an object or to modify production of the symbol on the basis of mother's acceptance or rejection (reward or punishment), since her behavior is arbitrary in terms of the accuracy of the production. Further, the acquisition of the meaning of the symbol does not seem to be a simple path from imitation to comprehension to production. In order to comprehend the meaning of a verbal symbol, a great deal more is required than association between the stimulus object and the symbol. A shoe not only is a physical object having a certain shape, color, and texture, but also has functional properties and can be manipulated in certain ways. This child responds to comments about the shoe before she produces the utterance.

Although these observations made of the exchange between the child and the parent probably occur to some degree in early communication situations—that is, objects being named by the mother, attempts at imitation by the infant, correction by the mother, etc.—it also seems highly likely that mother is using utterances containing the lexical item such as "Let me put your shoes on," "I have to take your shoe off," "Get me your shoe," etc. It is possible that comprehension of verbal symbols comes about by observation of the use of the symbols in environmental and syntactic contexts and that modification of the production of these symbols also comes about through these means. The game of imitation and correction may be just that—a game which has very little to do with the processes of either comprehension or production since the infant seems to pursue his own course regardless of parental rejection or acceptance. The infant in this study continued, for some time, to produce an utterance which the mother rejected and went on to further modify a production which the mother accepted.

The facts about how meanings or properties of lexical items are acquired are far from clear. A more thorough analysis of filmed and tape-recorded naturalistic data collected during the age period may more precisely map the sequence of events of imitation, comprehension, and production. There have been very few experimental studies of this important aspect of language development. One approach taken by Russian psychologists has been to attempt to teach new lexical items to children and to observe those conditions which lead to acquisition of meaning and those which do not. Kol'tsova (Slobin, 1966b, p. 138) took two groups of children aged 20 months and varied the conditions in which a new lexical item was introduced. The item was "doll," and it was introduced to one group in neutral sentences such as "Here is the doll" and "Give me the doll," and to another group in sentences such as "Rock the doll," "Feed the doll," in which the verb used was specifically contextually related to the item and might possibly exclude other items like "shoe," "ball," etc. When asked to identify the lexical item among a group of objects including several dolls, the children in the first group could identify only the doll used in the experimental situation, whereas the children in the second group identified all the dolls among the objects. The experimenter concludes that this difference can be explained by the fact that linguistic generalization comes about through observation of the variety of ways a lexical item can be used in sentences and actions. However, Mallitskaya (Slobin, 1966b, p. 139) successfully trained children 9 months to 1½ years to find the picture of a lexical item named. At about 11 to 12 months, these children could learn a new word after two or three repetitions and could identify eight pictures. After this stage children were presented with a set of three pictures, one of which was unfamiliar. The children were generally able to learn the unfamiliar name after one presentation. This is explained by the strong orienting reaction of the children to the new or novel picture. One could also explain this development by an increase in the memory capacity of these children.

This latter experiment indicates that under the experimental conditions described, children as young as one year of age can learn to differentiate and identify the pictures of lexical items. In other words, with sufficient practice they can be taught to accomplish the experimental task. However, the question still remains as to whether or not this is indeed the way in which children acquire an understanding of the meaning of lexical items. We have no indication from this experiment that these children could generalize from the picture to the object or category of objects. The former experiment (by Kol'tsova) indicated that the acquisition of the meaning of a lexical item for general differentiation and identification could only take place when the lexical item was used in utterances which defined the exclusive properties of the item and when the utterance was accompanied by appropriate actions.

ACQUISITION OF THE MEANING
OF LEXICAL ITEMS

In a study reported in 1926, it was found that during the period from 1½ to 6½ years the number of different vocabulary items in a child's lexicon or dictionary in terms of spontaneous usage grows from about 50 words to about 2500 words (Smith, 1926). Rather dramatic changes occur in the size of vocabulary during the first 4 years of life. At 2½ years the number of lexical items the child is using is six times the number he uses at 2, and at 3½ years it is three times the number he uses at 2½. These numbers, it should be remembered, are estimates only of what is produced at these ages, not what is understood. These children's comprehension vocabulary may exceed their production vocabulary. After 3½ years the size of vocabulary increases at a steady but diminished rate until 6½ years, the last age period sampled.

Since this study was conducted in the 1920s, it is very possible that these figures would be a modest estimate of the number of items in a child's lexicon at comparable ages today. There has been evidence from other types of studies indicating that the *extent* of vocabulary is greater for children at any age at present than it was for children several decades ago. For example, it has been found that the diversity of responses, number of idiosyncratic responses, and contrasting responses in the word associations of children have increased from 1916 to 1961 (Palermo and Jenkins, 1965). These results indicate that the number of available responses or number of different items in children's lexicons has probably increased. The fact that the gross numbers may now be different for children who are acquiring language normally, due to factors (the presence of television is cited as one by the experimenters) which are unrelated to a child's capacity to acquire a semantic system or his level of competence, makes it clear that *size* of vocabulary can tell us very little about developmental stages in the acquisition of this system. Like increases in mean length of response, size of vocabulary is merely a surface measure of what is occurring in linguistic development. We would like to determine the direction these changes take or, in other terms, the meanings lexical items have at various stages of development.

As has been indicated, the lexical items used at the stage of development when one-word utterances are primarily being produced can be classified as belonging to several grammatical classes. They are, however, not being functionally used as members of these grammatical classes, but syntactically as sentences, and often in conjunction with a particular action. Let us say that at this stage of development when the child says "X," he is really saying "Look at X!" or "That's X," or "Give me X," or "Is it X?" as defined by his actions and the prosodic features of the utterance. But what of the properties of "X"? The child's use of syntactic structures is quite unique at this stage of development, and the properties that he assigns to lexical items may also be unique. Our knowledge of the properties assigned to lexical items at this stage of development is extremely limited since it is derived from general observations about the child's use of language.

Vygotsky (1962, pp. 70–73) gives an example of how the meaning of a lexical item in a language changes over time and how this same general process occurs in the child's acquisition of the meaning of a lexical item. The lexical item used as an example of the change in the language is the word for "day" in Russian ("sutki"). In the language, "sutki" first meant a seam, then any junction (the corner of two walls of a house), then twilight (the joining of day and night), and finally the time from one twilight to another (24 hours or a day). The principle involved is that each new meaning of the word shares a property or properties of the previous meaning. The child assigns the same lexical items to objects or situations which share some property or properties. Vygotsky cites as an example the child's use of "quak." First it is used when talking about a duck swimming in a pond, then any liquid (including the milk in his bottle), then a coin with an eagle on it, and then any coinlike object.

The child, then, observes some properties when he uses a lexical item. However, it is not clear from this discussion whether or not there is a hierarchy in the properties he observes in his use of a lexical item. Ervin-Tripp (1966) indicates that the nouns used first often refer to items with characteristic sizes and visual contours and the verbs to animal or human movement. In other words, the overt or easily visible properties may be the first properties that are acquired by the child in his use of a lexical item. This may be an explanation for the behavior observed in the use of the item "quak" described above, and no hierarchy of properties other than the requirement that it be a visible attribute can be observed. However, in addition to "concrete" nouns and verbs, some of the early words used by children do not have easily visible properties. They use the adjectives "good" and "nice" and the verbs "want" and "see." It is, of course, possible that the properties of the words that are understood by the child at this stage are quite different from those understood at a later age.

Lewis (1963, p. 51) observed that a child, at first, used the word "tee" for the animals cat, small dog, cow, and horse, but not for his toy dog, which he pronounced to be "goggie." Later, other lexical items were used for these animals and finally different lexical items were used for each animal and "tee" was no longer used. This progression is shown in Figure 6–1, which is a rearrangement of Lewis' observations. The order of usage of the child's words for these animals during the period of approximately 1 year, 9 months to 2 years, 1 month is indicated by the numbers (1–11) in parentheses.

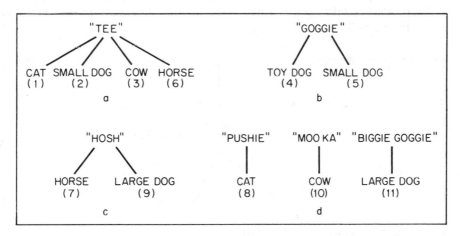

FIG. 6–1   Sequence in the acquisition of lexical items which label animals by a child.

Lewis terms this use of lexical items "expansion and contraction." That is, a familiar word which was used in one particular context (a particular cat) is now used in the context of other animals, but not for a *toy* animal. Some generalizations are being made at this early stage, although they may be quite primitive in nature. The behavior of the child at this stage is not similar to that observed in the use of "quak," even at the earliest point, since the use of the term "tee" is only applied to animals and a differentiation is observed between a toy animal and living animals.

Lewis states (1963, p. 52) that because of their functional similarity, or their manipulative similarity, objects and organisms in the environment may be grouped together and characterized by a single word. However, this appears to be an oversimplification. Outside of their overt physical dissimilarity, by no stretch of the imagination can one do with cows and horses what one does with dogs and cats, but one can play with toy dogs as well as living dogs, yet the former are grouped together while the latter are separated at an early stage. It is possible, then, that the generalization is being made in terms of a conceptual differentiation rather than merely in terms of a functional grouping. The child may have categorized "things" in his environment as ±human and ±animate on the basis of generalizations which do not stem from the functional or manipulative properties of these things alone, although at the early stages of development the basis for these generalizations may be in terms of purely visible attributes and, thus, quite different from those of older children and adults. Even further differentiation within a categorization takes place during these early stages with this set so that −human is differentiated into ±animate and +animate is differentiated into ±large. At the final stage complete differentiation of properties takes place. Some stages in this differentation are indicated in Figure 6–2.

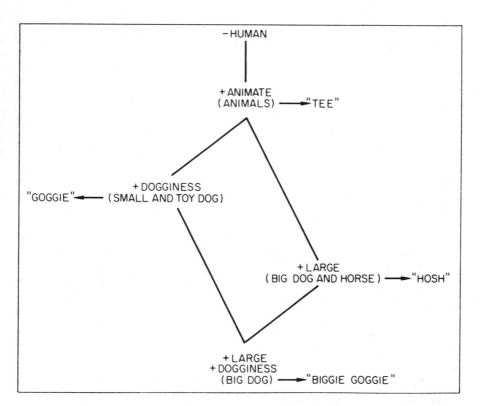

FIG. 6–2 Possible stages in the differentiation of the properties of the lexical items "TEE," "GOGGIE," "HOSH" and "BIGGIE GOGGIE."

Presumably, generalizations such as those observed with a set of animals take place within other semantic fields as well. For example, the child has been noted to use the lexical item "daddy" for all males observed. However, he does not use the term "mommy" for all females observed. It should be stressed, therefore, that the property understood does not seem to be based on the conceptual generalization (for example, +male) but probably on a set of specific and perhaps idiosyncratic observations.

Not all developmental changes in the acquisition of the meaning of lexical items can be described as overgeneralization and then differentiation. Some research has already indicated that the process of acquiring the meaning of lexical items may include behavior which cannot be labeled overgeneralization. Musseyibova (1964) noted that, although pre-school children were using both "left" and "right" in their everyday language, they were always talking about "right" and never "left." Sokhin (Slobin, 1966b, p. 140) found in an experimental study of the understanding of prepositions that understanding was limited to a specific attribute of the preposition. For example, when asked to put a block under a table the children could do so, but when asked to put a block under a ring on the table they could not do so and would often hold the block under the table directly under the ring. This behavior seems to represent a *partial* understanding of the preposition, although it was used quite freely and accurately in everyday language.

It is possible, then, that several degrees of understanding of lexical items can exist when the child uses these items in utterances: (1) same lexical item used when talking about different things—overgeneralization has taken place; (2) item used when talking about a specific thing—generalization has not taken place; (3) different lexical items used when talking about the same thing—differentiation has not taken place. Although these are all different types of behavior, in each of these instances the behavior results from the fact that not all the semantic properties of the lexical items used are understood by the child. It should be noted here that there may be a developmental difference in the stages at which the semantic properties of lexical items which belong to different semantic fields are acquired. For example, the properties of locative terms may be acquired before time terms.

Werner and Kaplan (1964, p. 149) discuss a type of linguistic behavior in early utterances which appears to be similar to that observed with the preposition "under." That is, a lexical item is used in a manner which indicates that the full set of semantic properties of the item is not understood. The example given is that the conjunction of two words in a typical predicate construction is understood by the child but only in specific sentence contexts. For example, "Brush mama" and "Brush papa" are understood but not "Brush hat." It might then be that entries in children's dictionaries are acts or phrases ("Brush mama" rather than "brush" and "mama"). This, however, seems to be an incorrect description since, although some items may appear only in specific contexts (brush [+human]), other items (papa and mama) appear in many contexts. For this reason, it appears to be more appropriate to describe this behavior as the result of a limited set of *unique* properties of lexical items which are derived from particular situational and sentence contexts. This set of properties is added to and/or modified as new sentences and situations are observed.

The data obtained on the comprehension of the meaning of lexical items at this stage of development are clearly limited and primarily anecdotal in nature. Again, the data indicate the interesting questions that might be asked rather than providing answers. The sentences children produce at this stage of development indicate that some semantic properties of lexical items are being observed. It was noted in Chapter 4 that certain combinatorial restrictions observed in the sentences produced are not merely sequential restrictions, but seem to be concerned with the choice of items under a structural heading as well. For example, not all the nouns appear with all the verbs in the child's lexicon. However, again, the data are limited.

THE DEVELOPMENT
OF DICTIONARY MEANINGS

During the age range at which most experimentation in the acquisition of dictionary meanings has taken place (5 years and up), the structure of children's sentences appears to be quite similar to that of adults, and new lexical items are added to spontaneous usage dictionaries apparently without difficulty. In addition, these items are incorporated into the grammar and used appropriately, in most instances, in the utterances that are produced. However, experimentation has indicated that these may be surface similarities and that the meaning of lexical items and structures may not be the same for children and adults, although both use them appropriately. Some questions that might be asked concerning this aspect of semantic development are: Do the lexical items used by children have the same properties as these same items in dictionaries? and, if not, what are the developmental changes that occur in the acquisition of dictionary meanings?

Werner and Kaplan (1964, p. 188) have described some studies of the definitions children use. At about age 6 there is an 82 percent usage of definitions in terms of concrete action (for example, "bottle" defined as "Where you pour something out of"). By age 15 there is 33 percent usage of these types of definitions. At age 13 a definition given for bottle is "a container in which all liquids go." In a study (Werner and Kaplan, 1950) requiring children 8½ to 13½ years of age to find the meaning of an artificial word (symbolizing an object or action) which appeared in six different sentence contexts, it was found that correctness of response increased from age level to age level. The experimenters categorized the children's responses as being (1) sentence contextual (the word carries the meaning of the whole or part of the particular sentence context in which it was found), and (2) nonsentence contextual (the word is differentiated from the particular sentence contexts but has a *broad* contextual meaning derived from a particular sentence context which is then applied in *all* contexts). The first type of behavior sharply decreases between ages 9 and 11 and the second type gradually decreases over the age range but is still evident at the oldest age. It was also observed that the younger children frequently altered the syntactic structure of a sentence so that the meaning they derived would fit a sentence structure. This last type of behavior abruptly dropped from 9½ to 10½ years, and the experimenters conclude from this result that the meaning of a word and the structure of the sentence become independent for the child at this stage of development.

There is, thus, a strong indication that lexical items do not have meanings separate from the sentence contexts in which the child uses them until somewhat after the age of 10. A conclusion that might be drawn, then, is that the item may not be an intact dictionary entry in the child's lexicon with all its semantic properties, but rather might be listed as an item with certain functional properties. For example, the noun "bottle" might be entered with the following properties: to drink out of, to pour out of, to put drinks in, etc.; and the verb "drink" might be entered as: to drink milk, to drink water, to drink juice, etc. This, however, would make for quite a cumbersome dictionary. Alternatively, since lexical items may have different properties depending on the context in which they are used, it is possible that children acquire only a limited or restricted set of properties for particular lexical items, which is derived from the syntactic context in which the child frequently finds or uses them. Therefore, for example, the child may store "bottle" as a thing which holds things you can pour or drink, and then give as a definition one of his readings of the word. The definition for this item given by one child aged 12 ("a hollow round glass vessel into which all liquids go") and the previously quoted definition given by a 13-year-old contain lexical items which are obviously yet to be acquired by most 6-year-olds, such as "hollow," "vessel," and "liquids." Further, the fact that younger children force the syntactic structure of a sentence to comply with their meaning of a lexical item indicates that they do have readings of lexical items separate from sentences, although these readings may be limited.

It has been found in word association studies that syntagmatic responses (responses that are *not* in the same syntactic class as the stimulus word but are usually found following the stimulus word such as "run"—"fast") are frequently given by children under the age of 8 years (Entwisle, 1966). The percentage of paradigmatic responses (responses in the same syntactic class as the stimulus word such as "run"—"jump") increases dramatically between the first and second grade and increases steadily from second grade through college. However, it has also been found that the syntactic class of the stimulus word affects the percentage of syntagmatic and paradigmatic responses that are produced (Palermo, 1965). Nouns elicit the greatest percentage of paradigmatic responses, adjectives and pronouns an intermediary amount, and adverbs, verbs, and prepositions elicit relatively few paradigmatic responses. It has also been found, in a study of the word associations of adults and of first, second, and third grade children (Brown and Berko, 1960), that count nouns and adjectives produce more paradigmatic responses than other classes at all age levels and that mass nouns and adverbs (except for adults in the case of adverbs) produce more syntagmatic responses than other classes.

It might be concluded, and some experimenters have so concluded, that younger children store the semantic properties of a phrase, rather than the properties of a word, in the lexicon. The supposition is that before the age of 6 children may enter properties under the headings NP and VP rather than Det, N, V, Prep, and Adv and, of course, these properties may also be limited and unique. However, the results of word association studies are far from consistent in terms of this hypothesis. Although the syntagmatic responses to verbs, adverbs, and prepositions seem to fit in well with this explanation, since VP can be composed of V + NP, V + Adv, and V + PP, the paradigmatic responses to adjectives do not fit as well, since adjectives are usually found within the NP on the surface at least. In addition to this, the percentage of paradigmatic responses to count nouns and mass nouns differs, and the percentage of paradigmatic responses to nouns and pronouns differs. All of these, of course, would be classified as the N of the NP although they differ from each other in terms of properties. Further, first-grade children give more paradigmatic responses to verbs than to adjectives and mass nouns (Brown and Berko, 1960). These differences indicate that the hypothesis that young children have a phrase dictionary is questionable. It is possible that NPs and Ps share semantic properties at some stage of development. Taking the examples cited before, the child may store "bottle" as a thing which holds something you pour or drink and the verb "pour" as taking something out of a bottle. Thus, the words "bottle" and "pour" may share a semantic property or properties although they are not classified in the child's lexicon under one syntactic heading with a single set of properties. Again, these results may be due to the child's having a unique and limited set of properties for lexical items.

Differences between the frequency of types of word association responses given by fourth-grade children when asked to give a response orally (as soon as they heard the stimulus word) and when asked to write their responses (Palermo and Jenkins, 1966) raise a great many questions about the processes involved in the task. There are marked differences in, for example, the percentage of these children giving superordinate (such as "red"—"color," "dog"—"animal") and contrast responses (such as "circle"—"square," "dark"—"light") in the two situations. Superordinate responses increase and contrast responses decrease in the written task. The time taken to respond may, therefore, play a role in the types of response given. First-grade children who responded orally give some indication that their responses may be impulsive reactions rather than involving some look-up procedure to match properties. (For example, "cottage" frequently elicits "cheese.")

Other results indicate that it is difficult to determine exactly what is happening in the word association task. Second-grade children not only dramatically more frequently produce paradigmatic responses than first-grade children, they also produce more contrast and superordinate responses. If it is considered that most contrast as well as superordinate responses include identity of the syntactic class as well as the observation of a general semantic property, then the shift to more frequent paradigmatic responses can be in part explained. A limited set of properties for a lexical item or a set of somewhat differing properties (from the standard) might not include those properties which link members of the same syntactic class. For example, the word "square" elicits "box" most frequently from first-graders and "round" most frequently from fourth-graders. It does not seem likely that "square box" is a lexical entry for these first-graders but only (1) that "square" is not listed in the dictionary with a property such as "shape," and (2) that "square" and "box" share a semantic property.

Such factors, plus impulsive responding, may account for what occurs in word association tasks. Figure 6–3 shows the mean percentage of all paradigmatic responses (based on the five most popular responses) and the percentage of subjects giving contrast and superordinate responses over the age range sampled by Palermo (1965). It should be noted how well the progression of contrast responses echoes the progression of paradigmatic responses. The experimenter further notes that the percentage of superordinate responses rises from first to sixth grade and then declines thereafter until the college level, whereas popular paradigmatic responses and contrast responses increase steadily from first grade to the college level. These results indicate that perhaps the usual explanations derived from word association experiments, such as children having a phrase dictionary or children being unable to make superordinate classifications of lexical items, do not explain the behavior of children in word association tasks, nor do they describe the developmental changes that occur.

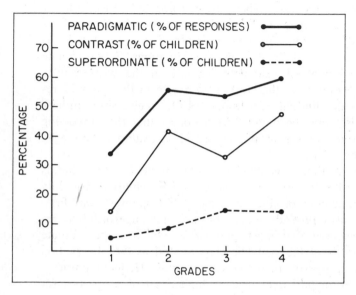

FIG. 6–3 Percentage of paradigmatic responses and percentage of children giving contrast and superordinate responses at various grade levels in a word association task.

The results of other studies indicate that (1) children have a restricted set of properties for lexical items until some level of maturation is reached, and (2) children have *a* reading for a lexical item until some level of maturation is reached. For example, it has been found that in children's labeling of physical materials, the properties of size, weight, and strength are correlated, and in their labeling of pictures of faces the properties of happy, good, and pretty are used synonymously (Ervin-Tripp and Foster, 1960). In comparing the performance of first-grade and sixth-grade children in this study, it was found that "contaminated" responses (i.e., responses that treat the adjectives as if they were synonymous) to physical objects and to faces still were being produced by sixth-graders, although they were reduced at the sixth-grade level. These results indicate that the younger children may have a set of properties which is identical or very similar and thus nondifferentiating for all the lexical items examined.

In another study it was found that the term "bigger" was almost always used in the context "taller" by 5 and 6 year olds (Lumsden and Poteat,

1968). For 10 out of the 12 stimulus displays, these children labeled as "bigger" the stimulus having the greater vertical dimension even when the surface area of the less vertical was four times as great. High school seniors performed significantly differently in this task. Indeed, the behavior of the younger children in this study and in the study cited previously indicates that they may assign different lexical items to the same or overlapping sets of properties in a manner similar to that of very young children, who are acquiring the meaning of lexical items in a semantic field. It is interesting to note that lexical items which have properties which are presumably easily visible (size, weight, height, etc.) are still nondifferentiated by sixth-grade children. Again, we wonder about developmental stages in the differentiation of properties of lexical items in various semantic fields.

In an interesting study examining the question of sets of readings, Asch and Nerlove (1960) explored children's understanding of double function terms. Terms such as "sweet," "hard," "cold," "crooked," etc., which could be applied to both objects and people, were examined and the following was found: (1) from 3 to 6 years the terms were used for objects and the physical properties of persons; (2) from 7 to 8 years there was a great increase in the use and understanding of each reading of these terms, but subjects could not formulate the relationship between the two uses of the terms; (3) from 9 to 10 years there was again a marked increase in understanding the dual function of these terms, plus some ability to state this dual function; and (4) from 10 to 12 years there was no further increase in understanding, but there was a marked increase in the ability to state this dual function. The experimenters conclude that double function terms are initially homonyms (that is, have a single set of properties or a single reading), and that this set of properties is composed of perceivable physical attributes and actions. Later it appears there are two sets of readings, but these sets are dissociated from each other, and finally the relationship or derivation of the personality term from the physical term is understood and expressed.

The results of a study of the semantic differential ratings of children in grades 2 through 7 (Di Vesta, 1966) indicate that the associative responses of second graders are similar to those of adolescents and adults. A shift occurs over the age range from a predominantly two-factor rating (Evaluation and Activity) to a three-factor rating (Evaluation, Activity, and Potency). The experimenter concludes that these factors are "reliable dimensions of the child's use of language." It is clear, however, from the results of the previous studies cited, that although the scaling factors tested in the semantic differential elicit similar types of responses from children and adults, children appear to understand these lexical items along a restricted dimension, whereas adults appear to understand these items along several distinct but related dimensions. Because of this factor the child's production and comprehension of these items may be limited.

COMPREHENSION OF RELATIONSHIPS IN SENTENCES

The expansion of the syntactic contexts in which lexical items are understood and produced leads to the addition and modification of properties and readings of these lexical items. For the most part, as was stated previously, children in their everyday language do not produce semantically peculiar sentences and thus give us clues to the structure of their semantic rules and lexicon. An examination of the sentences produced by children from 3 to 7 years shows that there are some exceptions (Menyuk, 1969, Chapter 3). On occasion the child will create a new word by changing the syntactic class of a word and adding appropriate grammatical markers (for example, "He is grouching" and "They are resters"). In addition, the child may create entirely unique words ("He is a bugiebooer"). The inherent possibilities of language for creating new words seem to be explored by the child from the pre-school period through first grade, although the frequency of these inventions sharply declines after the pre-school period. In these instances the sentence is grammatical but anomalous. That is, we have no reading in our dictionary for the lexical item used, but we can syntactically analyze the sentence. There are other instances in which the lexical items used are all in our dictionary, but their use in particular utterances violates some rule of co-occurrence. Again, the sentence can be syntactically analyzed and even understood, but only if we substitute according to the rules in our grammar. The following are some examples:

1. VP: They'll close him in jail
2. NP: They are kissing theirself
3. Adj: That's a tall school band
4. PP: I was at home in the weekend

In these instances the restrictions of the co-occurrence of (1) V + object, (2) V + Reflexive, (3) Adj + N, and (4) preposition + NP are not observed. Rules of co-occurrence are considered syntactic rules, and they operate in terms of the properties of lexical items used in a sentence. If the list of properties of a lexical item or of a class of items, such as a class of verbs, is incomplete, such anomalies can occur *because co-occurrence restrictions are based on the properties of items.* Thus, the sentence "The pin danced" is anomalous because the verb "dance" takes an animate subject. We have already observed that a limited and unique set of properties for a class of lexical items can result in the overlapping of adjectives such as "big," "strong," "heavy," and "tall." We can observe in the sentence examples given that restrictions of co-occurrence are not being observed in the use of verbs, prepositions, and adjectives. Therefore, both the properties of lexical items and the contexts in which they can occur must be observed by the child. As new syntactic structures and lexical items are acquired, additional rules of co-occurrence must be observed.

In addition to these aspects, there are restrictions on the co-occurrence of items in a string which are imposed by logical constraints. The sentence "The baby boy danced" is anomalous because of our knowledge that baby + dance expresses a false relationship although baby is +animate. In addition to adding to and changing the properties of lexical items and observing rules of co-occurrence based on the properties of lexical items, the child acquires knowledge of logical relationships. There is evidence in the sentences children produce that development takes place in all three directions, but the evidence is slight since, for the most part, the children do not produce semantically peculiar sentences.

In an experiment, children aged 5 to 8 years were asked to repeat strings which were (1) grammatical—for example, "Wild Indians shoot running buffalos"; (2) anomalous—for example, "Wild elevators shoot ticking restaurants"; and (3) agrammatical—for example, "Restaurants ticking shoot elevators wild." These strings were partially masked by noise (Mc-Neill, 1965). It was found that although children repeated anomalous strings slightly more frequently correctly than agrammatical strings, there were no marked changes over the age range. At 5 years, none of the agrammatical strings were correctly repeated whereas 6 percent of the anomalous strings were correctly repeated; at 8 years, 3 percent of the agrammatical strings and 9 percent of the anomalous strings were correctly repeated. It was also found that there was no marked difference between the percentage of anomalous and grammatical strings that were correctly repeated until age 7, although grammatical strings were more frequently correctly repeated throughout that age range. The differences in percentage of correct repetition between these two sets of strings was approximately 6 percent versus 11 percent at age 5, 6 percent versus 15 percent at age 6, 8 percent versus 20 percent at age 7, and 9 percent versus 49 percent at age 8.

The experimenter concludes that these results are consistent with the hypothesis that children have incomplete listings of properties of lexical items at a certain stage of development, and thus anomalous sentences are "as good as" grammatical sentences (McNeil, 1970). However, this conclusion does not seem to be completely explanatory. The rank ordering of correct responses from 5 through 7 years appears to indicate lack of understanding of the structure of the utterance rather than lack of understanding of the properties of lexical items per se. The agrammatical sentences were read essentially as word lists. The anomalous sentences were presented with natural stress and intonational patterns. This probably accounts for the somewhat better but very little better performance with anomalous sentences. The structure of the grammatical sentences might cause difficulties even at age 7, especially under noisy conditions, if they were all constructed as in the example given. The structure of these utterances involves the operations of adjectivalization of the verb and preposing, both of which are late acquisitions and are used by very few children even at age 7 (Menyuk, 1969, Chapter 3). Children below age 7 might have comparatively less difficulty in repeating utterances such as "Wild Indians shoot buffalos that run," and comparatively more difficulty in repeating utterances such as "Wild elevators shoot restaurants that tick," because they comprehend the structure of such utterances. Both the understanding of the properties of lexical items in a string and the understanding of the structures in which they occur are necessary for understanding a sentence and for producing an understandable sentence.

Fourth-graders were presented with nonsense CVC trigrams representing different syntactic classes (nouns, adjectives, adverbs and verbs): (1) in association with three pictured instances, (2) in a set of three sentences, and (3) with both types of stimuli (Prentice, 1966). Subjects trained with sentences were best able to use the trigrams in completion of sentences. Subjects trained with pictures were best able to match the trigrams to English equivalents. However, subjects trained in *both* situations did better than the "semantically" trained subjects in the semantic task and also did better than "syntactically" trained subjects in the syntactic task.

Rules of co-occurrence and logical relationships not only operate across class boundaries (Det + N, N + V, V + PP, P + NP) but also in terms of the relationship expressed in transformations on single and multiple underlying sentences. Children's understanding and generation of some of these relationships have been explored, but only to a limited extent. As has been seen, some of the earliest relationships are expressed by the conjunction of topic + modifier (as in "shoe off," "light on," "go up," "fall down"). This later evolves into the subject + predicate relationship ("That a ball," "Daddy drive car"), and the negative element + S ("no touch," "no bottle," "no write on") in contrast with positive utterances ("touch it," "that bottle," "write on").

In a study of the early utterances of three children (Bloom, 1970) a careful analysis was made of the situations in which these utterances were produced. The experimenter reports that the same two word utterance can be used to express different types of grammatical relationships depending on the situations in which it is used (Bloom, 1970). For example, "mommy sock" could be described as expressing the subject-object relationship when mother is putting on the child's sock and the possessive relationship when the sock belongs to mother. It was found that the negative morpheme in these utterances was used not only to express negation but also kinds of negation. Thus, the same two word utterance "no sock" could be described as expressing non-existence (when there is no sock in the situation), rejection (when there is a sock and the child doesn't want to wear it), and denial (when there is a sock but the child states that there isn't one). Presumably such differences are clearly marked by the objects present in the environment and the behavior of the speakers. Two important findings of this study are (1) children comprehend and attempt to express grammatical relationships in their utterances before they have acquired the appropriate forms, and (2) evidence that children have this knowledge can be obtained when careful study is made of the situations in which utterances are produced. In addition to these relationships, it has been observed (Werner and Kaplan, 1964) that early utterances can express sequential and simultaneous relationships. The child uses the convention of stringing words together which mirror the sequence of events ("tired, chair, sit") and grouping simultaneous actions by a pause between them ("papa horse —bottle kaput," meaning while or when papa was near the horse the bottle broke).

During later stages of development the syntactic rules for generating declarative, passive, and negative sentences as well as some types of conjunction and embedding have been acquired and are being used to express modification and conjunctive, causal, conditional, and disjunctive relationships. Utterances which involve a combination of structures are also being used. However, although such structures are being used, the question remains as to whether or not *any* sentence which might have these structures can be understood in terms of the relationships expressed. It is possible that there are only specific syntactic contexts (specific, AUX/ Mod + V forms) in which such relationships are understood. For example, children age 3 to 7 most frequently use the passive construction with get + V rather than be + V, and usually in the truncated form ("Blacky didn't get hit") (Menyuk, 1969, Chapter 3). It is also possible that these relationships are understood only in specific lexical contexts. For example, as has been seen, the specific verbs used influence the interpretation of the subject-object relationship in sentences ("I promised Bill to go"). Some relationships in sentences might be understood before others because of relative syntactic complexity or relative experience, or because of the concepts implicit in the sentences. A further question might be, can the child relate the logical relationship expressed in these structures to particular stimulus situations and thus give evidence of understanding them?

The dependency of *ease of* understanding on the relation between the statement heard and the situation has been explored in two studies. In the first study (Huttenlocher and Strauss, 1968) children aged 4½ to 5 years and 6½ to 7 years were asked to place a block above or below a fixed block (or above or below two blocks in the case of the older children), to fit a statement made by the experimenter (for example, "The red block is below the green block"). There were more errors and subjects took a longer time to respond when the block to be moved was the object in the sentence than when it was the subject. The experimenters concluded that the comprehension of the utterance was dependent on the relation between the statement and the situation described, since the same utterance was either easy or difficult to understand depending on which block had to be moved. On the other hand, one might interpret these results as being due to difficulty in comprehending a situation which did not fit the statement. When the movable block is the object in the statement, the subject needs time to reverse the actor and action in the sentence. Thus, in the statement "The red block is below the green block" and in the situation where the red block is movable, both actor ("red block") and action ("below") fit the statement. However, in the situation where the green block is movable, the actor ("green block") and action ("above") do not fit the statement.

In a second study (Huttenlocher, Eisenberg, and Strauss, 1968) fourth-grade children were asked to place a truck in front of or behind a fixed truck to match active and passive statements containing the verbs "push" and "pull," and reaction time was measured. With statements containing "pull" reaction time was longer than with "push." This, again, was probably due to the particular situation, since it would be possible to push against another truck but not possible to pull it in the experimental situation. Reaction time was always longer with passive than with active statements. For both active and passive statements subjects took less time to react when the movable truck was the subject or actor in the statement. Thus, with the following two statements—"The red truck is pushing (or pulling) the green truck," and "The green truck is being pushed (or pulled) by the red truck"—subjects took less time to react when the movable truck was the syntactic subject or semantic actor (red truck) than when the movable truck was the syntactic object or semantic acted upon.

It seems clear, then, that in analyzing sentences children, and probably adults as well, interpret some sentences as actor + action + acted upon, or interpret the subject in sentences as the actor, the verb as action, and object as acted upon, as described in Figure 6–4. When the situation is not congruent with this interpretation of sentences, time is needed to reverse the subject and object in the sentence to fit the situation.

The active-passive relationship, having the characteristics of being easily

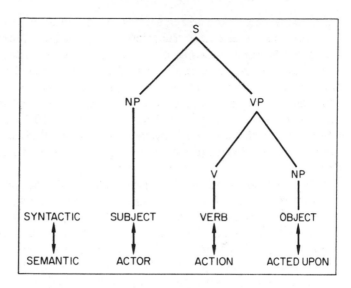

FIG. 6–4 Schematic representation of semantic interpretation of syntactic structure SVO.

picturable, appropriate for use in problem-solving experiments (as in the study cited above), and dependent for interpretation on lexical content as well as structure, has been the relationship most frequently explored in the child's comprehension of relationships expressed in sentences. In structural descriptions, passive sentences are transforms of actives. The sentence "Mary is loved by John" is derived from "John loves Mary," and the sentence "The house was painted" from "Someone painted the house." Both truncated passives ("The house was painted") and full passives ("Mary is loved by John") are used in English. Further, there are constraints on the co-occurrence of subjects, verbs, and objects in the underlying sentence to which the passive transformation can be applied. Thus, "The apple was eaten by John" is permissible but not "John was eaten by the apple." The relationship expressed in this sentence is nonreversible. However, both "the girl was hit by the boy" and "the boy was hit by the girl" are possible sentences. The relationship expressed in these sentences is reversible. The following are the questions previously put about the child's comprehension of relationships expressed in sentences, as specifically applied to the passive construction: (1) are all forms of the passive understood in the same way? (2) does the child understand that the actor and the acted upon remain the same in both active and passive sentences although their positions are reversed in some instances and the actor is missing in other instances? and (3) what is the effect of the lexical content on the comprehension of the expressed relationship?

In a recent study (Slobin, 1968), children (ages 5, 6, 8, 10, and 12) and adults were asked to retell stories that had been presented to them in the full passive and the truncated passive forms. There was a general tendency to retell stories in the active form by the entire population. The percentage of target sentences retold as actives was 62.4 percent in the case of full passives and 39.3 percent in the case of truncated passives. Full passive target sentences were retold in their original form 24.9 percent of the time, whereas truncated passives were retold in their original form 59.6 percent of the time by the total population. It should be remembered that full passives contain the actor ("by x") whereas truncated passives do not.

The question raised by the experimenter is whether or not there is a relationship between syntactic complexity and "psychological complexity." Truncated passives, according to structural descriptions, are generated by an additional rule in which the actor is deleted and, therefore, are "more complex" if degree of complexity is described in terms of number of rules. Since the full passives were more frequently recalled as actives, whereas truncated passives were more frequently recalled as passives, the experimenter concludes that there is no uniform relationship between syntactic complexity and psychological complexity; and that, for the purposes of comprehension of sentences, full and truncated passives are not stored in the same manner (i.e., active sentences + transformational rules).

However, if one divides the population, as the experimenter does, into two groups (5- to 8-year-olds and 10-year-olds to adults), one finds that although there is no significant difference in the percentage of instances in which full passives are retold in their original form by the two groups (24 percent versus 26 percent), there is a marked difference between the younger and older group in the percentage of instances in which truncated passives are retold in their original form (44 percent versus 74 percent). Truncated passives are recalled as actives in 55 percent of the instances by the younger group, despite the fact that the underlying actor in these cases is unmarked in the sentences heard. None of these data indicate that full and truncated passives are understood in different ways (that is, involving differences in the comprehension of the actor-acted upon relationship), and it is not clear from these data that full and truncated passives are stored in different ways by younger children. The more marked results with older subjects may, indeed, indicate that the two different types of passives are analyzed in different ways by these subjects *or* that recall strategies have changed over time.

How sentences are recalled (as active or passive) can be manipulated by the experimental situation. Pre-school through third-grade children were presented with active and passive sentences and with pictures graphically representing the subject or object in these sentences or the total content of the sentence (Turner and Rommetveit, 1968). The pictures were presented either when the sentence was given or when subjects were asked to recall the sentence. In general, pictures presented during the retrieval stage were more effective in producing recall of the sentences than were those presented during the storage stage. Pictures of the actor and the total sentence caused active sentences to be recalled as actives and passive sentences to be transformed into actives. Pictures of the object caused passive sentences to be recalled as passives and actives to be transformed into passives. In general, more active than passive sentences and more nonreversible passives than reversible passives were recalled correctly. The effect of reversibility disappeared when the sentence was encoded from a picture of the total sentence. Attention, then, can be focused on actor or object and influence the *form* in which sentences are recalled. In truncated passives attention is focused on the object. Preamble remarks as well as pictures can focus the attention of listeners on either actor or object and effect the recall of sentences (Tannenbaum and Williams, 1968). All of these data indicate that the active-passive relationship is understood by young children even though the active is used more frequently and the passive is more frequently generated in the truncated form. When attention is focused on the object, children can and do transform the active into the passive. This transformation is facilitated by particular situations.

Children (ages 6, 8, 10, 12) and adults were asked to verify sentences (state whether they were true or false) when they were presented in association with stimulus pictures (Slobin, 1966a). The sentence types presented were active declarative, active negative, passive declarative, and passive negative. These relationships were presented in reversible and nonreversible contexts. The sentences were (A) true or (B) false according to the stimulus picture. In the case of nonreversible relationships, the properties of subject, verb, and object would also indicate the falseness of the statement if the relationship were reversed ("The flowers are watering the girl"). An example of (A) and (B) statements in the reversible case is showing a picture of a dog chasing a cat and stating (A) "The dog is chasing the cat," "The cat is not chasing the dog," "The cat is being chased by the dog," "The dog is not being chased by the cat"; and (B) "The cat is chasing the dog," "The dog is not chasing the cat," "The dog is being chased by the cat," "The cat is not being chased by the dog." Latency of response in verifying the sentence was measured.

The amount of time it took to verify a sentence was dependent on a *combination* of factors: its structure, its truth, and the reversibility of subject and object. For the most part people were influenced by these factors in much the same way throughout the age range, although delay of response decreased with age. Therefore, in terms of the structures presented in the experiment, speed of analysis increased with age, but no developmental changes occurred in the pattern of response. In general, active sentences took less time to verify than passives, passives less than negatives, and negatives less than passive negatives. However, when true and false statements were separated it was found that the above rank ordering of time used by the total population to verify statements holds for *true* statements but not for *false* ones. In the latter instance, the order in terms of structure is active, negative, passive, and passive negative. Further, it was found that in the case of nonreversible sentences the active-passive time differences were eliminated. In general, false and nonreversible statements take less time to verify than true and reversible statements.

The question raised by the experimenter in discussing the results of this experiment is: does the listener obtain the meaning of an utterance (1) by regenerating the syntactic derivation of the utterance, or (2) by observing semantic rules, or (3) by his knowledge of the world (for example, his knowledge that cats and dogs may chase each other but girls and flowers do not water each other)? The fact that passive sentences take less time to verify than negatives, at least in true statements, is upsetting to one particular theory of how sentences are understood. This theory proposes that sentences are understood in terms of the underlying kernels plus transformational footnotes (Miller, 1962). We have already observed that the number of rules required for the generation of a structure is not completely explanatory in accounting for the observed sequence of development of syntactic structures, and it is obviously not completely explanatory of the differences in response time observed in this task. It is clear, however, that syntactic complexity does play some role in the time needed to verify sentences (passive negative sentences always take the greatest amount of time to verify), and it is clear that reversibility also plays a role (nonreversible utterances take less time to verify than reversible).

It is not clear whether it is the listeners' knowledge of the world or their knowledge of semantic rules that causes this time difference in verification. In the case of the young child, where experience may be limited, knowledge of the reversible nonreversible contrast may be gained primarily from the acquisition of properties of lexical items and rules of co-occurrence, which are derived from sentence structures, but, as was stated in the discussion on the acquisition of meaning, this is an open question. It is also clear that the situation affects the time needed to understand a sentence in a particular context. In this experiment negative sentences are more quickly verified than passives when the statement is false. In an experiment cited previously, the time needed to carry out a task was dependent on whether or not the situation was congruent with the sentence. The time needed by the listener to understand an utterance, then, is dependent on the syntactic and semantic structure of the utterance and the situation in which it is heard.

As stated previously, there are many relationships expressed in various types of sentence structure which have yet to be experimentally explored to any great extent. These are coordinate and subordinate structures derived from the conjunction of two sentences or the embedding of one sentence into another. The following are some simple examples of these structures. List *A* contains sentences which seem grammatical and list *B* contains sentences which do not because the relationship implied by the connective is not expressed in the sentence.

A	B
1. I like apples, and she likes bananas.	1. I like apples, and she drives a car.
2. I like apples, but I don't like bananas.	2. I like apples, but I like bananas.
3. I like apples because they taste good.	3. I like apples because bananas taste good.
4. I like apples, so I eat them.	4. She likes apples, so she eats bananas.
5. If I liked apples, I would eat them.	5. If I liked apples, I would eat bananas.
6. While I was in the orchard, I ate the apples.	6. While I was in the orchard, I played the piano.
7. I ate the apples; then I got sick.	7. I got sick; then I ate the apples.
8. I see the apples that he wanted to eat.	8. I see the apples that he ate.

Conjoined and embedded sentences express relationships which are logically or semantically dependent and also syntactically dependent. It was noted, in the discussion of syntactic development, that different kinds of conjunction and embedding are produced at different stages of development. There might, then, be differing levels of semantic competence expressed by the production of these types of structures. It is true, as has been seen, that various syntactic rules which must operate in the generation of these sentences are not always observed. In addition, some logical dependencies are also not being observed. Verb tense restrictions are not observed ("If he likes apples, he eat them"), pronoun restrictions are not observed ("The girl likes apples, so he eat them"), and the antithetical element ("no," "too," "also," "as well") does not appear ("I like apples, but I like bananas"). One might argue that in the last example of a syntactic rule not being observed, the peculiarity is really the result of nonobservation of semantic rules or lack of understanding of the meanings of the relationship expressed by various conjunctive terms and by embedding. For the most part, however, sentences such as those found in list *B* are not produced by children. The exceptions are *B1, B2,* and *B4,* which exemplify children's production of utterances which appear to be simply a stringing together of sentences without an understanding of the relationship expressed by the conjunctive terms used. Children, then, appear to use these terms before they understand the meaning implied by their use. This aspect of language development has received very little experimental attention.

Werner and Kaplan (1964) observed that conjunctions which combine events are used before conjunctions which express dependent relationships. Thus, "and" might be used before "because." Sequential relationships are expressed before simultaneous relationships. Thus, "then" might be used before "while." The antithetical relationship is expressed after the combination of events. Thus "but" would be used after "and." No detailed description of the sequential usage of connectives has been obtained, although it has been found that "and" is used by many more children before they use "because" and that "because" is used by many more children before they use "if" and "so" (Menyuk, 1969, Chapter 3). However, as was stated previously, use does not necessarily mean comprehension of relationships, and indeed some of the sentences produced indicate that production can precede comprehension.

First-grade and sixth-grade children's understanding and production of connectives was examined (1) by analysis of their spontaneous speech and (2) by asking them to select the sentence in a set of two which "sounds better" (Katz and Brent, 1968). The children were also asked (3) to tell why the sentences selected were better. College students were given tasks (2) and (3). The relationships and connectives examined were the following:

1. Explicit versus implicit causal—"because" versus no connective
2. Causal versus temporal—"because" versus "then" and "when," "therefore" versus "and then"
3. Inversion of cause and effect—using the connectives "and" versus "because"
4. Antithetic relationship—correct usage of "but" and "although" versus incorrect usage
5. Linguistic order and perceptual order—cause before result and result before cause examined in sentences with "and" versus no connective.

The experimenters found that the children's use of connectives in spontaneous speech and their selection of connectives in the choice situation were fairly well matched. The most marked developmental difference found between the two age groups of children was that the older children were able to explain their choices, whereas younger children often offered explanations which were merely repetitions of the sentences, or simply stated that the sentences "sound better." Both groups gave evidence of comprehending the causal relationship. There was no difference between the groups in their preference of the "because" connective over no connective. Sixth-grade children significantly more frequently than first-grade children selected "because" over "then." There was no difference between the groups in the choice of "therefore" over "and then," with all three groups preferring "therefore." However, all three groups preferred "when" to "because." Since children have great difficulty in explaining the temporal relationship and, in fact, often explain it in terms of a causal relationship, the experimenters suggest that temporal relationships are not as well understood as causal relationships—despite the fact that, in general, the temporal connective was more fr quently selected than the causal connective.

Both groups of children preferred sentences with "and" versus "because" in sentences containing an inversion of cause and effect, thus choosing the more appropriate sentences and again exhibiting their understanding of causal relationships. First-grade children chose sentences with incorrect usage of "but" and "although" significantly more frequently than sixth-grade children. More sixth-grade than first-grade children used "but" in spontaneous speech. Neither group used "although." However, sixth-grade children had great difficulty in explaining the relationship. This result indicates that even at the sixth-grade level, children have difficulty in understanding the antithetic relationship. In examining children's need for correlation between linguistic and perceptual order, it was found that in the presence of the connective "and," sixth-grade children preferred the cause-effect order rather than the reverse significantly more frequently than first-grade children. There were no significant differences when the connective was absent. The experimenters conclude that first-grade children can follow the perceptual order and do so in their spontaneous speech, but cannot make a direct link between perceptual and linguistic order, whereas sixth-grade children insist on this link. College students, on the other hand, do not insist on the cause-effect order to be marked linguistically, unless the *particular* connective used indicates that it is necessary.

The results of this experiment may be confounded by factors not accounted for, such as the syntactic structures ordinarily used to express temporal relationships. For example, sentences such as "We ran into the house when it started to rain" may be preferred to "It started to rain and then we ran into the house," and sentences such as "I lost my key and I couldn't get into the house" may be preferred to "I lost my keys and then I couldn't get into the house," not because of lack of understanding of relationships, but only because these are the structures ordinarily used to express the relationship. In these instances, preference may not really test comparative comprehension.

Further, there is a question about the attempt to equate explanation with comprehension. It is possible that such factors as extensiveness and depth of vocabulary (as in the definition of words) are being tested rather than comprehension. However, it seems clear from this experiment that the antithetic relationship is understood and produced long after causal and temporal relationships. The distinction between sequential (temporal) and causal relationships needs further exploration. It may indeed be the case that simultaneous temporal relationships ("when") are understood before sequential ("then"). These findings, however, contradict those of Werner and Kaplan (1964). This difference may be due to the fact that Werner and Kaplan observed much younger children, but it may also be due to the particular connective being used in this study ("then") and its comparative familiarity to the children.

The need for linguistic order to reflect perceptual cause and effect, which is evident at the sixth-grade level and then disappears at the college level, is an intriguing finding. It is possible that syntactic factors may be playing a role. The connective "and" in the youngest children's grammar may be considered to necessitate syntactic restrictions on verb tense and pronoun and some relationships between subject matter, but not necessarily cause-and-effect relationships. Absence of the connective may simply mean two sentences, not necessarily related, depending on how the sentences are read. The absence of a connective may give the oldest subjects freedom to choose connectives—for example, "We did not sit down (because) the benches were wet." But this does not explain the results obtained with sixth-graders.

Indeed, although Werner and Kaplan (1964), Vygotsky (1962), and Piaget (1926) have commented on the linguistic development of structures which express various relationships and how this sequence of development may be related to cognitive development, there have been few thorough studies of either (1) linguistic development of the use of structures which are derived from more than one sentence and express these relationships, (2) comprehension of the meaning of the relationships expressed in these structures, or (3) the relationship of the comprehension and use of these structures to cognitive development.

SUMMARY

The research on the processes involved in the acquisition of the meaningfulness of a speech signal has been limited primarily to observations of productions and, in some few instances, productions in certain situations. Imitation has been stressed as a necessary prerequisite to the comprehension of the meaningfulness of the signal and as an indication that the signal is indeed comprehended. However, it is not clear what is meant by imitation, since in many instances vocalization to vocalization is labeled imitation, yet during this stage of development vocalization is not the only stimulus which elicits vocalization. The presence of parents and dolls also elicits vocalizations. Further, given what has been observed about the sequence of processes involved in the acquisition of other aspects of the grammar, it is entirely possible that the child comprehends the meaningfulness of some utterances before he attempts either to imitate or to produce these utterances. The facts are, as yet, unavailable.

The Russian psychologists have begun to examine experimentally some of the conditions under which meaning is acquired. However, a great deal of their research is geared toward the question of how children can be taught the meaning of lexical items and other grammatical aspects, rather than how they do indeed acquire them. Therefore, their research has not fully explored the experimental possibilities, but has been limited to a restricted set of experimental conditions. The results of both observations and experimentation do not make clear how utterances become meaningful for the infant. It has been suggested that this acquisition may come about primarily by the naming of objects by adults, then practice in naming by the child. This is questionable, since there is evidence that many of the first lexical items produced are used as sentences and not as names of objects. It has also been suggested that the functional use of an object given a particular name by adults leads to an understanding of the word. However, many early words are not objects that can be used functionally ("in," "on," "off," etc.). Finally, it has been suggested that comprehension comes about through observation of the use of a lexical item in a sentence in association with a particular action. The research that has been carried out thus far reveals the myriad number of questions that have still to be answered concerning the acquisition of meaning.

Close observation of the development of semantic categorizations in very young children's language has not, as yet, been undertaken. The usual measures of the development of this aspect of the grammar have been counts of the number of differing lexical items used in the child's spontaneous production as he matures, or the proportion of differing types of items used to the total number of items used (type-token ratio). This is a surface aspect of the development of semantic competence and tells us very little about what the child knows or does not know about this aspect of the grammar at various stages of development. As might be suspected, the number of differing lexical items used increases over the developmental period (albeit at differing rates) into adulthood and during adulthood, since new vocabulary can always be added to one's dictionary or to the linguistic community's dictionary.

From the few data that have been gathered, several processes seem to occur in the child's early acquisition of the meaning of lexical items. The assignment of a set of properties to a lexical item may include properties that do not strictly pertain to the lexical item ("hosh" for both "horse" and "dog") or properties that do not pertain at all to the lexical item ("right" and "left" for "right") or a small set of properties that pertain to only some attributes of the lexical item ("under" for "below"). Because of this aspect of development, some lexical items are used only in specific sentence and situational contexts. Detailed observation, noting the progression from generalization to differentiation to acquisition of the standard properties of lexical items in sentence and situational contexts, supplemented with experimental testing of the child's understanding of lexical items, may reveal general trends in the sequence of development of lexical meanings and a possible hierarchy of acquisition of semantic categorizations, such as ±human, ±animate, etc.

Studies of children's definition of words, attempts to derive definitions of new words, word association responses, labeling of perceptual stimuli, and use of words in spontaneous utterances all indicate that children assign a unique and limited set of properties to the lexical items they use. As they mature this set of properties is modified and expanded. Since the reading of a particular lexical item is dependent on the sentence and situational context in which it is produced, the list of readings for a particular lexical item expands as it is observed in new structures that are acquired and comprehended. For this reason also, the structure of the child's lexicon continues to change and grow for a long period of time. An interesting question which has still to be answered is whether or not there are at some stage of development certain semantic fields whose lexical items share semantic properties and are used in substitution for each other (for example, the adjectives "big," "heavy," "tall," and the verbs "put," "take," "close"). Another interesting question is whether or not a developmental sequence can be observed in which members of certain semantic fields are differentiated before others. More detailed observations of utterances and experimentation may bring answers to these questions.

Research in children's comprehension of the underlying relationships expressed in transformations of a single underlying kernel sentence (primarily the passive transformation) indicate that very young children understand the subject-object relationship in these sentences and that in carrying out a task in association with sentences, the subject-object relationship is interpreted as actor and acted upon. Manipulation of the experimental situation causes children to recall sentences in either the active or passive voice. In carrying out tasks to fit statements, greater time is needed if the situation is not congruent with the statement. However, there does not appear to be any confusion about the relationship expressed in the sentence. Children's comprehension of the subject-object relationship has yet to be explored in many contexts. There are other types of utterances in addition to passives in which the subject-object relationship may not be clear. These are utterances in which the properties of lexical items as well as the structure need to be understood in order to comprehend the relationship (for example, utterances such as "Hay filled the wagon," "The window broke," "John opened the box with Bill," "John opened the box with a hammer").

It has been found in an examination of children's comprehension of the relationships expressed by various types of conjoined and embedded sentences that causal relationships are understood before temporal, and that both of these relationships are understood before antithetic relationships. However, in this area, again, the experimentation has been limited. Indeed, the questions that were posed about acquisition of other aspects of the grammar, and at least partially answered in current research, have yet to be broached in a rigorous and comprehensive manner in this aspect of language development. These are questions such as what is the sequence of development that can be observed in the structures that are produced and understood at various stages, and what factors lead to the sequence observed? Of course, a serious deterrent is the difficulty in determining the scope of the dimensions to be examined or what the semantic versus the syntactic structure of the language is. However, recent research has indicated that a systematic examination of the child's acquisition of the properties of lexical items and his comprehension of the relationships expressed in sentences can give us some understanding of the sequence of development in this aspect of the grammar.

7

DEVIANT
LANGUAGE
BEHAVIOR

IN THE PREVIOUS CHAPTERS we discussed research on the acquisition and development of aspects of the linguistic system (*the grammar*) by most children or by most children with whom research has been carried out. The only variables which appeared to affect the acquisition of the linguistic system by these children were age and the complexities of the system. Some children acquire certain linguistic structures at an earlier age than other children, but all acquired these structures at an age which agreed with the expectations of those they communicate with. None of the children within the group already discussed would be marked as exhibiting deviant linguistic behavior by any native speaker of his language. But the group or individual differences in patterns of language acquisition and development which will be dealt with in this chapter are those differences which would be marked by native speakers of the language. To be sure, using this as our criterion of deviant language behavior is an arbitrary procedure, since experience and situational variables can determine whether or not differences are marked. For example, a 3-year-old child talking to his mother, to somebody else's mother, and to an adult who has never spoken to a 3-year-old child would have his language performance evaluated differently by each listener. However, since there is wide agreement among native speakers of the language as to whether or not there is a marked difference in the language behavior of some children as compared to some model of normal language behavior, the definition appears to provide a valid categorization.

The factors contributing to these differences are physiological, environmental, both, or simply unknown. Studies of the linguistic behavior of children who are not acquiring language normally, in conjunction with studies of children who are, are of great interest to the student of language development, because it is hoped that these comparative studies can lead to a better understanding of the anatomical, physiological, and psychological bases of language acquisition and development. Further, it is hoped that these studies will indicate how the processes of perception and production of language are organized by the human being. Two questions have been explored in relation to studies of children who are developing language in a deviant manner: What factors lead to what type of deviant linguistic behavior? and What is the structure of the sentences that are heard and produced by these children? These questions will be discussed in this chapter.

The techniques used to examine developmental differences are all those techniques, previously described, which have been used to describe and examine normal language acquisition and development, such as descriptions of the utterances produced and understood, repetition of utterances, picture identification, and so on.

DESCRIPTIONS OF DEVIANT
LINGUISTIC BEHAVIOR

In a survey (Telford and Sawrey, 1967, p. 376) of the principal causes of "delay" in the production of language by a group of children (278 in number) who exhibited deviant linguistic behavior, it was found that deafness caused 40 percent of the incidents of delay, so-called developmental aphasia (some suspected damage to the central nervous system) caused 26 percent of the incidents, mental deficiency caused 25 percent of the incidents, cerebral palsy caused 8 percent of the incidents, and mental illness 1 percent of the incidents. Other causes for language production delay have been noted, such as lack of motivation and personality disorders.

It has been found (Telford and Sawrey, 1967, p. 371) that approximately 5 percent of school-age children exhibit deviant linguistic behavior. Of these, 81 percent have "articulation defects" and 6.5 percent stutter. All others display some form of language delay or severe articulation defect due to either known causes (for example, cleft palate) or unknown causes.[1]

What is "delayed speech" and what is an "articulation defect"? The categorization delayed speech can imply that the time at which a child

---

[1] For survey descriptions of various types of language disorders, see Travis, 1957.

starts to produce sentences is somewhat later than that observed with children who are labeled as normal, or it can imply that the child begins to produce sentences at approximately the average time, but proceeds at a much slower pace, and that at the stage when no further development in language behavior can be observed, his level of performance is below that of the average adult. The term usually implies all these aspects: delay in onset, slowness of the process, termination of the process before average adult linguistic performance is reached.[2] In between the onset and the termination of the process, the child is presumed to follow the course of development observed with children who are acquiring language normally. An articulation defect is viewed as some deviation from *acceptable* speech sound production. The defect may involve some few sound substitutions or be so severe that the child's speech is unintelligible.

Diagnostic classifications such as deaf and mentally retarded, and descriptive terms such as delayed speech and articulation defect tell us very little about the linguistic behavior which is marked as deviant. Both deaf and mentally retarded children presumably exhibit something called delayed speech, which may also include articulation defects; on the other hand, articulation defects can imply that there has been some delay in speech sound production acquisition due to known or unknown factors. In addition to the fact that the above terminology is unclear when being used, it is not even clear whether delay in language or articulation defects also necessarily implies delay in language comprehension or defects in speech sound discrimination. Indeed, it is frequently reported in the literature that no significant correlations have been found between difficulties in speech sound production and difficulties in speech sound discrimination (Eisenson, 1963).

In recent research, attempts have been made to describe structurally the utterances produced and understood by children who exhibit markedly deviant linguistic behavior. Children's use of morphological, syntactic, semantic, or phonological rules has been examined in various instances of deficit (for example, the performance of a group of mentally retarded children in a test of morphological rule competence). Simultaneous evaluations of various aspects of linguistic competence within a given population have been rarely undertaken. Comparisons are made between the performance of these children in a particular linguistic task and the performance of children who are acquiring language normally.

It should be noted that in each aspect of performance there may be degrees of deviance. These may pertain to the *number* of structures that are missing or are different, and also to which particular structures are

---

[2] For example, see Lenneberg, 1967, pp. 154–55.

missing or different. For example, if a child says (1) "I wearing a clean dress" or (2) "I wearing a cwean dwess," it is a comparatively simple task for listeners, who are members of the child's linguistic community, to use their knowledge of the language and retrieve "I'm wearing a clean dress." If a child, however, says (3) "Weh dean det," retrieving the utterance or comprehending its meaning is a complicated task. There are syntactic deviations from the fully grammatical form in sentences (1), (2), and (3) and phonological deviations in sentences (2) and (3), but the degree of deviation varies. The number of syntactic deviations in sentence (3) is greater than in sentence (1) and (2), and the number of phonological deviations is greater in sentence (3) than in sentence (2). However, if sentence (3) is uttered as (4) "Me weh kean desh," the sentence becomes more comprehensible because of the difference in the nature of the deviations, although the number of deviations remains approximately the same. In sentence (4) the subject of the sentence is known even though it is incorrectly marked (substitution versus omission), and the particular phonological deviations in sentence (4) preserve, to a greater extent than in sentence (3), the distinctive features of the underlying representations of items in the sentence (for example, "desh" versus "det").

There may, of course, be semantic deviations as well. There are children who produce utterances such as the following: (1) "I got new uh"; (2) "I got new fun"; (3) "I got new go fast." If phonological and syntactic deviations are also part of these children's grammars, and if sentences such as "dah new uh," "dah new pun," etc. are produced, then these children's utterances become even more incomprehensible. The degree of deviance, then, is dependent on the number and types of rules which differ in these children's grammar from the rules used by normal speaking children in all components of the grammar—syntactic, semantic, and phonological.

Degree of deviance is also dependent on one other factor, and that is the age of the child. For example, if a 10-year-old produces utterances such as "go car," "me shoe," "want baby," these utterances are marked as deviant by native speakers of his language although these same utterances would not be considered deviant if produced by a 2-year-old. If these same utterances were produced by a 19-year-old, the evaluated degree of deviancy would increase.

There are several questions, then, that one can ask about deviant language behavior: (1) What is its structure? (2) What is its degree of deviance? and (3) Is it deviant only in terms of age? One can then attempt to find relationships between answers to these questions and what is known about the physiological and psychological functioning of a child or group of children who exhibit a type of linguistic behavior. Through the definition of these relationships, as was indicated previously, a greater understanding of the bases of language behavior can be obtained.

DEVIANT LANGUAGE RESULTING
FROM KNOWN CAUSES

Some sensory-motor deficits appear to affect the acquisition of language and others do not. In any case, few studies of the sequence and structures of the language development of children with such deficits have been undertaken. Most studies of the language of these children have been survey studies of gross characteristics of language behavior. Studies comparing the language acquisition and development of blind children indicate that speech disorders occur with somewhat greater frequency in this population than in sighted children, and that blind children are somewhat slower in learning to speak (Telford and Sawrey, 1967, pp. 280–81). However, these studies indicate widely varying frequencies of incidence, and in addition, no studies of the structure of blind children's language at varying stages of development have been undertaken. Therefore, a question exists as to whether or not blind children's language development is different from that of sighted children to any marked degree. If it is indeed the case that there are marked differences, the nature of these differences has yet to be described.

The incidence of speech defects with cerebral palsied children is of course high because of the all-encompassing neurological effects which result in, for example, differences in breathing patterns and differences in motor patterns in the movement of tongue and lips for articulation. In addition to motor difficulties, the incidence of mental retardation, as measured by standard intelligence tests, is high in this population. It should be noted that the term "speech disorder" is used in describing the language problems of these children, and the exact nature of this speech disorder in any instance or group of instances is not clear. For example, in surveys of this population it is not clear whether speech disorder refers to articulation disorder or language delay or both.

Fuller (1966) conducted a study of the comprehension of some syntactic structures and morphological rules by two cerebral palsied children. Both children did not speak, and tests indicated that both were mentally retarded with I.Q.s of around 60 and 70. Their ages were 20 and 14 years. In comparing the performance of these two boys in a sentence comprehension test,[3] it was found that the order of difficulty of structures was comparable to that found with normal speaking 3- to 7-year-olds. Those structures which were understood all the time by the normal speaking children were also understood all the time by these boys; those that were

---

[3] Taken from Fraser, Bellugi, and Brown, 1963.

understood about half the time by the normal speaking children were understood half the time by the boys, and those understood by the normal speaking children about one quarter of the time were simply not understood by the boys. The morphological test [4] could only be used with one of the boys. Again, the order of difficulty was parallel for the cerebral palsied child and the normal speaking children. The experimenter concluded that the acquisition of the structures tested followed the same sequence as that observed with normal speaking children except that acquisition was stretched over a longer period of time. In addition, it appears that the ability to produce these structures is not necessary for understanding them.

This same kind of performance—that is, order of acquisition similar to that of normal speaking children but stretched out in time—has also been observed in the language behavior of a group of mongoloid children (Lenneberg, Nichols, and Rosenberger, 1964). The question of whether or not the process of acquisition continues throughout the developmental period is not answered in these studies. That is, it is possible that an asymptote is reached at some early stage of grammatical development. This occurrence would result in the same behavior that is attributed to a stretching out of the developmental period. Longitudinal studies are needed to resolve this question. It is clear, however, that comprehension of linguistic structures is not dependent on the ability to produce these structures. In addition to the results found in the study of two cerebral palsied boys, Lenneberg (1962) describes an 8-year-old boy who could not speak at all, but could comprehend sentences with quite complicated linguistic structures.

The morphological rules used by normal and educable mentally retarded children were examined (Newfield and Schlanger, 1968). There were 30 children in each group. The mean C.A. (chronological age) of the retarded group was 10.4 and the mean M.A. (mental age) was 5.1. The mean C.A. of the normal group was 6.1 and the mean M.A. was 7.9. The children were tested with real words and nonsense stems. Noun, verb, and possessive endings were tested. Both groups had more difficulty with the nonsense stems than with real words, but this difference was strikingly more marked with the mentally retarded group. Rules with real words had for the most part already been acquired by the normal group. There was a significant correlation only between success with nonsense stems and mental age for the normal group. There was a significant correlation between success with the total task, rather than only with nonsense stems, and mental age for the retarded group.

On the whole, the order of difficulty was similar for both groups, but there were some interesting differences, and these primarily involved verbs.

---

[4] Taken from Berko, 1961.

While normal children's performance was reduced with the past form of strong verbs (those requiring a memorized list), *ed* endings (such as "melted," "skated," etc.), and the third person, singular, present tense form, these "exceptions" did not cause anywhere near the difficulty experienced by the retarded group. These verb forms require memorization or the learning of rules which apply to unique subsets. This difference is even more marked when the performances of the two groups of children are compared in the application of rules which apply most generally and those which apply most specifically. The mean percentage of children applying the correct rule in the application of + ing tense rules and + z plural rules is 99 percent in the normal group and 93 percent in the retarded group. However, the mean percentage of children applying the correct rule in past tense of strong verbs and + ı z plural rules is 85 percent in the normal group and 33 percent in the retarded group. The differences, then, appear to be qualitative as well as quantitative. The position that the linguistic performance of mentally retarded children is like that of normal children only reduced is open to question and seems to be very dependent on the structure of the aspect of the grammar that is tested.

A sensory deficit such as deafness affects the acquisition and development of speech depending on the nature and degree of hearing loss,[5] but should not necessarily affect the acquisition and development of a visual symbol system or written language. A visual symbol system (or sign language) appears to be easily and naturally acquired by the deaf when they are exposed to it. There are studies now underway examining the semantic, syntactic, and phonological structures of sign language to determine whether they allow the expression of all the grammatical relationships encompassed by the spoken language.[6] It would be interesting to study the development of sign language over some maturational period to observe the sequential changes in structure that occur and to determine whether or not such developmental changes coincide with what has been observed in the acquisition of verbal language. No such studies have as yet been carried out, since the structure of the language has yet to be described. An additional problem is that presumably there are variations in the sign language used in this country depending on geography and the circumstances under which it is developed. Therefore, dialect studies are needed to determine the general characteristics of the language in a given place.

Because such a small percentage of the deaf population achieves average verbal skills, the linguistic competence of deaf children is usually studied by examining their reading and writing performance. It should be kept in mind that differences have been found in the written and spoken language

---

[5] For a discussion of "deaf" children who learn to speak, see Fry, 1966.

[6] We are aware of two such projects: Stokoe, 1960, and Schlesinger, 1967b.

of hearing children,[7] and the results of studies with deaf children are probably influenced by (1) the fact that 35 percent of the deaf population never
achieves functional literacy (Vernon, 1967), (2) the particular teaching
methods these children have been exposed to, and possibly (3) sign language and its structure.

The ability of deaf and hearing children to comprehend and produce
morphological rules has been examined (Cooper, 1967). Sizable populations of deaf children (140) aged 7 to 19 years and hearing children (176)
aged 7 to 18 years were compared. All were reading at the second-grade
level or above. Subjects' comprehension of morphological rules was tested
by requesting that they mark the picture which represented the form (for
example, "moggs"). Their production was tested by asking them to complete a sentence (for example, "Yesterday he hibb__"). It was found that
hearing subjects' performance was strikingly superior. Both a mental age
and chronological age comparison produced the same result.

The highest correlation existed between performance on the test and
reading scores for the total population. For hearing girls performance on
the test was more highly correlated with chronological age and mental age
than it was for deaf girls. For the most part, the same relationships were
observed with deaf and hearing boys. Despite the fact that performance on
the test was highly correlated with reading scores, it was found that when
the written test and an oral form of the test were presented to a subsample
of second-grade hearing children, no significant differences were observed
between performance on the oral and written tests. This indicates that there
is a correlation between written and verbal performance in this aspect of the
grammar. When the proportions of deaf and hearing girls passing each item
were compared across test items, it was found that the correlation was .68
for comprehension items and .78 for the productive items, thus indicating
that the patterns of difficulty for hearing and deaf children were similar.

Again, we appear to find evidence that the acquisition of a set of linguistic rules is similar for both sensorially handicapped children and those
who are not, but that it appears to take longer for the handicapped group.
However, two findings in this experiment challenge this simple conclusion.
The first is that increasing mental age and chronological age were not as
closely related to better scores for the deaf group as they were for the hearing group. Indeed, scores for deaf boys leveled off at age 9–10 years. The
second is that scores for both groups were closest in terms of morphological
markers (for example, past tense) and farthest apart for derivational rules
(for example, the comparative). Therefore, there is some evidence that
qualitative as well as quantitative differences exist in the performance of
these groups. These qualitative differences are due to the *types* of rules

---

[7] These are primarily differences in rate of occurrence per sampled time of various structures,
rather than differences in the structure used. See O'Donnell, Griffin, and Norris, 1967.

which the deaf group not only is slower in acquiring, but also appears to have marked difficulty in acquiring. These differences, of course, may be due to the particular language experiences of deaf children—that is, the particular content and method of their education, rather than their capacity to acquire structures.

It is important to note that the areas of primary difficulty for the deaf group and the mentally retarded group appear to be quite different. No direct comparisons can be made since there were differences in age range, the constructions tested, and the means of testing. However, in the production of rules for nonsense stems which apply to unique subsets (for example, the past form of strong verbs), the deaf population does as well as the hearing population, whereas the mentally retarded group does markedly more poorly than both deaf and hearing children.

Delay, then, is an encompassing term which may mean very different types of behavior, depending on the nature of the deficit and upon group and individual language experiences. When one looks at particular aspects of acquisition of the system and examines children's use of structures, the basis for the deviancy appears to cause differences in the types of structures which are acquired earlier or later by the group, and probably to determine whether or not some structures are acquired at all. The need for much further research comparing the linguistic competence of children with various types of deficits as well as comparing these children with normal speaking children is obvious.

A study (Schmitt, 1968) was undertaken to examine deaf children's ability to comprehend and produce certain types of syntactic structures: simple active declarative, negative, passive, and passive negative. Their ability to comprehend and produce progressive, past, and future tense verb forms in these structures was also tested. The deaf children were asked (1) to pick a picture among a set of four to match a printed sentence, (2) to pick a sentence among four to match a picture, and (3) to fill in a sentence by choosing among a set of fillers (for example, "Now the girl _____ by the dog"). These tasks were labeled (1) comprehension, (2) production selection, and (3) production construction. Eight-, eleven-, fourteen-, and seventeen-year-old deaf children were tested.

In comparing the performance of deaf and hearing children it was found that the combined task mean score of 8-year-old hearing children was significantly higher than that of 17-year-old deaf children. For the deaf group total scores (including all transformations and tense markers) generally increased over the age range. However, there were interesting exceptions in which older children achieved lower scores than younger children. For example, in the production-selection task 11-year-olds achieved lower scores than 8-year-olds in the use of future tense, and in the production-construction task 8- and 11-year-olds achieved higher scores with the active declarative construction than with the active negative construction, but the inverse occurred with 14- and 17-year-olds. The older children achieved higher scores with the negative construction than with the positive construction. The passive construction tended to be most difficult, followed by the passive negative, declarative, and negative in difficulty. The scores with the negative construction were equal to or *greater* than the scores obtained with the positive construction in three age groups.

In general, the performance of the deaf children reflected the presumed increasing complexity of the passive versus the active relationship. Thus, they performed in the manner of hearing children. However, it did not reflect the presumed increasing complexity of the negative versus the positive relationship. Thus, they performed in a manner somewhat different from that of hearing children.[8] Indeed, the performance observed may simply reflect the time at which a construction is taught (and forgotten) rather than competence in understanding and generating a sentence. Further, it appears that there may be some reflection of the structure of sign language in these children's responses. English subject-object order is presumably not maintained in sign language, and 8- and 11-year-old subjects reversed the subject and object in active declarative sentences. Although the present progressive is the tense marker first acquired by hearing children, it is, in general, the verb form most frequently deviant in the deaf population.

There are, therefore, particular aspects of the performance of the deaf children in this study which indicate differences in the sequence of acquisition of structures as compared to hearing children, and not simply a slowing down of the sequence of acquisition. In some instances, the performance of deaf children appears to be more critically affected by their particular language experiences than by the complexity of the linguistic structures. This, of course, may be true of all children who are involved in special language training programs. It would be most interesting to observe, especially with the young children in this population, the pattern of performance with a variety of structures when corrections are built into the experimental task. The differences in ease of acquisition among these structures, after a training period, may give some insight into what they know about language.

DEVIANT LANGUAGE BEHAVIOR RESULTING FROM UNKNOWN CAUSES

There is a group of children who do not speak or understand language or who have difficulty in producing or comprehending language to some

---

[8] This finding may have been the result of the situation in which, in many instances, the negative is clearly marked as being the only negative among four possibilities.

marked degree because of diagnosed brain damage. These children have been labeled aphasics. There is, on the other hand, a group of children whose verbal performance essentially matches that of brain damaged children, but who display no other sensory-motor deficits and who exhibit no positive signs in neurological examinations or EEG tests. Children within this group have been categorized as being "aphasoid" or "schizophrenic," implying that one subgroup's linguistic disability is due to organic factors while the second subgroup's linguistic disability is due to psychopathology.

In a summary of some of the findings with the two groups, Hirsch (1967) notes these distinctions: (1) the auditory memory span of aphasoid children is extremely short, whereas schizophrenic children have an excellent memory span for meaningless material; (2) the schizophrenic child produces bizarre and idiosyncratic language exhibiting lack of functional relationships between the words in the utterance, while the aphasoid child does not; and (3) the pitch, intonation, and stress of the utterances of schizophrenic children deviate markedly from the normal, whereas they do not in the case of the aphasoid child. Presumably large numbers of these children may have both neurological *and* psychological disfunctions. The dichotomization of this group may, therefore, be unfruitful for the purpose of studying their language production and comprehension. It is the language behavior itself which may lead to more clarifying categorization of members of this group. It should again be noted that in the population whose members exhibit no positive signs of organic damage, but do exhibit deviant language behavior, the language behavior observed ranges from the communicatively mute or incomprehensible to the comprehensible but deviant, and this deviancy may be in terms of syntactic, phonological, or semantic rules or some combination of these rules.

There have not been many studies of the structure of the language of these children at different stages of their development, or of the development of their language over some maturational period. Lee (1966) compared the syntactic structures in the utterances produced by a child of 3 years developing language normally with those in the utterances of a child of 4.7 years who had been diagnosed as being delayed in language development and was enrolled in a clinical program. The tape recorded utterances of the two boys were examined, and the presence or absence of certain structures were noted. Various levels of development were extrapolated from the results of studies of children who were developing language normally, and the structures of the utterances of the two boys were compared to these levels. Interpreting Lee's categorization, one finds that these levels can be represented as the development of the NP or S, as indicated in Table 7–1.

In comparing the structures in the utterances of the two children, it was found that the child with "delayed speech" was not using some of the

TABLE 7–1   LEVELS OF EARLY SYNTACTIC DEVELOPMENT

Level	Structure	Example
Noun Phrase		
Level I	NP $\longrightarrow$ (Art.) (Poss.) (Quant.) (Adj.) $+$ N	a, my, more, truck
Level II	NP $\longrightarrow$ $\left\{ \begin{array}{l} \text{Art.} \\ \text{Poss.} \end{array} \right\}$ $+$ Quant. $+$ Adj. $+$ N	the two red car
Sentence		
Level I	S $\longrightarrow$ S $+$ S	not ride, no truck
	S $\longrightarrow$ NP $+$ NP	That, it, truck
	S $\longrightarrow$ NP $+$ (Adv.) (Part.)	Truck there, Light off
	* S $\longrightarrow$ V $+$ NP	See truck
Level II	S $\longrightarrow$ above S_s $+$ expansion of NP	
Level III	S $\longrightarrow$ NP $+$ V	Truck go
	S $\longrightarrow$ NP $+$ Det. $+$ N	That big truck
	S $\longrightarrow$ Det. $+$ N $+$ Adv.	That truck in garage
	* S $\longrightarrow$ V $+$ NP $+$ Adv.	Take truck again
Level IV	S $\longrightarrow$ NP $+$ VP	That's a big car
Level V	S $\longrightarrow$ Q	Is that a truck, Where is the truck
	S $\longrightarrow$ Neg	The car is not broken
	S $\longrightarrow$ Do $+$ Neg	I don't see a car
	S $\longrightarrow$ $S_1 + S_2$	The car and the truck are broken
	S $\longrightarrow$ S_1 (S_2)	I wanna take a car

* These may be imperative sentences or sentences with *I* omitted

structures used by the child developing language normally. For example, sentences of the form NP $+$ VP, question sentences, and fully formed negatives were not being used by this child. In general, he appeared to be at Level I in sentence development, as indicated in Table 7–1, whereas the normal speaking child was at Level V. However, there were omissions of structures even at Level I by the child with delayed speech, and some structures used by this child appear at more sophisticated levels. The most interesting result disclosed by this analysis was not simply the fact that fewer or less developed types of structures were being used, but that in certain instances very different structures were being used. Most of the sentences produced by this child were predicate structures and very few were subject $+$ predicate structures. The following are some examples.

1. go school
2. drink water
3. want cookie
4. be here
5. be kitty cat

6. go no guess
7. want wake up
8. not coughing
9. do with hand
10. think no guess

Subjects of sentences were, for the most part, limited to "me," "I," "we," and they were used infrequently. Even the undeveloped subject + predicate constructions such as "There truck," "That hat," and "mommy sit" were not being used.

Some conclusions may be drawn from the linguistic behavior of this child. The first is that delayed speech, in this instance, does not simply mean producing language which is more appropriate for a younger child. The second is that it would be very difficult for this child to develop the rules of his language on the basis of the rules he has already acquired. He has not yet established the basic relationship of subject + predicate, and, as was observed in normal development, this is the first relationship to be established after topic + modifier and is necessary for the development of the transformational structures of negation and question. The third is that this child appears to have developed his own unique set of rules for generating sentences. His linguistic performance, although it might appear bizarre, was consistent rather than random.

This consistency has been noted in phonological deviancy as well (Menyuk, 1968b). An analysis of an 11-year-old's production of morphemes indicated that he was using a set of phonological rules which varied from that of his peers but was consistent nevertheless. All stop sounds which are normally produced at the middle or back of the mouth were produced as a voiced middle of the mouth stop (or /d/) in initial or medial position in the morpheme. In final position all such stops were unvoiced. Thus /k/, /g/, and /t/ were produced as /d/ in initial and medial positions and as /t/ in final position. Such a performance would appear to be inconsistent on the surface. It would appear that sometimes a sound would be accurately produced and at other times substituted by another sound. For example, the /t/ in some instances would be produced with voicing (/d/) and in other instances without (/t/). The word "tie" would be produced as "die" by these rules but the word "bit" would remain "bit." As Jakobson (1964, p. 22) has stated, "the disorders of language display their own peculiar order and require a systematic linguistic comparison with our normal verbal code."

A study by Menyuk (1964b) analyzed the structures in the sentences produced by children diagnosed as using infantile speech without any positive signs of physiological damage. These structures were compared to those produced by normal speaking children aged 3 to 6 years. The normals were matched with the deviant speaking group on I.Q., age, sex, and socioeconomic status. Once more, it was found that many of the structures used by the "infantile" speaking children's peers were not being used by these children. However, again, the most interesting findings were those of difference rather than simple delay.

Neither the 3-year-old nor the 6-year-old child in the infantile speech group was using structures which matched those used by a 2-year-old normal speaking child. They had developed a grammar that was more sophisticated in terms of some structures and different in terms of others. Therefore, these children were not simply a little delayed or even substantially delayed in their acquisition of structures. Further, after they had acquired the use of certain structures at age 3, there appeared to be very little change in the structures they used from age 3 to 6. The sentences produced by a group of these children were analyzed and the structures they contained were described (Menyuk, 1969, Chapter 4). Most of the sentences produced could be described in the following manner:

$$S \longrightarrow NP + VP \qquad\qquad \text{Mommy make}$$
$$S \longrightarrow NP + V + NP \qquad \text{Me have this one}$$
$$S \longrightarrow Q + NP + VP \qquad \text{Where you take?}$$
$$S \longrightarrow NP + Neg + VP \qquad \text{Blacky not talk}$$
$$S \longrightarrow NP + V + NP \qquad \text{Him want scratch}$$

The above rules comprise an extremely useful grammar, although there are many relationships which cannot be expressed by these rules (for example, various types of embedding and conjunction). It appears to be a basic "unmarked" grammar (tense, pluralization, and case are frequently unmarked), and the sentences generated are, for the most part, comprehensible if limited. However, in addition to these findings, it was observed that the particular expansions of this basic grammar used by these children restricted the possibilities for further development. For example, while these children produced negative, question, and declarative sentences, there is no indication of the development of the Aux/Mod node (can, will, tense, be + ing, etc.). Until this node is developed the transformational operations for the completed forms of these sentence types or for tense marker placement cannot be used. These children almost always use the marked form of the pronoun (him, me) as subjects of sentences, indicating that these are NPs, not pronouns.[9] Until this class is developed many of the techniques of reference cannot be employed. Indeed, many of the sentences produced could be described as simply S + S or NP + S. Lee

---

[9] For a discussion of the classification of marked pronouns in subject position, see Gruber, 1967a.

(1966) noted in her study that the child using deviant language produced utterances such as "Linda Debbie sick listen radio" (meaning presumably "When Linda and Debbie are sick *they* listen to the radio"), also indicating the use of NP + S and S + S structures by this child without marking time, reference, etc. It should be noted that, unlike the child in Lee's study, the children in this study (Menyuk, 1969) were expressing the subject + predicate relationship in their sentences. This is a good example of the fact that children who have been labeled as using delayed speech can use language with varying degrees of competence.

An important question, of course, is why these children acquire and use language in a manner different from that of normal speaking children. In a preliminary attempt to obtain some answers to this question, a group of these children were asked to repeat sentences containing various syntactic structures, and their repetitions were compared to those of normal speaking children (Menyuk, 1969, Chapter 4). The children with a language disorder repeated sentences with omission of whole phrases or with only the last words in a sentence, even though many of these sentences were based on transformations of a single underlying kernel. Only in some *few* instances were sentences modified according to rules in their grammar. Normal speaking children, on the other hand, consistently modified or repeated the structures of the sentence in accordance with the rules of their grammar. Both the length and complexity of the utterances affected the repetitions of the language disordered group, whereas length did not affect the repetitions of the normal speaking group. Increased complexity resulted in omissions of parts or almost the entire sentence by the language disordered group, whereas increased complexity resulted in simplifications by the normal speaking group.

It was also found that, whereas in their repetitions of sentences the normal speaking children exceeded to some degree the level of syntactic competence they displayed in their spontaneous utterances, the inverse was true of the language disordered group. This group did significantly more poorly in their repetition of structures than they did in producing them spontaneously. It appears, then, that whereas normal speaking children have the capacity to store and fully or at least partially analyze a sentence (depending on its structure), children using disordered language are incapable of this task *unless* the utterance is short enough and/or simple enough. This would account for the development of structures such as NP + S ("Where you take") and V + NP ("want wake up") for generating sentences, but for few other structures. Decoding parts of a sentence or only partial analysis of a sentence (restricted length and depth of analysis) could lead to such distortions and the storage of these types of rules in the grammar.

It has frequently been observed that children who appear to have syntactic problems, or who are labeled as language delayed, also have phonological problems. This was true of the group described above. It has not been so frequently observed that children who have problems in acquiring the phonological system of their language also have syntactic problems.

The issues raised in these studies are interesting ones, since they bear on questions concerning the processing of language and how it is organized. Is it indeed organized, as some linguistic description would imply, in the manner indicated in Figure 7–1. If this is the case, then syntactic deviation would lead to phonological and semantic deviation but the inverse would not be true.

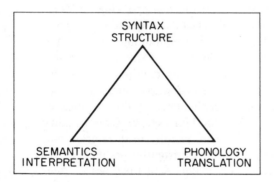

FIG. 7–1 Possible organization of the three components of the grammar from some linguistic points of view.

If the child's syntactic rules are deviant, does this necessarily mean that his phonological and semantic rules will be deviant? If his phonological rules are deviant, does this necessarily mean that his syntactic and semantic rules will be deviant, etc.? Answers to these questions will perhaps tell us more about how language is organized.

A study (Shriner, Holloway, and Daniloff, 1969) comparing the structure of the utterances produced by children with severe articulation disorders and those with normal speech in grades 1 through 3 indicated that there were structural differences between the utterances of the two groups, but they were of a proportional kind. Picture stimuli were used, and in each instance 50 to 60 utterances were analyzed in response to these pictures. The mean number of words per response was significantly higher among children without articulation problems, and the occurrence of expanded subject NPs ("the cat"), Vs ("did eat"), object NPs ("the mouse"), and VPs ("did eat the mouse") was significantly greater in their utterances. However, the children in both groups did produce all such structures. Only the proportion of usage differed. Articulation problems seemed to depress the frequency of occurrence of expansion but, according to the measures used, they did not alter the structure of the grammar used.

A study of the language and articulation performance of 22 "echolalic" 3-year-olds and a matched group (matched in terms of the I.Q. scores obtained when they were 4 years old) of normal speaking children was undertaken (Fay and Butler, 1968). The echolalic group was defined as those who gave 10 or more echoic responses to 50 consecutive speech-evoking stimuli in an interview session. This group was further divided into "pure" echoers and "mitigated" echoers. The latter group introduced some modifications into the echoic response (an example given is the response "I sleep" to the question "Where do I sleep?"). The language and articulation measures used to test these children were some of the subtests to be found on the Speech, Language, and Hearing Examination of the Collaborative Perinatal Study.[10]

It was found that the echolalic children performed significantly more poorly than the normal speaking children on the language subtests, although the groups were matched in terms of I.Q. They did not, however, perform significantly more poorly in terms of the articulation test, in which children were asked to imitate single-syllable words. Mitigated echoers achieved higher I.Q. scores than pure echoers and also achieved higher scores on the language measures, although their scores were consistently lower than those of their matched normal speaking controls. The experimenters conclude that the audio-motor system represented by articulation is nonconvergent with the syntactic-semantic system of these echolalic children. They can regenerate speech sounds correctly, but they cannot, presumably, generate sentences. Of course, articulation performance in generating sentences was not measured, and decoding and regeneration of a single syllable is far from what is actually required in articulating language. We have observed previously that if a sequence is short enough it can be repeated successfully. Further, it is possible that the syntactic and semantic competence of these children was not adequately tested since the language subtests used were quite similar in nature to the verbal subtests of the standard I.Q. test used (a short form of the Stanford Binet). The language subtests measured object naming and two aspects of behavior grossly labeled "verbal comprehension" and "verbal expression." It is possible that an intelligence test performance, rather than syntactic and semantic competence, was being more intensively measured in the "language" examination.

---

[10] The Speech, Language, and Hearing Examination of the Collaborative Study of Cerebral Palsy, Mental Retardation, and other Neurological Disorders of Infancy and Childhood. National Institute of Neurological Diseases and Blindness, National Institutes of Health.

SUMMARY

The findings of some studies of the linguistic performance of children who, because of known or suspected physiological conditions, develop language in a deviant manner indicate that all these children, despite differences in cause of deviancy, develop language in the normal sequence but stretched out in time. However, a closer look at these data indicates that differences, as well as delays, occur in the types of rules with which groups of these children have especially marked difficulty and in the specific rules they acquire and use. It appears that their linguistic behavior is deviant either because of their distorted experience, as in the case of the child who does not have the capacity to analyze complete sentences in the way the normal speaking child does; or because the techniques for acquiring language are different, as in the case of the child who cannot spontaneously use the auditory-vocal channel. There are, therefore, differences in linguistic behavior among groups of these children as well as between groups of these children and their normal speaking peers. It should be noted, however, that although the linguistic performance of these children is deviant, it is not random. These children search for and find linguistic rules, which they use.

Grossly speaking, it appears that the child can have an articulation problem and not a syntactic problem or a syntactic problem without an articulation problem, indicating perhaps that the syntactic and phonological components of the grammar are separated and not dependently related in the generation of language. However, the studies cited do not fully test these questions. It is true that some children can uncomprehendingly repeat a sequence if the sequence is short enough, but the relationship of this performance to the use of language at any level of the grammar, including the phonological level, is not clear. These studies also do not address themselves to the problem of comparing comprehension and production. The results of some studies indicate that even when no language is produced some linguistic structures are understood. Again, this latter question has not been fully explored. If the child produces utterances which are syntactically deviant to a marked degree, they will appear to be anomalous (for example, the sentence previously cited "Linda Debbie sick listen radio"), but little research has been done on these children's understanding of semantic properties and rules. Many of the questions which pertain to the organization of the grammar and the relationships between comprehension and production at the various levels of the grammar, and which might be in part answered by experimentation with deviant speaking populations, have, thus far, been merely touched upon.

8

DIALECT
VARIATIONS

IN ADDITION TO those differences in linguistic behavior which would be marked as deviant by members of a child's linguistic community, there are differences between linguistic communities within a language group. These differences have been termed dialect variations. Dialect variations may or may not create problems in communication between members of different linguistic communities. The magnitude of the problem is determined by how widely the grammars of each community deviate from each other and, also, by factors which have nothing to do with the structure of the language, but are concerned with relative social classifications of linguistic performance and the structure of the communication act within each community. This latter aspect includes such sociolinguistic factors as: (1) the roles and status of the speakers, (2) the environmental circumstances in which communication is taking place, (3) the purpose or function of the communication, and (4) the topic and content of the communication (Ervin-Tripp, 1969). Each linguistic community may have its own social classification scale of linguistic performance and its own unique rules concerning the structure of the communication act. If these aspects differ widely between communities, members of these communities will have difficulty in communicating with each other. It should be emphasized, however, that members of linguistic communities that share a wide range of grammatical and communication rules will not experience difficulty in speaking to each other.

DESCRIPTION OF THE POPULATION

Of great interest, in recent research, has been the effect of dialect variations on the structure of the language that is acquired and the effect of this structure on language use and cognitive development. An important reason for this interest is the necessity of considering possible educational approaches in the light of differing degrees of educational success supposedly due to differing kinds of linguistic performance. The research to be reported here has been directed primarily toward describing the differences in the acquisition of the "native" language (American English) due to socioeconomic status and race, rather than the effect on the structure of language acquisition and development due to (a) bilingualism (for example, English and Lithuanian), or (b) the acquisition of a second language on entrance to school (for example, English after Lithuanian), or (c) geographic displacement within the country (for example, a white middle-class child moving from the north to the south and entering school).

Some data indicate that bilingualism can create advantages in cognitive performance. In a study by Peal and Lambert (1962) it was found that bilingual children performed as well as monolingual children on tests of verbal performance, and performed better than monolingual children on nonverbal tests of symbol manipulation. The experimenters conclude that "training" in two languages makes bilingual children more adept at concept formation and abstract thinking, since they learn to conceptualize the environment in terms of general properties without reliance on linguistic symbols. A similar type of advantage has not, as yet, been found with children who are exposed to and presumably acquire a new dialect at school age. Of course, this may be due to the age at which the different dialect is acquired as well as to factors of confusion. There would obviously be many similarities between the case of a child exposed to a second language at school age and the case of a child exposed to a different dialect at school age. There would, however, be differences as well. For example, when two languages are considered to be totally dissimilar, less confusion seems to be created for both the teacher and the student than when they are considered to be only partially dissimilar. The specific effect of geographical displacement alone, with all other factors held constant, has not been examined.

Given the differences in the prenatal, neonatal and developmental experiences of children from differing economic backgrounds, one may find differences in the proportion of instances in which language deviancy from the language of the community occurs within these populations. Birch states,

. . . it is . . . dangerous to treat cultural influences as though they were acting upon an inert organism. Effective environment is the product of the interaction of organic characteristics with the objective opportunities for experience. The child who is apathetic because of malnutrition, whose experience may have been modified by chronic illness (or tiredness) or whose learning abilities may have been affected by some "insult" to the CNS cannot be expected to respond to opportunities in the same way as does the child who has not been exposed to such conditions [Birch, 1968, p. 580].

Birch concludes that available health information indicates that children who are economically and socially disadvantaged and exposed to discrimination are also exposed to excessive risks for maldevelopment. However, and very importantly, Birch also suggests that children with particular ethno-economic experiences *cannot be considered a homogeneous group,* but must be differentiated for the purposes of remedial, supplemental, and habilitative education.

It has been assumed, in the research to be reported, that the primary differentiating factor in the description, measurement, and comparison of linguistic performance between children from different socioeconomic and racial backgrounds has been their language experience—the language of their community and how it is used. Presumably those children whose language behavior deviated markedly from that of their age peers within a community because of prenatal, neonatal, and developmental experiences would not be a part of the experimental population in these studies, but rather would be a part of the populations described in the previous chapter.

STUDIES OF STRUCTURAL DIFFERENCES

Although there has been a great deal of interest in the language development of children from low income families and, especially from low income black families, there have been few studies of the structure of the language used in these communities. Most of the research has been concerned with describing how the language of these children differs from that of middle-class children at various stages of development, and with attempting to describe differences in the function of language in these communities.

There is little question that structural differences in the language to be acquired exist between communities. Some of these differences may be concerned with only phonological aspects of the grammar, while others may be concerned with phonology, semantics, and syntax. One might ask why structural differences from standard English exist to any marked degree in any linguistic community in this country, given the amount of exposure to this dialect that each community supposedly receives via the school room, radio, and television. Several factors have been suggested (Ervin-Tripp, 1969). Natural barriers, such as geographical distance and isolation from the speakers of the standard dialect, preserve differences. Social barriers against such things as marriage, friendship, or working relationships between members of the linguistic communities, although geographically near each other, will perpetuate dialect differences. How speakers of a nonstandard dialect are spoken to and the punishment resulting from attempts at using the standard dialect may also perpetuate differences. There is the added factor of language loyalty. Dialect differences rise from a particular ethnic, religious, and cultural experience, and are sometimes maintained as a group's internal effort for self-identification and for acceptance from society.[1]

On the whole, comparisons of the middle income black and middle income white dialects have not revealed any significant differences. Low income black and low income white dialects differ from each other, and both may differ from middle income dialects. It should be kept in mind that low income dialects, both white and black, differ from each other depending on the derivation and history of the dialect.

Labov, Cohen, and Robins (1965) found phonological differences in the low income dialects of New York City. The following are some examples. It should be noted that reduction of /l/ and /r/ is a widespread occurrence in New York City, but it appears to cover a wider range of phenomena in low income dialects.

1. Reduction of /r/ intervocalically (as in "Carol"), before a consonant (as in "work"), and finally (as in "her").
2. Reduction of /l/ before a consonant (as in "felt"), finally (as in "fell"), and intervocalically (as in "all right").
3. Reduction of final consonant (as in "told," "don't," "lost")
4. Substitution of initial /ð/ by /d/ (as in "this")
5. Substitution of initial /θ/ by /t/ (as in "think")
6. Substitution of final /θ/ by /f/ (as in "bath")
7. Substitution of final /ð/ by /v/ (as in "with")

Context plays a role in the simplification of final clusters. Clusters containing /t/ and /d/ are simplified before a word beginning with a consonant but may be preserved, depending on the vowel, before a word beginning with a vowel. Phonological changes in the dialect may appear to be syntactic. The experimenters point to the changes produced as a result of the final /r/ rule as examples of this fact. "Their" is changed to "they" and "your" is changed to "you" because of a phonological rule

---

[1] For a discussion of this aspect of dialect maintenance, see Fishman, et al., 1966.

difference and not because of a lack of syntactic distinction between subject and possessive pronouns in the dialect. There are other instances in which the basis of change is syntactic rather than phonological. The final /z/ in plurals before a word beginning with a vowel is preserved, but in marking third person singular, in this same context, it is not.

Baratz (1969a) has reviewed some of the findings of studies of "American Negro" dialect. The following kinds of phonological differences have been found.

1. The vowels /ɪ/ and /ɛ/ are not differentiated before a final nasal ("pin" and "pen" are produced as "pin").
2. The liquids /l/ and /r/ are reduced ("carrot" is produced as "cat" and "toll" as "toe").
3. Final clusters are reduced ("bold" is produced as "bol").

The following are some of the syntactic differences from standard English that have been isolated in various low-income black American dialects (Stewart, 1967) and found in the language of children in these communities (Baratz and Povich, 1967).

1. Verb forms

He playing	Present Participle
He be playing	Present Participle
He was spend the night	Past
They was playing	Past Participle
He play a game	Third, singular
She pretty	Copula
She be pretty	Copula

2. Transformations

Why he do that	Q
She don' have no toy	Neg.
He don' do nothing	Neg.
My cousin, she live down the street, and she don' like me	Rel. Cl.
Muvver was beat him for he didn' go outside	Causal
Dey go way up dere dey go fall	Conditional
Them the children toy	Possessive

The fact that differences exist between the dialects of low income communities is clear when one examines the data collected from different communities. For example, although causal and conditional are frequently not marked by "because" and "if" in the sentences produced by adults and children from one low income environment, as in the sentences above, they are produced by a 3-year-old child from another low income environment, as in the following example sentences: [2] "If that dog bite me, man, I beat his brains out"; "I know he like us cause he give us dat." The adults in this latter environment consistently mark causal and conditional with "because" and "if."

Several factors should be noted about the descriptions produced thus far of low income dialect differences. It should be noted that differences have been found between dialects, not deficits in one as compared to another. It is evident in the structural differences described that there is no grammatical relationship which can be expressed in one dialect that cannot be expressed in another, although different techniques may be employed to express these relationships. There appear to be syntactic categorizations of tense which differ between dialects just as these categorizations may differ between languages. However, the examples of dialect differences in syntactic categorizations found thus far are not clear. An example of such a difference between dialects is that in some low income black dialects a time dimension is categorized into two parts, whereas in the standard dialect there is no division of this dimension. Two forms are used for the present participle and the present tense of the copula to indicate two aspects of time, whereas in standard English there is only one form. Stewart (1967) describes the meaning of the two forms, in each case, in the following manner:

He sick—right now
He be sick—habitually
He playin the piano—right now
He be playin the piano—habitually

In standard English the same types of distinctions between *now* and *all the time* appear to be made:

He's sick—right now
He's always sick—habitually
He's playing the piano—right now
He plays the piano—habitually

Again, this seems to be an instance in which the same meanings are expressed, but in different syntactic ways, although it is possible that subtle differences exist. In addition to the phonological and syntactic rule differences, there are, presumably, fairly wide differences between dialects in

---

[2] These are sentences based on those collected by Claudia Mitchell, University of California at Berkeley, in preparation for a doctoral dissertation.

the properties they assign to shared lexical items, and there are lexical items which are not shared at all. This aspect of dialect differences has yet to be structurally described.

Another factor should be noted about the structural descriptions of dialect differences that have been presented. These descriptions present data only on the production of language, and distinctions have to be made between production and comprehension grammars. There appears to be a certain amount of variability in the rules that are use⁴ by black adults of a certain environment, depending on the context in which the language is produced and depending on their own linguistic e⸱ ⸱ience (Labov and Cohen, 1967). In general, there are differences between the phonological rules used in careful and in casual speech. Repetition of sentences by adolescent subjects indicates that various structures are understood and then either translated into the speaker's syntactic rules or simply understood and repeated. The following are some examples given by the experimenters.

1a. "I asked Alvin *if he* knows how to play basketball" repeated as "I asks Alvin do he know how to play basketball."

1b. "Nobody *ever*" repeated as "Nobody never"

2a. "Money, *who is eleven,* can't spit as far as Boo can" repeated as given

2b. "Larry *is stupid*" repeated as given

This behavior indicates that the structures of the standard dialect are understood and can, in some instances, be reproduced. It is concluded that the ability to reproduce the standard forms is dependent on how near the surface structure a particular rule is. Copula omission appears to be a late rule in the grammar and therefore the copula is repeated as given in (2a), whereas the embedded question appears to be a deep structure rule and is not repeated as given in (1a). In observing the sentences produced by an adult from a particular low income environment, one can find instances in which the auxiliary verb is produced and those in which it is not ("What are you gonna do?" and "What you gon do?"). However, omission of the auxiliary verb is consistent for a 3-year-old child in this environment (Menyuk, 1970). With phonological rules, black adolescents do not show the same differences in formal and casual speech as are exhibited by adults, and they do not appear to perceive such differences (Cohen, 1966). Therefore, one should observe not only the possibility of differences between the comprehension and production grammars of speakers of low income dialects, but also the possibility that these differences are dependent upon the age of the speakers as well as the nature of the rule and the situation in which a linguistic structure is produced.

It should also be noted that certain phonological rules seriously affect syntactic markers. Some examples of this were given previously. Reduction of final /r/ precludes the formation of the plural contracted form of the auxiliary and copula ("we're") as well as changes "their" to "they." Reduction or replacement of /l/ before a consonant precludes the formation of contracted forms of the modal "will" ("he'll sing"), and reductions in final clusters containing /s/, /z/, /t/, and /d/ obviously affect formation of plural, possessive, and past tense markers.

An important question is: can these phonological sequences be perceived even though they are not produced? A perception test, administered to children who speak a dialect in which the final /t/ is reduced, examined these children's ability to observe the difference between "mess" and "messed" and between "mess up" and "messed up" (Cohen, 1966). Although the past tense marker is more often preserved when preceding a vowel in these children's production of language, it was not perceived any more often. Less than 50 percent of the nearly 200 children tested distinguished between the present and past tense forms. On the other hand, when these children were asked to read and correct sentences containing malformations or omissions of tense markers ("He pick me," "Last week I kick" and "throwed") they behaved quite differently. There was no correlation between the perception and correction test, and several children obtained 100 percent on one test and 0 percent on the other. It appeared to the experimenter that distinction of isolated morphemes does not indicate knowledge of standard forms, whereas contextual performance may indicate this knowledge. It is also possible, given these results, that speakers of a low income dialect, in addition to having a comprehension grammar which differs from a production grammar, may also have a reading grammar which differs from both the comprehension and production grammars.

In summary, some structural differences between the standard English dialect and various low income dialects have been described. These descriptions are, at the moment, quite limited. However, they do indicate that low income black and white dialects differ from each other as well as from the standard dialect. They also indicate that differences, not deficits, exist in one dialect as compared to another. These differences may operate on all levels of the grammar, and there may be differences which are restricted to either the comprehension or the production grammar of the speaker, depending upon the speaker's age and his experience with the standard dialect. These latter factors have been scarcely touched upon in research.

Finally, it should be noted that no evidence has been found that low income black or white children exhibit greater difficulty in acquiring the language of their community than do white or black middle income children. That is, it does not take the low income child a remarkably longer time than the middle income child to acquire his linguistic system (Menyuk, 1970). However, here again the available information is very limited. No studies or structural descriptions of the acquisition of language by low income children from various communities, comparable to those done with white middle income children, are reported in the literature.

COMPARATIVE STUDIES

In attempting to evaluate the results of comparative studies of the linguistic performance of low and middle income children, one must keep in mind that the dialects acquired by children from different low income communities are different from each other. This factor of difference is consistently observed in the performance of black and white low income children. However, this factor of difference may be equally true of both black and white low income children from Baltimore as compared to black and white low income children from Boston. Therefore, some of the generalizations drawn from these studies may hold only within the city boundaries.

The free word associations of black and white elementary school children in the first, third, and fifth grades were compared (Entwisle, 1970). The population was divided into children from low income urban families and children from middle income suburban families (with incomes double those of the families of the inner-city children). The rate of paradigmatic responses (same syntactic class as stimulus word) at each grade level was measured since, as was discussed previously, a shift from syntagmatic to paradigmatic responses appears to be an indication of maturation of the semantic system. It was found that first-grade urban children of average measured intelligence give paradigmatic responses to about the same extent as suburban children of above average measured intelligence. Urban black first-graders of average measured intelligence did not respond paradigmatically at the same level as white urban children, but they give more paradigmatic responses than white suburban children of average measured intelligence. By third grade, however, the suburban child leads in paradigmatic responses. No differences in rate of paradigmatic responses are evident at the fifth grade. In essence, the low income inner-city child, including the black inner-city child, in terms of rate of paradigmatic responses, exceeds the suburban child at first grade, falls behind at third grade, and both groups are equal at fifth grade.

It is difficult to explain these trends. The experimenter notes that television is viewed with great frequency by the urban child, whereas the suburban child has more restrictions placed on his viewing. This difference, therefore, might account for his greater "sophistication" at first grade. However, this does not account for the subsequent lag at third grade, since presumably this difference continues to exist. The experimenter points out that it is possible that the particular educational experience encountered by each group of children between first and third grade—that is, their comparative success at tasks such as learning to read—may account for the trends observed.

In addition to the quantitative measures, it was also found that, although paradigmatic rates were comparable between urban black and white children, black children differed from white children, both urban and suburban, in the number of different responses given to a word. This occurred most noticeably for frequently used words. Apparently the associations elicited by a word were different for each group of children. For example, the word "wing" most frequently elicits "fly" and "bird" from the white population but elicits "fly" and "chicken" from the black population; the word "music" elicits "sing" and "song" from the white population but only "dance" from the black population; the word "black" elicits no responses pertaining to human beings from the white population but elicits "child," "girls," "hand," "man," and "yes" from the black population. There are, therefore, indications that the sets of properties of lexical items understood by the two groups of children differ.

Phonological differences also produced differences in performance. Black third-grade children respond to the word "since" with the words "money," "dumb," and "five," indicating that the word is understood as "cents" or "sense." By the fifth grade "money" is still the most frequent response but "when" and "yesterday" are also used. Both conflicting semantic properties of lexical items and conflicting lexical categorizations of words due to phonological differences may obviously affect the relevancy of the educational experience for these children. These factors seem to affect their performance in the word association task. By grade 5, presumably, at least at the level of word associations, these conflicts have been somewhat resolved and the children—white and black, urban and suburban—are performing in a comparable manner to word association stimuli.

Some of the results of studies using a Cloze procedure [3] can be explained in terms of the findings of the previously cited study (Entwisle, 1970). Others cannot. In one study (Peisach, 1965) white and black, low and middle income, first- and fifth-grade children were asked to fill in the words in samples of teachers' speech. The fifth-grade children were also asked to fill in samples of children's speech. There were differences between the responses of the socioeconomic groups at both grade levels to teacher's speech, but the differences were more marked at the fifth-grade than at

[3] The technique used in the Cloze procedure is to delete every nth word and ask subjects to replace the word.

the first-grade level. Low income children did more poorly than middle income children in supplying the exact or semantically related or grammatically equivalent missing word. Low income children did as well as middle income children with samples of low income children's speech, but did significantly more poorly with samples of middle income children's speech. This latter result produced significant group differences, but there were no significant differences between the performance of white and black children on the whole. However, the low income black children, relative to their income group, gave the least adequate performance. The middle income black children did as well as white children and as well as low income black children with black children's speech samples.

In another study (Williams and Wood, In Press) using the Cloze procedure, black junior high school students from low and middle income families were asked to replace words in samples of middle income and low income speech. The middle income children did equally well with the low and middle income speech, but the low income children did poorly with the middle income speech.

To fit the findings from the Cloze procedure studies and the word association study together into a coherent picture of possible differences in the linguistic competence of low income and middle income children is a difficult task, although presumably some of the same aspects of semantic competence are being tested with both techniques. In the Cloze procedure studies cited, low socioeconomic status appears to have an effect in producing poorer responses, whereas in the word association study children of low income families performed better than children of middle income families at an early age. Further, whereas differences in rate of paradigmatic responses between socioeconomic groups disappeared at the fifth-grade level in the word association study, differences between socioeconomic groups in supplying a grammatically equivalent word became more marked in a Cloze procedure study at the fifth-grade level. Finally, although there were no significant differences between the performances of white and black children, using either type of testing technique, black low income children performed as well or better than white middle income children in the word association study at two grade levels, whereas black low income children performed more poorly in a Cloze procedure study.

Obviously the two types of tasks and measurements of performance cannot be equated, although they both may be considered by some as a means of estimating semantic competence. The specific task differences may account for the differences in the effect of socioeconomic status on the developmental trends in performance observed over the age range of first to fifth grade. One technique measures only children's ability lexically to categorize words, whereas the other technique, in addition, measures children's ability to predict the lexical items in a sentence. Therefore, one technique is concerned only with examining acquisition of properties, primarily syntactic, whereas the other technique is also concerned with examining comprehension of possible relationships in sentences. It is also possible that socioeconomic status affects performance more or in different ways in some studies as compared to others, not only because different techniques of measurement are used, but also because these studies are conducted in different parts of the country. Dialect differences between socioeconomic groups can be greater in one area than in another. It is clear that many more studies need to be undertaken to examine the effect of socioeconomic status on developmental trends in semantic competence, and that studies of dialect difference within a community have to be undertaken before the results of such developmental studies can be generalized. This, of course, is also true of studies which examine other aspects of linguistic competence.

There is one result that raises questions about whether or not these techniques do indeed sample linguistic competence. They may be sampling some other kind of competence. The fact that in the Cloze procedure task middle income children deal as adequately with low income children's language as they do with their own has yet to be explained. The difference in scores between the black and white populations in the Peisach (1965) study using samples of the teacher's language could largely be accounted for by fifth-grade low income black children's performance. Therefore, it was suggested that these children's acquisition and use of two dialects created conflict and interfered with the performance of the task. It was the case that this latter group of children did better than white children with boys' language samples, and this difference could be accounted for by the fact that one of the boys' language samples was "non-Northern" speech.

Again, however, this does not account for the results obtained. Dialect differences can account for differences in performance, but logically these differences should work in both directions (Baratz, 1969b). That is, each group of children should do better with the language sample of their own community. Alternatively, it is possible that having both dialects might lead to better overall performance. In that case low income children who are exposed to both dialects for a long enough period of time should do better overall than middle income children who are exposed to only one dialect, and this difference should be more marked at the fifth grade than at the first grade. Exactly the opposite happened. Although it is possible that having two dialects may create confusion, since there supposedly will be many instances of overlapping linguistic generalizations, as well as divergent instances, it does not seem logical that children who are unfamiliar with a dialect, in general, produce as good a performance with this dialect's samples as children who are familiar with it. Conflicts other than linguistic ones may produce these differences, and these conflicts may very well be brought about by the educational experience of low income children, since the difference in performance between the socioeconomic groups becomes more marked at the fifth-grade than at the first-grade level in at least one of the tasks.

Another hypothesis which might account for the results obtained in the Cloze procedure studies is that low income children's memory span for verbal material may differ from that of middle income children. In one study (Eisenberg, Berlin, Dill, and Frank, 1968) 160 low income black and white children and middle income black and white children, 8 to 10 years of age, were asked to identify monosyllabic words spoken by four women. Each female speaker came from approximately the same linguistic environment as that of the four groups of listeners. None of the children in the study had a hearing loss which would affect performance and none had a "speech disorder." It should be noted that monosyllabic words do not place any immediate memory strain on normal speaking children.

It was found that the education of the speaker (number of years of schooling) was the most significant variable in speaker intelligibility. However, white speakers were significantly more intelligible than black speakers. Black listeners were significantly poorer listeners than white listeners, and low income listeners were significantly poorer listeners than middle income listeners. Low income listeners had significantly better scores when listening to low income speakers of their own race than they did when listening to low income speakers of another race. When 40 teachers from the inner-city schools were asked to identify the monosyllables produced by 64 of the children who had listened, it was found that white children were significantly better understood than black children, girls were better understood than boys, and middle income children were better understood than low income children. A significant correlation was found between the listening scores of children and the intelligibility of their speech both for the whole group and for the white and black subgroups. The lowest intelligibility scores were obtained by the black low income children as were the lowest listening scores.

Clearly, the differences between the groups cannot be accounted for by differences in memory span. Monosyllables were well within the memory capacity of all the children. Dialect differences can account for some of the results obtained. The differences between the performance of the low income groups of children when listening to monosyllables generated in their own dialect and their performance when listening to monosyllables generated in another dialect can be attributed to dialect differences. The reason for black low income children's speech being least intelligible and for them being the least accurate listeners could be the fact that their dialect represents the greatest departure from each of the other three dialects of the subgroups. However, the reason for white middle income speech being, on the whole, more intelligible than that of any other sample of speech to every group is not obvious. It was not the case that each group did best when listening to the sample of speech from its own linguistic community. The results of this study cannot be related to dialect differences alone.

The repetition and comprehension abilities of 16 low income black children and 16 white middle income children were compared in another study (Osser, Wang and Zaid, 1969). The mean age of both groups of children was 5 years. The sentences used in the repetition and comprehension tasks were the same. In the repetition task a total error score (total number of deviations from the sentence presented) and a critical error score (number of deviations which changed the syntactic structure of the sentence) were obtained. The results of the repetition task were "corrected" to account for dialect differences frequently found in the language of these children. It was found that black low income children repeated sentences with a significantly greater mean number of total errors and critical errors than did the white middle income children, even when errors due to known dialect differences were eliminated. They also incorrectly identified the appropriate picture in the comprehension task with significantly greater frequency. It should be noted that difficulty in repetition of a structure was not significantly correlated with difficulty in comprehension of a structure, indicating that the two tasks were not testing the same competence.

It was found that the length of the critical structure was not significantly correlated with the number of errors for that structure; therefore, differences in memory span or an "attention deficit" could not account for the differences obtained. It was concluded that the differences found could probably be attributed to (1) dialect differences not accounted for which would require the black children to recode the sentence into the familiar dialect for repetition, and (2) differences in the availability of common (shared) standard English structures by the two groups. Thus, differences between the performances of the two groups of children might be accounted for by postulating both a difference and a deficit in the language acquired by the black low income children as compared to the language acquired by white middle income children.

Concerning the deficit hypothesis, the question, of course, is whether or not these "missing" structures are a part of the dialect of both linguistic communities represented by the children and, therefore, should have been acquired by the black low income children as well as the white middle income children. In reviewing the error categories in which sharp differences in frequency occur between the groups, outside of the identified forms of dialect difference, one is struck by the possibility that many such types of errors are a reflection of dialect difference. For example, omission of the *Do* support verb (as in "He does play") as well as Aux omission were found in the dialect of a black adult from an inner-city environment

(Menyuk, 1970). *Do* omission sharply differentiated the groups. As has already been indicated, both tense and number may be marked differently in certain black American dialects. Since number may be marked in a particular way, determiners in general and articles in particular may, in these dialects, involve unique rules. The type of errors found with articles and determiners as well as tense and number also sharply differentiated the groups. Again, possible dialect differences have to be completely determined before valid comparisons can be made. Perhaps having adults from the different communities represented by the children perform the tasks might be a way of determining dialect differences in contrast to developmental differences.

In a study (Baratz, 1969b) examining the repetition ability of third- and fifth-grade black low income children and white low-middle income children, it was found that white children did significantly better with certain standard English forms, whereas black children did significantly better with certain forms restricted to their own dialect. White subjects repeated significantly more successfully than black subjects the third person singular, copula, embedded *if* question ("I asked him if he wanted to go"), and standard negation constructions. Black subjects repeated significantly more successfully than white subjects the embedded question ("I ask him do he want to go") and the double negative constructions. These results are in keeping with the hypothesis that dialect differences produce differences in the performance of linguistic tasks.

It was also found that age plays a significant role in the repetition of certain standard English forms for the entire population. Older children more successfully preserve the copula and the past marker, and more older children are able to repeat the embedded *if* question and standard negation. However, fewer of the older children preserved the third person singular, possessive, and plural markers. Age was not a significant factor in the repetition of the forms restricted to the black dialect. These latter findings are very interesting if the upward and downward trend in the use of certain markers can be accounted for primarily by the performance of black subjects.

It may be the case that certain standard English forms are not available to black low income children of pre-school age. It has been found that when these children are exposed in an intensive fashion to a standard English dialect for a short period of time, changes do occur in their repetition of sentences (Cazden, 1965). Some examples of these changes are the use of past tense and third person singular markers and the copula. Certain phonological differences, however, appear to become more firmly established as these children mature, and this may be due to the fact that some dialect differences become more deeply entrenched at an older age.[4]

---

[4] For some brief examples, see Menyuk, 1970.

A certain period of exposure may make some standard English rules available to children who speak another dialect. As they mature, some of their own dialect rules may become more deeply entrenched. These two factors may account for the upward and downward trends in the repetition of certain structures that was observed in the bi-dialectal repetition study. Studies that examine children's repetition ability at various ages in a variety of communities that use dialects different from standard English may give us a much more complete picture of the effect of age on the use of certain structures and the critical times for the acquisition of new and different rules at various levels of the grammar.

It should be noted that the results of studies examining the comparative performance of black and white low income children in the various tasks discussed indicate that exposure to standard English dialect within the usual school setting does not appear to interfere with the entrenchment of their dialect differences. Nor does this exposure make available to these children standard English forms which can be adequately used in various school tasks.

What of the case where no dialect differences have been found between the groups of children tested? Do differences in performance still occur? The sentence repetition of 44 black and white low, middle, and upper-middle income, pre-school, first- and fifth-grade children was examined (McCaffrey, 1968). The experimenter states that with this population dialect differences were not frequently found, and therefore dialect differences were not examined in the analysis of the data. The following average ranking of the performance of the 11 subgroups in the repetition task was found:

1. White, upper fifth
2. Black, low fifth
3. White, upper first
4. White, middle pre-school
5. Black, middle first
6. White, low first
7. Black, middle pre-school
8. White, low pre-school
9. Black, low first
10. White, upper pre-school
11. Black, low pre-school

The experimenter states that age, socioeconomic status, and race all play a role in children's ability to repeat sentences containing various syntactic structures. Fifth-grade white upper-middle income children perform most accurately and pre-school black low income children perform least accurately. Indeed, this latter group produces the most marked differences in performances. This group achieves 30 percent correct responses, while the next higher score (that of pre-school white upper-middle income children) is 60 percent. However, if we compare the percentage of correct responses of each group in the total population and include the score of the pre-school black low income group, we find in a chi square comparison that no difference between groups on the basis of race or socioeconomic status is significant at the .05 level. The only difference that is significant is due to age. There is a significant difference ($p < .01$) between fifth-grade and pre-school children's scores. The difference between the scores of fifth-grade and first-grade children approaches significance ($X^2 = 3.38$, $p < .10$). If the score of the pre-school black low income group is eliminated, then even *trends of difference* on the basis of race and socioeconomic status almost disappear. They are nonexistent at the fifth-grade level where upper-middle income white children achieve a score of 98 percent and low income black children achieve a score of 95 percent. Figure 8–1 indicates and compares the scores of age, socioeconomic status, and racial groups. The scores above each heading both include and exclude the score of the black pre-school low income group to indicate the very marked degree to which the score of this group causes differences.

The reason for the dramatically less accurate performance of the pre-school low income black children must be determined. The experimenter suggests that differences among the groups are not due to basic linguistic capacity differences, but rather to differentially developed ability to release basic knowledge, and possibly to differential rates of language acquisition between groups. This in turn may be related to the type of language stimulation received by the differing groups. Since no really marked difference between the groups in repetition ability exists, except that found with the pre-school black low income children, the above explanation does not seem adequate. It seems clear that dialect differences cannot account for the difference in performance. Perhaps the dramatic difference is due to differences in experience with carrying out particular tasks, linguistic and nonlinguistic, between this group and the other groups. It is perhaps this difference in task orientation which accounts for the difference in school performance which is observed between groups at a later age and becomes increasingly marked as new tasks based on the accomplishment of old ones are presented to these children. Some of the differences observed in performance may clearly be accounted for by dialect differences. Other differences are unrelated to either the capacity to acquire a language or linguistic performance per se, but may be related to differing experiences with types of tasks.

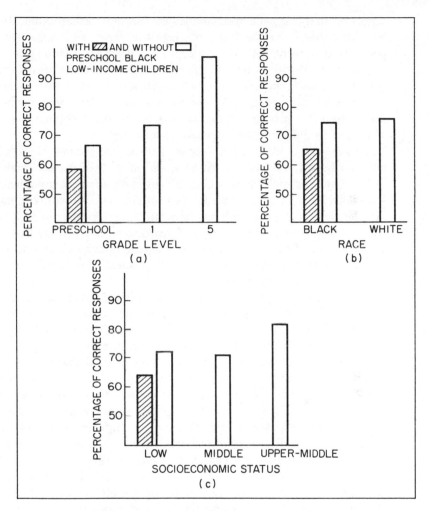

FIG. 8–1 Percentage of correct responses in a repetition task by various grade levels, black and white and upper-, middle- and low-income children including and excluding the responses of pre-school, black, low-income children.

USE OF LANGUAGE

Style of speaking may vary from speaker to speaker as well as from linguistic community to linguistic community. "Societies and persons differ in the extent to which they choose this modality [speech], the situations in which they choose it and their evaluation of it. They differ in the ways speech enters into the definition of situations, conception of personality types, the socialization of the child" (Hymes, 1967, p. 83). It has been suggested that linguistic communities of varying socioeconomic status can be differentiated on the basis of linguistic style, and this suggestion is perfectly congruent with the concept that different communities will use language in differing ways for different purposes. It has been further suggested that differences in linguistic style also involve differences in the comparative effectiveness of these various styles for communication purposes. And it has been still further suggested that differences in linguistic style lead to differences in cognitive functioning.

Some recent studies of low income and middle income black and white children have been focused on the question of how socioeconomic status affects linguistic style, how differences in style affect communication, and how differences in style might lead to differences in cognitive functioning. A great deal of this research has been motivated by the work of Bernstein (1964) who studied the language of low and middle income British speakers. He described and compared the language of the two groups and found that low income language was more "restricted" and middle income language was more "elaborated."

Three types of hypotheses have been derived from the results of this research. The first is that the socioeconomic status of a linguistic community affects the types of linguistic structures that are used by that community. That is, restricted language involves the much more frequent use of syntactic structures which are generated from simple underlying structures (one simple underlying kernel sentence), whereas elaborated language involves the use of syntactic structures which are generated from more complex underlying structures (conjunction and embedding).

The second hypothesis is that restricted language is difficult to understand outside of the situational context in which it is being produced and is only easily understood in context by other members of the same linguistic community, whereas elaborated language can be understood even when it is produced "at a distance" from the situational context and can be understood by all—both members and nonmembers. One of the reasons cited for elaborated language being more effective in communication is that greater use of modification ("the tall, old, gray-haired man") and reference ("the tall man, who is old and gray") is presumably found in this style. Another reason cited is that elaborated language is presumably more redundant than restricted language. For example, number and tense may be marked twice in the elaborated style, whereas it is only marked once in the restricted style.

The third hypothesis is that the frequent use of simple active declarative sentence types leads to simple active declarative thinking, whereas use of conjunction and embedded sentence types leads to thinking in which differentiations and relationships are observed. Some representative research carried out from these points of view will be discussed.

For example, the sentences elicited in home interviews with 40 fifth- and sixth-grade children from low and middle to high income black and white families were analyzed (Williams and Naremore, 1969). In the interviews the children were asked to discuss three topics: games, television, and aspirations. In the analysis, measures such as proportion of frequency of usage of conjunction, embedding, and elaboration of base structure rules (prepositional phrases, objects, etc.) were made. In general, it was found that socioeconomic status and the topic of the discussion were more significant factors in the proportion of usage of certain elaborated structures than race, despite the fact that low income black children used these structures substantially less frequently than low income white children. Indeed, on six of the eleven measures used, black high to middle income children scored highest. The experimenters stress the fact that the topic of discussion was a significant factor in the elicitation of the types of structures measured. This seems reasonable given the nature of the topics. These appear to vary widely in terms of their potential in eliciting gross amounts of language (television and games versus aspirations) as well as their relevancy to the various groups of children (television versus games and aspirations).

The experimenters make one further comment, which they identify as a subjective comment. Frequency of usage of certain structures elicited in the television discussion indicated that high to middle income children tended to narrate or tell a story about a program, whereas low income children tended to list instances of things seen. It is concluded that this difference is related to a greater tendency of low income children to employ a "particularistic and concrete style of speaking" and the greater tendency of middle to high income children to assume "a more general and abstract perspective."

It should be noted that in the usual description of linguistic style differences the term *more* is used, which indicates that one cannot speak of any group using either restricted or elaborated language exclusively. Indeed, in her review of some of the studies of Basil Bernstein and his co-workers, Cazden (1968b) states that these experimenters have found that the distinction made between low and middle income children's use of language in terms of a "restricted" versus an "elaborated" code must be qualified. Under certain conditions low income children use an elaborated code, or, to be more precise, under certain conditions low income children use more elaborated structures than they use ordinarily. These same kinds of results—i.e., differences in frequency of usage of certain structures— have been found in studies comparing individual children in the same linguistic community. Both child A and child B may at some stage of development have the competence to use certain syntactic structures. However, within a given sampled time, child A may use a given structure (X)

three times as frequently as child B uses (X), while child B, within this same sampled time, uses a given structure (Y) three times as frequently as child A uses (Y). This difference in frequency of usage of structures (X) and (Y) may be a reflection of individual style, cultural linguistic style (there are other factors outside of socioeconomic status), the situation in which language is being produced, or some convolution of these factors. The types of sentences produced by children during ages 3 to 7 years clearly indicate the early acquisition of individual variation in the linguistic style of children who are acquiring language in the same linguistic community. The frequency with which a child will use, for example, negations, imperatives, or embedded constructions is a function of individual style once such a structure has been acquired (Menyuk, 1969, p. 38).

Since, in general, no unequivocal differences in linguistic capacity—that is, the capacity to acquire a language—and no differences in linguistic competence—that is, the ages at which the rules of the language, either restricted or elaborated, are acquired—can be found between differing socioeconomic or racial groups, the important question appears to be, what are the consequences of differences in the frequency of usage of various structures on the performance of certain linguistic and cognitive tasks?

In a study [5] of the ability of low income and middle income British children, aged 5 to 7 years, to tell a story about a picture, describe a picture, and describe and explain a mechanical toy, certain differences in the predicted direction were found. Middle income children who displayed high verbal ability on standard tests also scored higher on a measure of form-class usage. Middle income children used nouns to a greater extent than did low income children. The latter used pronouns to a greater extent than did middle income children. Both groups used pronouns with anaphoric reference (for example, "The boy kicked the ball and it broke the window"), but the low income children more frequently used pronouns with exaphoric reference (for example, "They're playing football and he kicks it").

Obviously, the latter sentence is more difficult to understand outside of the context of the picture, and, therefore, communicates less information. Nouns carry more information than pronouns unless the reference is clear. One consequence, then, of differences in frequency of usage of certain structures might be the amount of information either heard or conveyed in a verbal exchange between members of a linguistic community. This is a thought provoking tidbit, but it is just that—a tidbit. A more thorough structural analysis of the sentences produced in tasks of this kind may reveal further differences. However, it should be kept in mind, as an ex-

---

[5] For a review of this study, see Cazden, 1968b.

ample, that certain rules of reference which are confusing to nonspeakers of the dialect may be perfectly clear to speakers of the dialect.

Krauss and Glucksberg (1967) studied the ability of kindergarten, first-, third-, and fifth-grade children to communicate information to a peer. The speakers were required to describe to the listeners the characteristics of an abstract figure so that the listeners could select the correct figure from an array of six such figures. The mean number of errors over the first eight trials is presented in the report of the study. Initial performance did not differ markedly at the four grade levels. However, by trial 8, third and fifth graders were making fewer than one error, whereas kindergartners showed virtually no improvement over trials and first graders were making a mean number of errors that was between that of kindergartners and third graders. It had been found previously that pre-school children were able to communicate effectively about familiar forms for which common names were available, but were unable to do so about abstract figures (Glucksberg, Krauss, and Weisberg, 1966).

The results of the above study suggested that it was the speakers' failures in encoding the messages which led to errors rather than the listeners' failures in decoding the messages. To assess this possibility further, 90 adults were asked to identify the figures when given the descriptions provided by children on the first trial. It was found that accuracy of identification significantly increased as the age of the describers increased from kindergarten through fifth grade. This result indicates that encoder ability increases over this age range and also that decoder ability increases from fifth grade to adulthood, since adults did better than fifth graders with trial 1 descriptions. It has been suggested that the increased effectiveness of older children to encode is due to the fact that the younger a speaker is, the more "private" is the language he uses to describe an abstract figure (Krauss, 1968). The example given is the following: a 4-year-old speaker calls a figure "sheet." When asked why he calls this figure a sheet he states, "Have you ever noticed when you get up in the morning the sheet is all wrinkled? Well, sometimes it looks like this."

It appears, then, that the content as well as the structure of the language used to communicate in such tasks changes as a function of age. The younger the child, the greater the probability that the properties of lexical items used to encode the characteristics of a strange object will be unique to the speaker. In a number of tasks, Flavell [6] and his co-workers have found that the ability to analyze the needs and characteristics of the listener and to use this analysis in a communication task increases with age, reaching a peak in middle childhood and early adolescence; at this

---

[6] Reviewed briefly in Flavell, 1966.

stage communication becomes more effective. However, the fact that the above skills are dependent not only on the age, experience, and characteristics of the child, but also on the characteristics of the listener, perceived and real, and on the nature of the task is stressed by the experimenter.

It has been hypothesized that because of certain structural differences in their language or proportional differences in the use of certain structures, or because of the possibility of unique semantic systems, children from low income communities do not communicate about their environment as well or as accurately as middle income children do, either with themselves or with others. Some of the techniques that have been developed to examine the communication effectiveness of children as they mature are now being used to compare the communication effectiveness of children from differing socioeconomic communities. Such studies, thus far, are few in number.

Low income and middle income children in a British community were asked to look at *a* set of pictures and then to look at another set and indicate how this set differed from the original.[7] Again, low income children used less elaborated language to describe differences than did middle income children. However, the low income children made fewer pointing errors than did middle income children. It was hypothesized that low income children do as well or better than middle income children in perceiving differences, but have greater difficulty in conceptualizing these differences and reporting them.

Heider, Cazden, and Brown (1968) examined the ability of low income white and black children and middle income white children to encode the properties of the abstract figures used in the Krauss and Glucksberg studies and the properties of pictures of faces. The population was composed of 143 10-year-old boys and girls. The experimenters found sharp differences in the encodings of middle income and low income children. The middle income children were much more fluent and gave many more images per picture. Encodings were classified as (1) whole-inferential (for example, "It looks like a star"), and (2) part-descriptive (for example, "It has a point on top and a point on the bottom"). Low income children much more frequently gave whole-inferential encodings than did middle income children (80 percent versus 33 percent), whereas middle income children much more frequently gave part-descriptive encodings than did low income children (53 percent versus 13 percent). Middle income children's encodings were, on the whole, more accurately decoded by all the children regardless of their socioeconomic status. There was no evidence that children of one economic group communicated more accurately with each other

---

[7] For a review of this study, see Cazden, 1968b.

than with children from another group. However, there was evidence that the *style* of encoding most successfully decoded by each group was the style primarily used by that group for encoding.

In a further analysis of the data it was found that fluency, part descriptions, and "descriptive language" were significantly correlated with each other. A combination of high scores on these three factors was defined as an "analytic" style and low scores as a "wholistic" style. Both low income and middle income children more successfully decoded wholistic encodings than analytic encodings. The only case in which the reverse was true was that middle income children more successfully decoded the analytic encodings of children of their own group than did the children of the other groups. The low income black children did best when decoding the wholistic encodings of abstract figures by white middle income children and did poorest when decoding the analytic encodings of abstract figures produced by black low income children. That is, black low income children had the greatest difficulty in decoding the encodings of children of their own group which departed from the style of the group. The low income white children did equally best when decoding the wholistic encodings of figures by black low income children and when decoding low income white children's encoding of faces. They did almost equally poorly when decoding the analytic encodings of faces by white and black low income children. Obviously, those factors which lead to communication effectiveness (accurate decoding in this experiment) by each group cannot be described and explained in simple terms. The experimenters conclude that analytic encoding is more redundant and impersonal (not tied to personal references), and thus may convey more information. But the question is, who does the encoding convey more information to? It seems that analytic encodings only convey more information when they are both encoded and decoded by white middle income children.

Some other factors in the process of communicating with oneself as well as with others were examined in this study. A subtest which required children to find small differences between parts of figures indicated that low income children did almost as well as middle income children when specifically asked to attend to parts, and that both low and middle income children did not value part descriptions more than whole-inferential ones. It was thought that perhaps low income children might be more impulsive than middle income children in encoding, and that this factor might lead to greater inaccuracy. However, reaction time data showed that children within each group who were more analytic, and middle income children in general, had faster reaction times. In the decoding process, middle income analytic children were slower than low income nonanalytic children. They were slower with decodings of analytic descriptions and when giving responses which did not match the selection of the encoder.

This reaction time data suggested to the experimenters that middle and low income children might have, as a group, different strategies for processing decodings and different criteria for deciding on an answer. As part of this difference in strategy, it was also possible that middle income children had somehow learned to a greater degree than low income children to parcel up their environment in terms of attributes and dimensions, and that this could account for the differences found in part-descriptive versus whole-inferential encodings between the economic groups.

To test the above hypothesis, 18 white boys, 9 of whom were middle income children with high part-descriptive scores, and 9 of whom were low-income children with high whole-inferential scores, were asked to encode a picture of an animal. Each picture had two values of three attributes: number of spots, position of face, position of body. It was found that the density of critical attributes (distinguishing attributes) given by both groups did not differ. However, listeners to low income children's encodings requested a significantly greater number of additional comments than did listeners to middle income children's encodings. Is it again a dialect difference, real or imagined?

The experimenters conclude that "there are undoubtedly class differences in dispositional and motivational variables; and there are undoubtedly class differences in cognitive abilities as well" (Heider, Cazden, and Brown, 1968, p. 10). The results obtained may be related to the first conclusions. They do not seem to warrant the last conclusion. One can state that in the particular tasks given, subjects varied in terms of the descriptive style used, and that the differences in style and perhaps strategy led to unequal performance in the communication task, but made no difference in the observation of criterial attributes. It was not the case that a greater use of the part-descriptive style led to more accurate distinguishing and reporting of critical differences between pictured stimuli.

Although the hypotheses underlying this type of research are intriguing, it should again be stated that it is clear that one needs a greater understanding of the linguistic structure of differences in style, a much greater understanding of how these structural differences may relate to communication tasks, and a much deeper analysis of various kinds of communication tasks and of the attitudes and roles assumed by groups of children in these tasks before conclusions can be drawn. It is conceivable that certain communication tasks can be performed better by low income children than by middle income children because these are tasks which are more pertinent to the roles that they more frequently assume (for example, alerting a younger sibling to possible danger). It should also be kept in mind that in the presence of white middle class experimenters the performance of low income black and white children has been found to vary from their performance in the presence of experimenters whom they recognize to be of their own community.

SUMMARY

It has been found that there are differences in the syntactic, phonological, and semantic rules used in various linguistic communities. The dialect of a linguistic community can be either markedly different from the standard dialect of the language or superficially different, depending on the history of the dialect (its derivation) in that community and the amount and frequency of communication between speakers of that dialect and speakers of the standard dialect. It is not the case that there is a low income dialect or a low income black dialect which can be found in all low income and all low income black communities.

It has also been found that rules for all the grammatical relationships that can be expressed in the grammar of the standard English dialect can also be found in the grammar of dialects which are different from standard English. For example, rules for negation, question, imperative, relative clause, conjunction, etc., and rules for marking tense, pluralization, etc. exist in all communities, although the rules may be somewhat different between dialects. It has not been found that the rules for the expression of certain types of grammatical relationships (perhaps universal in nature) are available in the grammar of one dialect and are not available in the grammar of another.

Further, it has been found in those few studies that have examined aspects of the acquisition of language by pre-school children growing up in linguistic communities in which the dialect is different from that of standard English, that these children acquire these aspects in a sequence and at a rate that are commensurate with that of children growing up in communities that use the standard English dialect. In comparative studies of spontaneous production it has not been found that low income children or black children are slower in acquiring their grammar than are middle income white children in acquiring theirs.

In comparative studies of word association, ability to fill in deleted words (Cloze procedure), and repetition of sentences, both socioeconomic status differences and racial differences have been found in the performance of children. Some of these differences can be accounted for by dialect differences. It is the case that children can more accurately repeat sentences generated by rules unique to their own dialect than they can sentences generated by rules outside their dialect. However, some of the results of these studies cannot be accounted for solely on the basis of dialect differences or even the conflict created by the possible acquisition of two dialects.

Depending on the nature of the task, and on the dialect of the subjects, these differences in performance tend either to become more marked as the children mature or to disappear. The rate of paradigmatic responses of low income children in a word association task is greater than that of middle income children at first grade, becomes less than that of middle income children at third grade, and is equal to that of middle income children at fifth grade. The difference in accuracy of sentence repetition between low and middle income groups and between black and white children is most marked at the pre-school level but has disappeared by the fifth grade. On the other hand, differences between socioeconomic groups become more marked at the fifth-grade level when a Cloze procedure technique is used. It certainly seems to be the case that the nature of the task, the aspect of linguistic performance which is being tapped in each task, and the age of the subjects affect whether or not socioeconomic and racial groups will differ in performance. It is not the case that socioeconomic and racial differences consistently either produce differences in the performance of linguistic tasks or produce the same pattern of differences in the performance of various tasks at various ages.

It has been found that the proportion of usage of various types of syntactic structures is different in various linguistic communities, and these differences are concerned primarily with structures that define and explain relationships to the listener. Proportionately greater use of prepositional phrases and other expansions of NP, of conjunction and embedding, and of nouns as compared to pronouns has been found in the language samples of middle income children as compared to the language samples of low income children.

It has, in turn, been hypothesized that this difference in frequency of usage of certain structures can affect cognitive abilities. However, the relationship of the use of differing styles of language to cognitive abilities is not clear. When the task is concerned with perceptual differentiation of aspects of pictured stimuli, children from linguistic communities in which "elaboration" is less frequently used perceive these differences and encode these differences as well as or better than children from linguistic communities in which "elaboration" is used more frequently. Children from a low income community do not encode as effectively—that is, more errors occur in decoding their encodings—as children from a middle income community when abstract figures or faces must be described. Again, the particular linguistic task that children are engaged in may affect whether or not socioeconomic groups or racial groups perform differently.

The fact that socioeconomic status and race produce differences in performance, depending on the dialect differences of the children, their age, and the particular linguistic task they are asked to engage in, may obviously lead in turn to differences in the performance of certain school tasks. Since many of these school tasks are based on middle income models of performance, these differences can create difficulties for low income children. It has been consistently observed that children from low income communities encounter difficulty in learning to read because of the dialect differences, motivation, or both. It is important to note that certain school tasks may also create difficulties for groups of middle income children, since they may also use a cognitive style which is different from the average model postulated and may differ markedly from the postulated average in terms of experience relevant to the performance of these tasks, and in terms of motivation. The problems that have been encountered in the education of children from low income families and the questions these problems have raised cause us to reevaluate the nature of the tasks that children are given to perform in home and school situations and the way in which they are taught to accomplish these tasks. Research into these questions and the answers obtained can, potentially, benefit all children.

9

EXPLANATORY
THEORIES

THEORIES OF LANGUAGE acquisition obviously should be evaluated in terms of how adequately they predict and explain the behavior that is observed. Despite the fact that a detailed description of language acquisition has not yet been obtained, a lengthy and controversial discussion has taken place in the literature concerning theoretical explanations of children's language acquisition and development. Only a brief summary of some of the main theoretical positions that are held will be presented here. This summary will allow us to review some of the principal research questions still to be answered. The theories proposed address themselves to three questions: Why do children acquire a language? How do they go about acquiring it? and What is it that they acquire?

If we attempt to characterize the various theoretical positions taken, in an admittedly oversimplified manner, they appear to fall into two categories, each of which has two subcategories. These categorizations and subcategorizations are presented in Figure 9–1.

The main subdivision separates those theories which hold the position (a) that the human organism, like other organisms or in a manner different from other organisms, has the capacity to generalize about input stimuli; and those which hold the position (b) that the human organism has the capacity to abstract from the input signal. Under the heading of theories which propose that children acquire language because of stimulus-response-reward conditions are two subheadings: (a_1) those theories which propose acquisition of stimulus-response-reward equivalences, and (a_2) those which

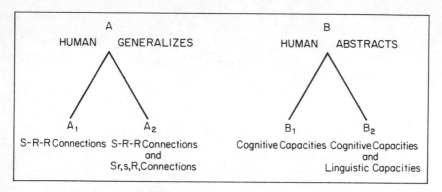

FIG. 9–1   Schematic representation of theoretical explanations of language acquisition.

propose stimulus-response-reward equivalences *and* the governing principles of mediated association and the feedback control of behavior. Under the heading of theories which propose that children acquire language because they are endowed with specific biological mechanisms which allow them to conceptualize are two subheadings: (b_1) those theories which propose that language acquisition is a reflection of the child's capacity to hypothesize about any type of phenomenon, and (b_2) those which propose that language acquisition is both a reflection of the child's capacity to hypothesize *and* specifically the capacity to search for and discover certain regularities in natural language. Again, the theory that will adequately describe the behavior that has been observed and thus lead to logical answers to each question is the theory that would, of course, be most explanatory.

WHY IS LANGUAGE ACQUIRED?

There appear to be three primary theoretical explanations concerning the question: why do children acquire a language? One is that the child essentially acquires language because it is there, a part of his environment, and because vocalization is part of his repertoire of behavior. He acquires language because he learns that vocal behavior brings rewards, just as other animals learn that certain behaviors within their repertoire will bring them rewards. The infant produces some vocal behavior which causes a change in the environment which then leads to the reduction of some physiological drive (hunger, thirst, pain, fear). The environmental consequences reward the infant for this vocal behavior. To account for further development after the crying stage it has been suggested that since this vocal behavior is rewarded it becomes functionally autonomous; there need no longer be a physiological drive which triggers off vocal behavior. Once behavior has been established, it is shaped by the fact that undesirable responses (inadequate or perhaps nongrammatical) at given stages of development are not reinforced and, therefore, become extinguished (Dollard and Miller, 1950).

The above theory does not seem to adequately account for the fact that although crying and screaming are the most rewarded vocal behaviors of the infant, since they are the vocal behaviors he primarily produces at the early stage of development, he does not persist in this behavior but spends greater and greater amounts of time in another kind of vocal behavior—cooing and babbling—as he matures. One might hypothesize from the above theoretical position that the mother decides at some point that crying is inadequate and only reinforces noncrying behavior. But the facts would refute this, since crying is rewarded to some extent throughout childhood and, in addition, we do not know how the mother can decide that time is up for the infant to spend most of his time crying unless the infant produces vocalizations which cue the mother to this fact.

A second theory tries to circumvent the above problems by proposing that children acquire language because of the principles of identification. Crying receives primary reinforcement by the fact that via this vocalization a physiological drive is reduced. The infant, during this period, identifies with the mother and, therefore, begins to imitate the vocal behavior of the mother. The infant, in turn, is rewarded for this imitation by signs of approval during the babbling period. Because of this secondary reinforcement, noncrying vocalization is established (Mowrer, 1960). This process might, then, establish a set for imitation which includes larger and larger chunks of verbal behavior (possibly from syllable to word to sentence). Although this theory is superficially reasonable, it does not adequately describe the sequence of development that has been observed in the linguistic behavior of the infant and child. One can only suggest that noncrying vocalization is a better match of mother's vocalizations than crying vocalizations. At the babbling stage the child does not produce imitations of the consonant vowel segments he hears and, in fact, these productions differ markedly from adult models until physiological maturation of the vocal mechanism is attained. The role of any form of imitation in language acquisition, as we have seen, has yet to be clearly defined. However, the child does produce identifiable and acceptable phonological sequences long before he produces sequences which are acoustically like those of an average adult.

The theory is equally inadequate in describing the child's production of sentences. The child does not produce sentences which are imitations of what he hears or even exact bits of what he hears. For example, the child does not imitate the last things heard and proceed from "boy" to "bad boy" to "a bad boy" to "are a bad boy" to "you are a bad boy"; nor does he imitate first things heard and proceed from "you" to "you are," etc. Developmental changes cannot adequately be described by simply stating that as children mature more complete approximations to adultlike strings of speech sounds of increasing length occur. The child appears selectively to produce certain parameters of sounds, speech sound sequences, and word sequences which are acceptable to himself and others at certain stages of development, and which he may or may not have heard produced by others in his environment. This selection changes in a very orderly way over the developmental period.

The two theories discussed above leave unanswered the following questions: How does the child determine, either consciously or unconsciously, what he is being rewarded for? and How does the parent determine what to reward? If these theories are to account for the facts of language development, this reward must be related to specific productions rather than to simply vocalizing or speaking. Otherwise one cannot account for the child's getting beyond crying and proceeding through the other stages of development. Thus far these theories have not specified the parameters of the stimulus-response-reward chain which will explain why children will acquire and develop a complex system called language.

Since reduction of either a primary or a secondary drive does not seem to be an adequate or even clear explanation for the child's acquiring the complex grammar of a language, a third theory proposes that the capacities for language acquisition are structurally present at birth and that maturation of these structures brings about changes in the child's use of language throughout the acquisition period. The language environment remains relatively constant but the child modifies his use of the input stimuli as his capacities are modified over the maturational period. All that is needed in the environment is language to institute the process. Presumably there are indications of a language-specific maturational scale that is peculiar only to speech and language and independent of other maturational processes, and indeed of other cognitive processes (Lenneberg, 1967).

A somewhat different version of this theory proposes that although man's capacity for cognition is not found in other animals, and although this capacity is probably based on either unique structures or functions of man's nervous system, it is not the case that the behavior observed in language acquisition deviates in any marked manner from other types of cognitive acquisitions involving perception and hypotheses formation.

In examining the relationships and dependencies between language and cognition, children have been used who presumably lack language but are intellectually intact (deaf children), or who presumably have limited language (young children), or who have different linguistic categorizations for phenomena (children from different language groups). Experimental results, thus far, have not settled arguments concerning relationships. Varying the experimental task brings about varying results. If the task involves remembering a set of classifiable perceptual dimensions (color, size, etc.) or compositions (pictures of objects) for which there are easily available linguistic categories, then language appears to aid in the task. In other tasks, which involve some cognitive operations on a list of linguistic categorizations, easily available categories are not used by some children (age is a factor) or, if they are used, they interfere with carrying out the task. It appears that different strategies for task solution are used in different tasks, and also that the strategies used by children are affected by their age and their particular language experiences.

A reasonable approach, then, to examining the questions raised in arguments concerning the relationships between language and cognitive functioning appears to be the analysis of particular types of tasks. As was stated, most of the tasks that have been used in experiments thus far have been those which tap only the child's labeling system or lexicon. In acquiring the semantic system of his language the child must learn, for example, how conjunctive, disjunctive, and dependent relationships are expressed in the language. Although the child's understanding of these types of relationships at various stages of development has been examined in cognitive tasks, the correlation between the child's understanding of utterances expressing certain relationships and his performance in cognitive tasks testing comprehension of these relationships has not been examined in any systematic manner.

The approach to exploring the theory that man acquires language because he is pre-programmed to do so has taken two directions. The first is to attempt to distinguish structural and/or functional and/or maturational differences in man's nervous system which may be correlated with his language-specific capacities. The second is an attempt to distinguish the linguistic behavior which is different from other types of cognitve behavior.

It is the case that various stages of language comprehension and production seem to occur universally. Regardless of the language spoken in the child's linguistic community, he babbles, produces words and sentences. Further, it has been found that the developmental course of the content of these babblings and presumably the structure of early sentences show great similarity in the language produced by children from different linguistic communities. Regardless of his personal environment during the early years of life, the structure and order of the linguistic behavior observed is not altered, although it is the case that gross output and proportion of usage of different structures vary with the particular child in a particular environment. The only restriction to this statement that seems clear at the moment is that the child must have those nervous system structures and mechanisms necessary to language acquisition if he is to develop language normally. However, researchers attempting to find those structures and mechanisms have not come up with any conclusive findings.

It has also been suggested that there are certain peripheral capacities unique to man which play a role in *instituting* language behavior and which also form the bases for later development. Some very preliminary research with the human neonate suggests that perhaps the human organism may be pre-programmed to respond differentially to sounds within the speech spectrum and those outside it, just as other animals are pre-programmed to respond differentially to sounds which are cues for escape and approach responses. Some research also suggests that, contrary to previous opinions, the vocal mechanism of other primates differs somewhat from that of human beings. However, the questions of grammar acquisition and development obviously pose more complex problems than that of determining peripheral capacities, since a great deal of what the child must know is not in the acoustic signal and cannot be processed by peripheral mechanisms. Nevertheless, it would be important to determine if there are perceptual-motor mechanisms which are species-specific and which underlie the use of language. Research in this direction has just begun and, in general, research into the biological structure of language is in its infancy. Many of the questions concerning the correlation of structure, the functioning of structures, and the acquisition of language have yet to be precisely answered.

Whether language learning is unique to the human is still a question that is being asked. Recently an experiment has been undertaken to teach a chimpanzee to use language (Gardner and Gardner, 1969). Evidence has indicated that chimpanzees cannot articulate sounds as humans do because of the restrictions on their vocal mechanisms. Therefore, the experimenters are attempting to teach the chimpanzee to use a sign language. The chimpanzee has learned to sign words and strings of words. These strings are now up to three or four "words" in length. However, several striking differences exist between the "utterances" of Washoe the chimp and those of a child at this same stage of development. The first is that although both questions and negatives are used by the experimenters with Washoe, they are not used by the chimpanzee. Indeed, most of the utterances are limited to what might be termed imperatives. The second is that in combining words into a string, the relationship between words observed in children's utterances is not evident or certainly not clear in Washoe's utterances. Most of these strings appear to be a joining together of separate imperatives. For example, when signing "open/drink," presumably the chimpanzee means "Open the refrigerator door!" "Give me a drink!" and when signing "Open/flower," presumably the chimpanzee means "Open the gate!" "I want a flower!" This type of behavior does not appear to be very different from the natural communication of chimpanzees when using gesture and vocalization to indicate locations, demands, etc.

HOW IS LANGUAGE ACQUIRED?

As was indicated earlier, theories not concerned with biological structure and functioning but which still maintain that the human is unique from other organisms in his capacity to think and learn and to acquire language have taken two positions. One position is that language acquisition is "like" other human learning, and the other position is that language learning is different from other learning in that a very unique system of categorizations and rules has to be learned when the child acquires language.

Taking the former position, Schlesinger (In Press) states that it is possible to posit psychological constructs (such as actor and action) which are isomorphic to the underlying categorizations of items in sentences (such as noun and verb). Utterances produced by children are produced directly from these psychological categorizations (called "intention markers"). They represent the intentions of the child in a given situation and, therefore, do not have to be initially learned in conjunction with distinct representations of their syntactic class. The intention markers are unspecified as to grammatical categories. Intention markers representing a situation are associated with the utterances heard, and realization rules determine the syntactic categories (such as adjective, verb, noun) in which *concepts* are produced in utterances. It is not clear from this discussion how realization rules are derived from intention markers; nor is it clear, if associations are formed between the situation, the intention markers, and an utterance, why certain types of utterances are produced by children. For example, if the intention marker includes the intention to declare that something is a sock and in a particular situation the child hears "That's your sock," why does the child say "Me sock!" Further, certain types of utterances that are heard appear to be good matches to the situation, so that associations may be made, and other types of utterances do not appear to be good matches. For example, declarative sentences seem to be possibly good matches ("That's a sock"), but negative ("That's not a sock") and question sentences ("Is that a sock?") do not. The latter two types seem to be extrapolations from the situation.

Taking a compromise position, McNeill (1969) suggests that there are "weak linguistic universals" and "strong linguistic universals." Linguistic universals are those categories and rules which can be found in all languages. Weak linguistic universals are defined as those linguistic structures which reflect universals in cognition or perception. As an example of this category, McNeill gives the verb category which indicates action. Strong linguistic universals are defined as those structures which may have as their underlying basis cognition or perception, but this basis is not a *sufficient* explanation for the appearance of a structure in the grammar. As an example of this category, he gives a type of noun.

Presumably association with an action is a necessary and sufficient condition for a word to be a verb but some *additional* linguistic property is needed to make a word into a noun, since association of a word with an action does not block the classification of the word as a noun. An example of this is a word like "playing" in an utterance like "Playing is fun." However, as is noted, association with an object is in some instances sufficient for words to become nouns. Therefore, it seems, linguistic universals should be parceled into weak, strong, and "erratic" types. Presumably nouns might fall into the erratic category, since both association with the cognitive categorization of an object and a specific linguistic ability can make a word into a noun. McNeill points out the possibility of determining which structures in the grammar of languages are so-called weak or strong universals by determining those structures which are direct reflections of cognitive categorizations and those which are not. It appears to be a task "easier said than done" if the discussion of the structure noun is an example. However, the procedure suggested seems to be a reasonable one.

It is clear from the above discussion that explanations of how the child acquires a language or an explanation of the techniques used to acquire a language are natural outgrowths of the theory of "why." To take into account the fact that the structure of the language is not evident in the acoustic signal heard and the fact that children nevertheless acquire this abstract structure, it has been suggested that children *have* various kinds of preliminary linguistic information (McNeill, 1968b). That is, they are pre-programmed to acquire language and that is why they acquire it. More specifically the following has been stated (Chomsky, 1965, Chapter 1):

1. The child has the capacity to detect and recognize abstract features in the physical environment.
2. The child has a technique for representing abstract features of input signals.
3. The child has a way of representing structural information about these signals.
4. The child has some initial information about limiting a class of possible hypotheses about language structure.
5. The child has the capacity to test his hypothesis.

Because the child *has* the above capacities, this is "how" he goes about acquiring language. The procedure might work in the following manner in an analysis of an input signal:

1. This is a sentence.
2. We will label this S.
3. S contains a noun phrase and a verb phrase.
4. Because S contains NP + VP it fits the hypothesis about what is an S.
5. S_1 fits this hypothesis, S_2 partially fits this hypothesis, S_3 does not.

The child, in essence, must have some method for deriving the grammar of his language which reasonably explains the grammar he acquires. The child ". . . must possess . . . a linguistic theory that specifies the form of a possible human language, and, second, a strategy for selecting a grammar of the appropriate form that is compatible with the primary linguistic data" (Chomsky, 1965, p. 25).

The primary difficulty that other theorists have with this position is that there is as yet no definition of (1) possession of a linguistic theory, or (2) a strategy for selecting a grammar. Schlesinger (1967a, p. 397) states, "The linguist constructs a model of language competence and it remains for the psychologist to explain what makes the linguistic model work. . . . It would be just as reasonable or unreasonable to argue that a theory specifying how language is learned can serve to evaluate theories describing what is learned." This appears to be a very logical argument. In response, it has been argued that although at present there are no sufficiently detailed hypotheses about the functioning of the human organism in acquiring language, this should not preclude the search for such hypotheses or the acceptance of present inadequate ones.

From the above discussion it appears that explanations of how a child acquires language seem to be very much bound up with explanations of what he acquires. However, some theoreticians consider that what is acquired is dependent on *how,* whereas other theoreticians consider that how language is acquired is dependent on what is acquired.

WHAT IS ACQUIRED?

According to stimulus-response-reward theorists, the child establishes a response repertoire by the conditions of the stimulus-response-reward situation *plus* his capacity to identify recurrent regularities in the environment. What he acquires, then, are conditioned responses. The process of dictionary acquisition, one aspect of the acquisition of semantic rules, is often referred to as demonstrating the validity of this theory. Staats (1967) has discussed the acquisition of word meaning through the process of conditioning which involves the systematic pairing of the word with some aspect of the environment. That is:

Hurt _____ pain _____ CR
Bad _____ punishment _____ CR
Sweet _____ sensory response _____ CR

The problem with such an explanation is that there is no description of how the child determines what is a word and what aspects in the environment should be associated with a word. These words usually appear in phonetic strings, so that even the first task of isolating the word from the string is not described by this explanation. Further, the affective meaning can be colored by the context, as in the following examples:

"Did you hurt yourself?" versus "Did you hurt Timmy?"
"He's a bad boy" versus "You're a bad boy" versus "You're a bad boy today."
"The cars are blue" versus "The cars are going too fast."
"Sugar is very sweet" versus "Sugar is always sweet."

To confound the situation even further, the affective meaning can be changed as well as colored by the context, as in the following examples:

"She is a good girl" versus "She is too good for words."
"That girl is beautiful" versus "A beautiful girl is often stupid."
"This laundry smells sweet" versus "You've made the coffee too sweet."
"I had dinner at 7" versus "You have to finish your dinner."
"I'm very happy about what you did" versus "He's a happy dope."
"I need a dollar" versus "It costs a dollar."

All the above present a meaning in a context. The question is, how does the child parcel out the general properties of a morpheme, when they are presented in various contexts, by any stimulus-response condition? This he must do if he is to use and understand the word. What is the stimulus ("very sweet," or "too sweet," or "smells sweet")? What is the response— sensory response (taste or smell), or affective response (good or bad)— and what is the reward for the response?

The same problem occurs in trying to set up the stimulus-response-reward conditions for "sentence types" where one cannot clearly define the evoking stimulus (is it a syllable, word, phrase, sentence, or paragraph?) or clearly define a "sentence-type response" which is dependent on the parameters of the stimulus or which can be predicted by the stimulus. We are still left with the problem of determining an objective characterization of the stimulus and response in any instance of verbal behavior or exchange. The assumption of stimulus and response generalizations

doesn't help us because we have still to determine what the child is generalizing about, and this brings us back to the necessity of characterizing the stimulus and response.[1]

It has been stated that the child may possibly generalize about the number of words in a string, the word sequence they share, their acoustic similarity, etc.—in other words, the surface aspects they share. There are obviously many questions involved in this kind of characterization. Some of them are: Do the children count words in a string? If they do count, does a set of a certain response class share the same number of morphemes? What are the limits of a similar sequence for determining the response class (a word, a noun phrase, a noun phrase + verb phrase, etc.)? What characterizes acoustic similarity, since repeated productions of the same morpheme by the same speaker will produce acoustic outputs that differ to some degree?

To counteract the problems posed by the above theoretical explanation of syntax acquisition, the mediation theorists have proposed that although single words are established by S-R-R connections, through verbal labels and salient features in the environment, sentence types and grammatical classes are formed by associations. Oversimply stated, the sequences A-B-C and A-B-D imply that C and D are members of the same class (Jenkins and Palermo, 1964). The frequency of occurrence of A-B or B-C indicates a structure. Both class and sequential structure are learned simultaneously and interdependently. Words are connected with others in sequence, and ordering or structuring begins. The sequence is as follows: (1) the child imitates or attempts to imitate what he hears; (2) he acquires lexical items through stimulus-response connections between the word and some features within himself or in the environment; (3) words are attached to each other in sequences and structures are formed; (4) particular structures are used more than others because of their utility or effectiveness in bringing about positive responses; (5) classes of lexical items are formed because of their position in the utterance; (6) through stimulus-response equivalence mechanisms, within class substitutions are made; (7) transformations are initially learned independently but are facilitated by semantic mediation.

The above theory does not depart very drastically from a simpler S-R-R model, except by virtue of the fact that an attempt is made to parcel out the limits of the stimulus into classes of words and structures. According to this theory, sequential ordering and position in the string are two important principles in determining class and structure. However, first,

---

[1] Stimulus and response generalization presumably means that response classes can be grouped together under several headings: they have a common effect or consequence; they are elicited by a common stimulus; they are common responses (Salzinger, 1967).

we do not see the child following the principles of ordering in the strings he produces. Second, the structure of the language prevents the child from determining correctly by its position in the string the class in the language to which a word belongs. The child may hear the following sequences: (1) "The baby is sick," (2) "The baby is crying," and (3) "The baby likes crying." The last word in each sentence plays a very different grammatical role in the sentence. In sentence (1) it is a predicate adjective, in (2) the main verb, and in (3) a noun. To attempt to determine what the class of a word is by its position in the sentence would not take the child very far in understanding or using language.

Taking into account the fact that children do not mirror exactly the ordering observed in adult utterances, it has been suggested that positional rules nevertheless play a role in children's production of utterances. By learning the positions of various categorizations, the child may then learn relationships (Schlesinger, In Press). Some of the positional rules have been categorized in the following manner:

1. Modifier + Head —More nut
2. Agent + Action —Airplane bye
3. Action + Object —See sock
4. Agent + Object —Eve lunch
5. Negative + X —No wash
6. X + dative —Throw daddy
7. X + locative —Baby room

or

locative + X —Here ball
8. Introducer + X —See boy

Although the above examples are differentially labeled, it is not clear how the child determines the difference between examples *1* and *2, 2* and *3, 3* and *4*, etc., and especially *3* and *8* by positional rules. If it is additionally posited that word classes are learned as acquired stimulus-response equivalences, the situation becomes even more confused since, for example, modifiers in the so-called modifier + head construction produced by children can be determiners ("pretty baby"), nouns ("daddy tie"), and negatives ("no pencil"). Although it has been argued that linguistic rules describe language, but not human behavior, and that the rules of behavior may be quite different from those found in a description of language, research in learning has not clarified these rules of behavior as they pertain to language.

This research has shown that in specific situations human subjects can be conditioned to emit certain types of verbal and nonverbal responses. For example, they can be conditioned to increase the proportion of negative

or aggressive statements they make, and they need not necessarily be consciously aware of the stimulus-response-reward conditions designed by the experimenter. But the relationship of these results to language acquisition is highly questionable for the following reasons: (1) the kind of behavior that is shaped has already been established and only the amount or degree changes (for example, the amount of vocalization produced for a sampled period); (2) the behavior which can be shaped must be very limited (for example, labeling stimulus objects), but the linguistic system which is acquired is of much greater complexity and is composed of interdependencies of the structure of sound, word, phrase, and sentence; (3) the number of trials needed to establish a small bit of behavior seems to be disproportionately large in terms of real time acquisition of language; and (4) behavior established in a laboratory is maintained for only a short period of time after the laboratory sessions are over if it is contrary to usual linguistic behavior.

Further, although the view is often held that the procedures used in the language laboratory are also the procedures used by parents and children— for example, "Parents teach by stressing a word which is normally unstressed" (Palermo, 1966, p. 13)—evidence for such adherence to the rules has yet to be found. Human beings can be conditioned and can learn to associate, but the fact that they are conditionable and can learn to associate is not evidence that either of these processes is necessary and sufficient for language learning.

Theories which have been categorized under the heading "Human Generalizes" (in Figure 9–1) do not logically describe the sequence of development observed in language comprehension and production at various stages. They do not adequately account for the fact that the child progresses in an ordered sequence through the babbling period to sentence production; that he is able to produce not only words and sentences he may have heard but also unique words and sentences which reflect different hypotheses about the structure of the language at various stages of development; and that these sentences involve a variety of structure, word, and sound sequential patterns. Also, these theories do not account for the fact that, given similar linguistic stimulus situations (the same sentence or paraphrase of the sentence), a particular verbal response cannot be predicted. Given the possibility of extra-linguistic stimulus situations, experimenters have employed the questionable procedure of defining the stimulus situation by observing the response and then attempting to generalize about aspects of the situation which may have elicited the response.

Theories which have been categorized under the heading "Human Abstracts" (in Figure 9–1) appear more adequately to account for the sequence of development that is observed, but they do not explain it. They do not describe how the child proceeds from sequence to sequence.

It has been stated that "the basic processes and relations which give verbal behavior its special characteristics are now fairly well understood" (Skinner, 1957, p. 3). It is evident, from the preceding discussion, that these processes and relations have in fact not been clearly specified for the acquisition and development of language or its mature use—at least, to the satisfaction of all. It has been assumed by many in current research that a more precise description of what occurs over the language acquisition period in terms of what the child understands about language and can produce at various stages of development will lead to more adequate explanations of the process. The research discussed in this book provides examples of the directions now being taken and the experimental procedures now being used to obtain this detailed and meaningful description.

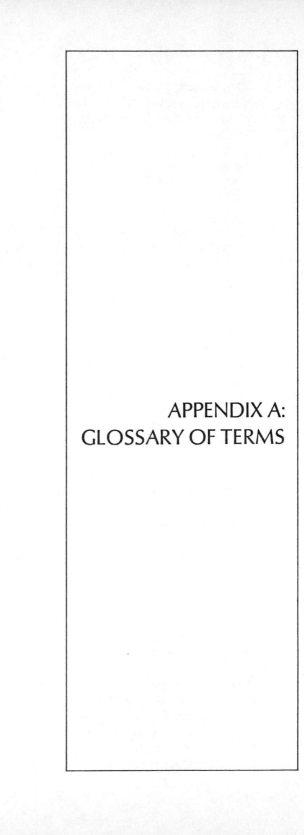

APPENDIX A:
GLOSSARY OF TERMS

Adj	Adjective
Adv	Adverb
Art.	Article
Aux	Auxiliary
C	Consonant
Comp	Complement
Det.	Determiner (Article, Adjective, Quantifier, etc.)
Emp	Emphatic
Imp	Imperative
Mod.	Modal ("can," "do," "will," etc.)
N	Noun
Neg	Negative
NP	Noun Phrase
P	Preposition
Part	Particle
Pass	Passive
Perf	Perfect
Poss	Possessive
PP	Prepositional Phrase
Pred	Predicate
PreS	Pre-sentence
Prog	Progressive
Q	Question

Quant	Quantifier
Rel. Cl.	Relative Clause
S	Sentence
SVO	Subject–Verb–Object
Trans	Transitive
V	Verb
V	Vowel
VP	Verb Phrase
Wh	"Who," "what," "where," etc.
$\longrightarrow$	Is rewritten

APPENDIX B:
KEY TO
PHONOLOGICAL
SYMBOLS

Symbol		Key Word
b		*b*ig
p		*p*at
m		*m*ouse
d		*d*oll
t		*t*oy
n		*n*ice
k		*k*ick
g		*g*ate
ŋ	(only medial and final)	thi*n*k si*ng*
X		*ch*utzpah (German)
f		*f*at
v		*v*ase
θ		*th*ing
ð		*th*at
s		*s*ip
z		*z*oom
š		*sh*y
ž	(only medial and final)	mea*s*ure gara*g*e
j		*j*ump
č		*ch*air
w		*w*et

r	*r*ed
l	*l*ike
h	*h*ot
y	*y*et
a	m*a*
u	t*oo*
i	m*e*
ɪ	s*i*t
e	m*a*te
ɛ	s*e*t
ə	*u*mbrella
ɔ	pa*w*
æ	p*a*t

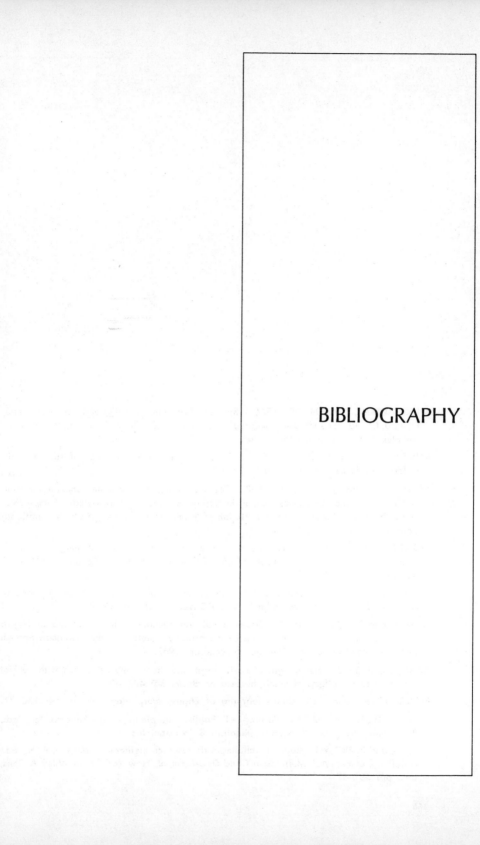

BIBLIOGRAPHY

AJURIAGUERRA, JULIAN DE. 1966. Speech disorders in childhood. In Carterette, Edward C., ed., *Speech and Language Communication, Brain Function,* Vol. III. Los Angeles: University of California Press, pp. 117–40.

ANISFELD, M., and G. R. TUCKER. 1967. English pluralization rules of six year old children. *Child Development,* **38**: 1201–17.

ASCH, S. E., and H. NERLOVE. 1960. The development of double function terms in children: an exploratory investigation. In Kaplan, B., and S. Wagner, eds., *Perspectives in Psychological Theory: Essays in Honor of Heinz Werner.* New York: International Universities Press, pp. 283–95.

BARATZ, JOAN C. 1969a. Language and cognitive assessment of Negro children: assumptions and research needs. *ASHA, A Journal of the American Speech and Hearing Association,* **11**: 87–91.

————. 1969b. A bi-dialectal task for determining language proficiency in economically disadvantaged Negro children. *Child Development,* **40**: 889–902.

————, and E. POVICH. 1967. Grammatical constructions in the language of Negro pre-school children. Paper presented at the national meeting of the American Speech and Hearing Association, Chicago, November, 1967.

BASSER, L. S. 1962. Hemiplegia of early onset and the faculty of speech with special reference to the effects of hemispherectomy. *Brain,* **85**: 427–60.

BERKO, JEAN. 1958. The child's learning of English morphology. *Word,* **14**: 150–77.

————. 1961. The child's learning of English morphology. In Saporta, S., ed., *Psycholinguistics.* New York: Holt, Rinehart & Winston, Inc.

————, and R. BROWN. 1960. Psycholinguistic research methods. In Mussen, P. H., ed., *Handbook of Research Methods in Child Development.* New York: John Wiley & Sons, Inc., pp. 531–57.

BERNSTEIN, BASIL. 1964.   Elaborated and restricted codes: their social origins and some consequences. In Gumperz, J., and D. Hymes, eds., *The Ethnography of Communication. American Anthropologist Publication,* **6.**

BIRCH, HERBERT G. 1968.   Health and the education of the socially disadvantaged child. *Developmental Medicine and Child Neurology,* **10:** 580–99.

BLASDELL, RICHARD C., and PAUL JENSEN. 1968.   An approach to the study of first-language acquisition. Paper presented to the Communication Sciences Laboratory Annual Seminar, Transformational Grammar as a Model of the Human Language User.

BLOOM, LOIS M. 1970.   *Language development: Form and function in emerging grammars.* Cambridge, Mass.: M.I.T. Press.

————, 1970.   *Early language development: What children mean by what they say.* Draft of paper presented at Seminar for Research in Mental Retardation and Human Development, Lawrence, Kansas.

BOSMA, J. F., H. M. TRUBY, and J. LIND. 1965.   Upper respiratory actions of the infant. *American Speech and Hearing Association Reports,* No. 1, 35–49.

BRAIN, RUSSELL. 1961.   The neurology of language. *Brain,* **84:** 145–66.

BRAINE, M. D. S. 1963.   The ontogeny of English phrase structure: the first phase. *Language,* **39:** 1–13.

————. 1965.   Three suggestions regarding analysis of children's language. Paper presented at the 10th Annual Conference on Linguistics, of the Linguistic Circle of New York.

BRAZIER, M. A. B. 1967.   Neurophysiological contributions to the subject of human communication theory. In Dance, Frank, ed., *Human Communication Theory.* New York: Holt, Rinehart & Winston, Inc., pp. 61–69.

BRICKER, W. A. 1967.   Errors in echoic behavior of pre-school children. *Journal of Speech and Hearing Research,* **10:** 67–76.

BROWN, ROGER. 1968.   The development of Wh questions in child speech. *Journal of Verbal Learning and Verbal Behavior,* **7:** 279–90.

————, and U. BELLUGI. 1964.   Three processes in the child's acquisition of syntax. *Harvard Educational Review,* **34:** 133–51.

————, and J. BERKO. 1960.   Word associations and the acquisition of grammar. *Child Development,* **31:** 1–14.

————, C. B. CAZDEN, and U. BELLUGI. 1969.   The child's grammar from I to III. In Hill, J. P., ed., *1967 Minnesota Symposium on Child Psychology.* Minneapolis: University of Minnesota Press, **2:** 28–73.

————, and C. FRASER. 1964.   The acquisition of syntax. *Monographs of the Society for Research in Child Development,* **29:** 43–79.

————, and C. HANLON. 1968.   Derivational complexity and order of acquisition in child speech. Paper presented at Carnegie-Mellon Symposium on Cognitive Psychology, Pittsburgh.

————, and E. H. LENNEBERG. 1954.   A study in language and cognition. *Journal of Abnormal and Social Psychology,* **49:** 454–62.

BRUCE, D. J. 1964.   An analysis of word sounds by young children. *British Journal of Educational Psychology,* **34:** 158–70.

BULLOWA, M., L. G. JONES, and A. DUCKERT. 1964.   The acquisition of a word. *Language and Speech,* **7:** 107–11.

CARMICHAEL, LEONARD. 1964.   The early growth of language capacity in the individual. In Lenneberg, E. H., ed., *New Directions in the Study of Language*. Cambridge: M.I.T. Press, pp. 1–22.

CAZDEN, C. 1965.   Environmental assistance to the child's acquisition of grammar. Unpublished Doctoral Dissertation, Harvard University.

————. 1967.   The acquisition of noun and verb inflections. Paper presented at the Society for Research in Child Development, New York, March 1967.

————. 1968a.   The acquisition of noun and verb inflections. *Child Development*, **39**: 433–48.

————. 1968b.   Three sociolinguistic views of the language and speech of lower class children—with special attention to the work of Basil Bernstein. *Developmental Medicine and Child Neurology*, **10**: 600–611.

CHASE, RICHARD A. 1967.   Verbal behavior: some points of reference. Annual Report, Neurocommunications Laboratory, The Johns Hopkins University School of Medicine, pp. 63–102.

CHOMSKY, CAROL S. 1969.   The acquisition of syntax in children from 5 to 10. Cambridge, Mass.: M.I.T. Press.

CHOMSKY, N. 1965.   *Aspects of the Theory of Syntax*. Cambridge, Mass.: M.I.T. Press.

————, and M. HALLE. 1968.   *The Sound Patterns of English*. New York: Harper & Row, Publishers.

COHEN, PAUL. 1966.   Outline of research on the English of Negro and Puerto Rican speakers in New York City. *Project Literacy Reports, No. 7*. Ithaca, N.Y.: Cornell University, pp. 13–17.

COLE, M., J. GAY, J. GLICK, and D. SHARP. 1968.   Linguistic structure and transposition. Paper presented to Psychonomic Society meeting, St. Louis, Missouri, October 1968.

COOPER, R. L. 1967.   The ability of deaf and hearing children to apply morphological rules. *Journal of Speech and Hearing Research*, **10**: 77–85.

CULLEN, J. K., N. L. FARGO, and P. BAKER. 1968.   Delayed auditory feedback monitoring: III. Delayed auditory feedback studies of infant cry using several delay times. Annual report, Neurocommunications Laboratory, The Johns Hopkins School of Medicine, pp. 79–93.

CULLEN, J. K., N. L. FARGO, R. A. CHASE, and P. BAKER. 1968.   The development of auditory feedback monitoring: I. Delayed auditory feedback studies on infant cry. *Journal of Speech and Hearing Research*, **11**: 85–93.

Di VESTA, F. J. 1966.   A developmental study of the semantic structure of children. *Journal of Verbal Learning and Verbal Behavior*, **5**: 249–59.

DOLLARD, J., and N. E. MILLER. 1950.   *Personality and Psychotherapy*. New York: McGraw-Hill Book Company.

ECCLES, JOHN C. 1966.   Brain and the development of the human person. *Impact of Science on Society*, **16**: 93–112.

EISENBERG, L., C. I. BERLIN, A. DILL, and S. FRANK. 1968.   Class and race effects on the intelligibility of monosyllables. *Child Development*, **39**: 1077–90.

EISENBERG, RITA B. 1964.   Auditory behavior in the human neonate: a preliminary report. *Journal of Speech and Hearing Research*, **7**: 245–69.

————. 1965.   Auditory behavior in the human neonate: methodological problems and the logical design of research procedures. *Journal of Auditory Research*, **5**: 159–77.

————. 1966.   Habituation to an acoustic pattern as an index of differences among human neonates. *Journal of Auditory Research*, **6**: 239–48.

————. 1967.   Stimulus significance as a determinant of newborn responses to sound. Paper presented at meeting of the Society for Research in Child Development, New York, March 1967.

EISENSON, JOHN. 1963.   The nature of defective speech. In Cruickshank, W. M., ed., *Psychology of Exceptional Children and Youth*, second ed. Englewood Cliffs, N.J.: Prentice-Hall, Inc.

ENTWISLE, DORIS R. 1966.   The word associations of young children. Unpublished Paper, Johns Hopkins University.

————. 1970.   Semantic systems of children. In Williams, F., ed., *Language and Poverty: Perspective on a Theme*. Chicago: Markham Publishing Co., pp. 123–39.

ERVIN-TRIPP, S. M. 1963.   Structures in children's language. Paper presented at the International Congress of Psychology, Washington, D.C.

————. 1964.   Imitation and structural changes in children's language. In Lenneberg, E. H., ed., *New Directions in the Study of Language*. Cambridge: M.I.T. Press, pp. 163–90.

————. 1966.   Language development. In Hoffman, L. W., and M. L. Hoffman, eds., *Review of Child Development*. New York: Russell Sage Foundation, pp. 55–105.

————. 1969.   Sociolinguistics. In Berkowitz, L., ed., *Advances in Experimental Social Psychology*, Vol. 4. New York: Academic Press, pp. 91–166.

————, and G. FOSTER. 1960.   The development of meaning in children's descriptive terms. *Journal of Abnormal and Social Psychology*, **61**: 271–75.

FAY, W. H., and B. V. BUTLER. 1968.   Echolalia, I.Q. and the developmental dichotomy of speech and language systems. *Journal of Speech and Hearing Research*, **11**: 365–71.

FISHMAN, J. A., et al. 1966.   *Review of Language Loyalty in the U. S.*, Janua Linguarium, series maior 21. The Hague: Mouton.

FLANAGAN, J. L. 1965.   *Speech Analysis, Synthesis and Perception*. New York: Academic Press.

FLAVELL, JOHN H. 1963.   *The Developmental Psychology of Jean Piaget*. New York: Van Nostrand Reinhold, pp. 85–121, 150, 155.

————. 1966.   Role taking and communication skills in children. *Young Children*, **21**: 164–77.

————, D. R. BEACH, and J. M. CHINSKY. 1966.   Spontaneous verbal rehearsal in a memory task as a function of age. *Child Development*, **37**: 283–300.

FODOR, J., and M. GARRETT. 1966.   Some reflections on competence and performance. In Lyons, J., and R. J. Wales, eds., *Psycholinguistic Papers*, Chicago: Aldine, pp. 135–63.

————, and T. BEVER. 1968.   Some syntactic determinants of sentential complexity: II. Verb structure. *Perception and Psychophysics*, **3**: 453–61.

FRASER, C., U. BELLUGI, and R. BROWN. 1963.   Control of grammar in imitation, comprehension and production. *Journal of Verbal Learning and Verbal Behavior*, **2**: 121–35.

FRIEDLANDER, BERNARD Z. 1967.   The effect of speaker identity, inflection, vocabulary and message redundancy on infants' selection of vocal reinforcers. Paper presented at meeting of Society for Research in Child Development, New York, March 1967.

FRISHKOPF, L. S., and M. H. GOLDSTEIN. 1963.   Responses to acoustic stimuli in the 8th nerve of the bullfrog. *Journal of Acoustic Society of America*, **35**: 1219–28.

FRY, D. B. 1966.   The development of the phonological system in the normal and deaf child. In Smith, F., and G. A. Miller, eds., *The Genesis of Language*. Cambridge: M.I.T. Press, pp. 187–206.

FULLER, MARGARET. 1966.   Understanding English grammar without the ability to speak. Unpublished Paper, University of California at Berkeley.

FURTH, HANS. 1964.   Conservation of weight in deaf and hearing children. *Child Development,* **35**: 143–50.

GARDNER, R. A., and B. C. GARDNER. 1969.   Teaching sign language to a chimpanzee. *Science,* **165**: 664–72.

GESCHWIND, NORMAN. 1965.   Disconnection syndromes in animal and man. *Brain,* **88** (Part II): 237–94.

GLEASON, HENRY A. 1961.   *An Introduction to Descriptive Linguistics*. New York: Holt, Rinehart & Winston, Inc.

GLUCKSBERG, S., R. M. KRAUSS, and R. WEISBERG. 1966.   Referential communication in nursery school children: method and some preliminary findings. *Journal of Experimental Child Psychology,* **3**: 333–42.

GREENBERG, JOSEPH, ed. 1963.   *Universals of Language*. Cambridge: M.I.T. Press.

GRUBER, J. S. 1967a.   Topicalization in child language. *Foundations of Language,* **3**: 37–65.

————. 1967b.   Correlations between the syntactic constructions of the child and of the adult. Paper presented at the Society for Research in Child Development, New York, March 1967.

HALLE, MORRIS. 1961.   On the role of simplicity in linguistic descriptions. *Proceedings of Symposia on Applied Mathematics: XII. Structure of Language and Its Mathematical Aspects*, pp. 89–94.

HEIDER, E. R., C. B. CAZDEN, and R. BROWN. 1968.   Social class differences in the effectiveness and style of children's coding ability. *Project Literacy Reports, No. 9*. Ithaca, N.Y.: Cornell University, pp. 1–10.

HIRSCH, KATRINA DE. 1967.   Differential diagnosis between aphasic and schizophrenic language in children. *Journal of Speech and Hearing Disorders,* **32**: 3–10.

HOCKETT, CHARLES F. 1963.   The problem of universals in language. In Greenberg, Joseph H., ed., *Universals in Language*. Cambridge: M.I.T. Press, pp. 1–29.

HUTTENLOCHER, JANELLEN. 1964.   Children's language: word-phrase relationship. *Science,* **143**: 264–65.

————, K. EISENBERG, and S. STRAUSS. 1968.   Comprehension: relation between perceived actor and logical subject. *Journal of Verbal Learning and Verbal Behavior,* **7**: 527–30.

————, and S. STRAUSS. 1968.   Comprehension and a statement's relation to the situation it describes. *Journal of Verbal Learning and Verbal Behavior,* **7**: 300–304.

HYMES, DELL. 1964.   Directions in ethno-linguistic theory. *American Anthropoligist,* **66**: 6–56.

————. 1967.   The functions of speech. In De Cecco, J. D., ed., *The Psychology of Language, Thought, and Instruction*. New York: Holt, Rinehart & Winston, Inc., p. 83.

IRWIN, O. C. 1946.   Infant speech: equations for consonant-vowel ratios. *Journal of Speech Disorders,* **11**: 177–80.

————. 1947.   Infant speech: consonant sounds according to the manner of articulation. *Journal of Speech Disorders,* **12**: 397–401.

————. 1960.   Language and communication. In Mussen, P. H., ed., *Handbook of Research Methods in Child Development.* New York: John Wiley & Sons, Inc., pp. 487–516.

JAKOBSON, R. 1962.   *Selected Writings I.* The Hague: Mouton and Co., pp. 317, 328–402, 491–503, 538–46.

————. 1964.   Toward a linguistic typology of aphasic impairments. *Ciba Foundation Symposium on Disorders of Language.* London: J. and A. Churchill, Ltd.

————, C. G. M. FANT, and M. HALLE. 1963.   *Preliminaries to Speech Analysis.* Cambridge: M.I.T. Press.

————, and · M. HALLE. 1956.   *Fundamentals of Language.* The Hague: Mouton and Co.

JENKINS, J., and D. S. PALERMO. 1964.   Mediation processes and the acquisition of linguistic structure. In Bellugi, U., and R. Brown, eds., *The acquisition of language. Monographs of the Society for Research in Child Development,* pp. 141–69.

KAGAN, JEROME, and MICHAEL LEWIS. 1965.   Studies of attention. *Merrill-Palmer Quarterly of Behavior and Development,* **11**: 95–127.

KAPLAN, ELEANOR L. 1969.   The role of intonation in the acquisition of language. Unpublished Doctoral dissertation, Cornell University.

KATZ, E. W., and S. B. BRENT. 1968.   Understanding connectives. *Journal of Verbal Learning and Verbal Behavior,* **7**: 501–9.

KATZ, J. J., and J. A. FODOR. 1963.   The structure of a semantic theory. *Language,* **39**: 170–210.

————, and P. M. POSTAL. 1964.   *An Integrated Theory of Linguistic Descriptions.* Cambridge: M.I.T. Press.

KENDLER, TRACY S. 1963.   Development of mediating responses in children. In Wright, J. C., and J. Kagan, eds., *Basic Cognitive Processes in Children. Monographs of the Society for Research in Child Development,* 28, pp. 33–48.

KIMURA, D. 1961.   Cerebral dominance and perception of verbal stimuli. *Canadian Journal of Psychology,* **15**: 166–71.

KLEIN, ROBERT P. 1969.   Acoustic analysis of the acquisition of acceptable /r/ in American English. Paper presented at the Society for Research in Child Development, Santa Monica, Calif., March 1969.

KLIMA, E. S., and U. BELLUGI. 1966.   Syntactic regularities in the speech of children. In Lyons, J., and R. J. Wales, eds., *Psycholinguistic Papers.* Chicago: Aldine, pp. 183–208.

KOENIGSKNECHT, R. A., and L. L. LEE. 1968.   Distinctive feature analysis of speech sound discrimination in 3 year old children. Paper presented at the American Speech and Hearing Association, Denver, Colo.

KRAUSS, R. M. 1968.   Language as a symbolic process in communication. *American Scientist,* **56**: 265–78.

————, and S. GLUCKSBERG. 1967.   The development of communication: competence as a function of age. *Child Development,* **40**: 255–60.

LABOV, W., and P. COHEN. 1967.   Systematic relations of standard and non-standard rules in the grammars of Negro speakers. *Project Literacy Reports, No. 8.* Ithaca, N.Y.: Cornell University, pp. 66–82.

————, and C. A. ROBINS. 1965. A preliminary study of the structure of English used by Negro and Puerto Rican speakers in New York City, final report. *Cooperative Research Project*, No. 3091. Office of Education.

LANTZ, D. L., and E. H. LENNEBERG, 1966. Verbal communication and color memory in the deaf and hearing. *Child Development*, **37**: 765–80.

LEE, LAURA. 1966. Developmental sentence types: a method for comparing normal and deviant syntactic development. *Journal of Speech and Hearing Disorders*, **31**: 311–30.

LENNEBERG, E. H. 1962. Understanding language without the ability to speak: a case report. *Journal of Abnormal and Social Psychology*, **65**: 419–25.

————. 1966. The natural history of language. In Smith, F., and G. A. Miller, eds., *Genesis of Language*. Cambridge: M.I.T. Press, pp. 221–27.

————. 1967. *Biological Foundations of Language*. New York: John Wiley & Sons, Inc.

————. 1969. On explaining language. *Science*, **164**: 635–43.

————, I. A. NICHOLS, and P. F. ROSENBERGER. 1964. Primitive stages of language development in mongolism. *Disorders of Communication*: XLIII. Research Publications, A.R.W.M.D. Baltimore, Maryland: Williams and Wilkins.

LEWIS, M. M. 1963. *Language, Thought and Personality*. New York: Basic Books, Inc.

LEWIS, MICHAEL, J. KAGAN, and H. CAMPBELL. 1966. Studies of infant attention: I. The six-month old. Unpublished Manuscript, Fels Research Institute, Yellow Springs, Ohio.

LIBERMAN, A. M., F. S. COOPER, K. S. HARRIS, and P. F. McNEILAGE. 1962. A motor theory of speech perception. *Proceedings of the Speech Communication Seminar*, Speech Transmission Laboratory, Royal Institute of Technology, Stockholm.

LIEBERMAN, PHILLIP. 1967. *Intonation, Perception and Language*. Cambridge: M.I.T. Press.

————. 1968. Primate vocalizations and human linguistic ability. Unpublished Paper, Linguistics Department, University of Connecticut, Storrs, Conn.

LIND, J., H. M. TRUBY, and J. F. BOSMA. 1965. *Newborn Infant Cry*. Upsala: Alquist and Wiesells.

LUMSDEN, E. A., and B. POTEAT. 1968. The salience of the vertical dimension in the concept of "bigger" in 5 and 6 year olds. *Journal of Verbal Learning and Verbal Behavior*, **7**: 404–8.

LURIA, A. R. 1965. *Higher Cortical Functions in Man*. New York: Basic Books, Inc.

McCAFFREY, ARTHUR. 1967. Speech perception in infancy: a test of some hypotheses and some results. Unpublished Manuscript, Harvard University.

————. 1968. The imitation, comprehension and production of English syntax: a developmental study of the language skill of "deprived" and "non-deprived" children. Progress Report No. 2, A Research Project of the Language Group, Harvard Graduate School of Education.

McCARTHY, DOROTHEA. 1930. Language development of the pre-school child. *Institute of Child Welfare Monograph No. 4*. Minneapolis: University of Minnesota Press.

————. 1954. Language development in children. In Carmichael, L., ed., *Manual of Child Psychology*, 2nd Edition. New York: John Wiley & Sons, Inc., pp. 492–630.

MacKAY, DONALD G. 1968. Metamorphosis of a critical interval: age-linked changes in the delay in auditory feedback that produces maximal disruption of speech. *Journal of the Acoustical Society of America*, **43**: 811–21.

McNEILL, DAVID. 1965. Development of the semantic system. Unpublished Paper, Center for Cognitive Studies, Harvard University.

————. 1966. Developmental psycholinguistics. In Smith, Frank, and G. A. Miller, eds., *The Genesis of Language*. Cambridge: M.I.T. Press, pp. 15–84.

————. 1968a. Empiricist and nativist theories of language. Paper prepared for the Symposium on New Perspectives in the Science of Man, Alpbach, Austria, June 1968.

————. 1968b. On theories of language acquisition. In Dixon, T., and D. Horton, eds., *Verbal Behavior and General Behavior Theory*. Englewood Cliffs, N.J.: Prentice-Hall, Inc., pp. 406–20.

————. 1969. Explaining linguistic universals. Paper presented at the XIXth International Congress of Psycholinguistics.

————. 1970. The development of language. In Mussen, Paul H., ed., *Carmichael's Manual of Child Psychology*, New York: Behavioral Science Book Service, **1**: Chap. 15.

————. 1971. The capacity for the ontogenesis of grammar. In Slobin, D. I., ed., *The Ontogenesis of Grammar*. New York: Academic Press, pp. 17-40.

MASSON, GEORGINA. 1957. *Frederick II of Hohenstaufen*. London: Secker and Warburg, p. 230.

MENYUK, P. 1963a. Syntactic structures in the language of children. *Child Development*, **34**: 409–630.

————. 1963b. A preliminary evaluation of grammatical capacity in children. *Journal of Verbal Learning and Verbal Behavior*, **2**: 429–39.

————. 1964a. Alternation of rules in children's grammar. *Journal of Verbal Learning and Verbal Behavior*, **2**: 480–88.

————. 1964b. Comparison of grammar of children with functionally deviant and normal speech. *Journal of Speech and Hearing Research*, **7**: 107–21.

————. 1964c. Syntactic rules used by children from pre-school through first grade. *Child Development*, **35**: 533–46.

————. 1965. Cues used in perception and production of speech by children. *Research Laboratory of Electronics Quarterly Progress Reports*, No. 77.

————. 1967. Children's perception of a set of vowels. *Research Laboratory of Electronics Quarterly Progress Reports*, No. 84.

————. 1968a. Children's learning and reproduction of grammatical and nongrammatical phonological sequences. *Child Development*, **39**: 844–60.

————. 1968b. The role of distinctive features in children's acquisition of phonology. *Journal of Speech and Hearing Research*, **11**: 138–46.

————. 1969. *Sentences Children Use*. Cambridge: M.I.T. Press.

————. 1970. Language theories and educational practice. In Williams, F., ed., *Language and Poverty: Perspective on a Theme*. Chicago: Markham Publishing Co.

————, and S. ANDERSON. 1969. Children's identification and reproduction of /w/, /r/, and /l/. *Journal of Speech and Hearing Research*, **12**: 39–52.

————, and N. BERNHOLTZ. 1969. Prosodic features and children's language production. *Research Laboratory of Electronics Quarterly Progress Reports*, No. 93.

————, and D. KLATT. 1968. Child's production of initial consonant clusters. *Research Laboratory of Electronics Quarterly Progress Reports*, No. 91.

MESSER, S. 1967. Implicit phonology in children. *Journal of Verbal Learning and Verbal Behavior*, **6**: 609–13.

MILLER, GEORGE A. 1962. Some psychological studies of grammar. *American Psychologist*, **17**: 748–62.

MILLER, G. A., E. GALANTER, and K. PRIBAM. 1960. *Plans and Structure of Behavior.* New York: Holt, Rinehart & Winston, Inc.

MILLER, W., and S. ERVIN. 1964. The development of grammar in child language. *Monographs of the Society for Research in Child Development*, **29**: 9–34.

MOFFIT, ALAN R. 1969. Speech perception by 20 to 24 week old infants. Paper presented at the Society for Research in Child Development, Santa Monica, Calif., March 1969.

MOREHEAD, DONALD M. 1968. Processing of phonological sequences: a distinctive feature analysis. Unpublished Manuscript, University of California, Berkeley.

MOWRER, O. H. 1960. Hearing and speaking: an analysis of language learning. *Journal of Speech and Hearing Disorders*, **23**: 143–53.

MURAI, JUN-ICHI. 1960. Speech development of infants. *Psychologia*, **3**: 27–35.

———. 1963/64. The sounds of infants. *Studia Phonologica*, **3**: 21–24.

MUSSEYIBOVA, T. A. 1964. The development of an understanding of spatial relations and their reflection in language of children of pre-school age. In Ananyev, B. G., and B. F. Lomov, eds., *Problems of Spatial Perception and Spatial Concepts* (NASA Technical Translation). Washington, D.C.: NASA.

NAKAZIMA, SEI. 1962. A comparative study of the speech developments of Japanese and American English in childhood. *Studia Phonologica*, **2**: 27–39.

NEWFIELD, M. U., and B. B. SCHLANGER. 1968. The acquisition of English morphology by normal and educable mentally retarded children. *Journal of Speech and Hearing Research*, **11**: 693–706.

O'DONNELL, R. C., W. J. GRIFFIN, and R. C. NORRIS. 1967. *Syntax of Kindergarten and Elementary School Children.* Champaign, Ill.: National Council of Teachers of English, Research Report No. 8.

OHMAN, S. E. G. 1966. Coarticulation in VCV utterances: spectrographic measurements. *Journal of the Acoustical Society of America*, **39**: 151–68.

OSSER, H., M. WANG, and F. ZAID. 1969. The young child's ability to imitate and comprehend speech: a comparison of two sub-cultural groups. *Child Development*, **40**: 1063–76.

PALERMO, DAVID. 1965. Characteristics of word association responses obtained from children in grades 1 through 4. Paper presented at Society for Research in Child Development, Minneapolis, Minnesota.

———. 1966. On learning to talk. *Research Bulletin No. 61*, Department of Psychology, Pennsylvania State University.

———. 1966. Oral word association norms for children grades 1 through 4. *Pennsylvania State University Research Bulletin No. 60.*

———, and J. J. Jenkins. 1965. Changes in word associations of 4th and 5th grade children from 1916 to 1961. *Journal of Verbal Learning and Verbal Behavior*, **4**: 180–87.

PEAL, E., and W. LAMBERT. 1962. The relation of bi-lingualism to intelligence. *Psychological Monographs*, **76**.

PEISACH, ESTELLE C. 1965. Children's comprehension of teacher and peer speech. *Child Development*, **36**: 467–80.

PENFIELD, WILDER, and LAMAR ROBERTS. 1959. *Speech and Brain Mechanisms*. Princeton: Princeton University Press.

PIAGET, JEAN. 1926. *The Language and Thought of the Child*. New York: Harcourt Brace Jovanovitch.

POSTAL, P. M. 1968. *Aspects of Phonological Theory*. New York: Harper & Row, Publisher.

POWERS, MARGARET. 1957. Functional disorders of articulation: symptomatology and etiology. In Travis, L. E., ed., *Handbook of Speech Pathology*. New York: Appleton-Century-Crofts, p. 716.

PRENTICE, J. L. 1966. Semantics and syntax in word learning. *Journal of Verbal Learning and Verbal Behavior*, 5: 279–84.

PRESTON, MALCOLM. 1967. Perception of voiced and voiceless stop consonants in 3 year old children. *Haspinks Laboratories SR–11*.

————, and GRACE YENI-KOMSHIAN. 1967. Studies of development of stop consonants in children. *Haskins Laboratories SR–11*.

ROSENBAUM, MILTON E. 1967. The effect of verbalization of correct responses by performers and observers on retention. *Child Development*, 38: 615–22.

ROSENBLITH, WALTER A. 1965. Sensory coding in the nervous system. In von Hippel, A., ed., *Designing of Materials and Devices*. Cambridge: M.I.T. Press, p. 263.

ROSS, J. R. In Press. On declarative sentences. In Jacobs, R., and P. Rosenbaum, eds., *Readings on Transformational Grammar*.

SALZINGER, K. 1967. The problem of response class in verbal behavior. In Salzinger, K., and S. Salzinger, eds., *Research in Verbal Behavior and Some Neurophysiological Implications*. New York· Academic Press, pp. 35–54.

SCHLESINGER, I. M. 1967a. A note on the relationship between psychological and linguistic theories. *Foundations of Language*, 3: 397–402.

————. 1967b. Problems of investigating the grammar of sign language. The Hebrew University of Jerusalem in cooperation with the Association of the Deaf and Mute in Israel and the Helen Keller House. Working Paper No. 2.

————. 1971. Production of utterances and language acquisition. In Slobin, D. I., ed., *The Ontogenesis of Grammar*. New York: Academic Press, pp. 63-102.

SCHMITT, PHILIP. 1968. Deaf children's comprehension and production of sentence transformations. Unpublished Doctoral Dissertation, University of Illinois.

SCHOLES, R. J. 1968. The role of grammaticality in the imitation of word strings by children and adults. Paper presented at meeting of the Linguistic Society of America, New York, December 1968.

SHANKWEILER, DONALD, and MICHAEL STUDDERT-KENNEDY. 1966. Identification of consonants and vowels presented to left and right ears. *Haskins Laboratories SR 5/6*, 6.1–6.9.

SHEPPARD, W. C., and H. L. LANE. 1968. Development of prosodic features of infant vocalizing. *Journal of Speech and Hearing Research*, 11: 94–108.

SHIPLEY, E. F., C. S. SMITH, and L. R. GLEITMAN. 1965. A study in the acquisition of language: free response to commands. Technical Report VIII, Eastern Pennsylvania Psychiatric Institute.

SHRINER, THOMAS H. 1967. A review of mean length of response as a measure of expressive language development in children. Submitted to *Journal of Speech and Hearing Disorders*, December 1967.

———, R. G. DANILOFF, and J. M. NEMEC. 1969. Resynthesization of meaningful and non-meaningful CVC syllables by children. Unpublished Manuscript, University of Illinois.

———, M. S. HOLLOWAY, and R. G. DANILOFF. 1969. The relationship between articulatory deficits and syntax in speech defective children. *Journal of Speech and Hearing Research,* **12**: 319–25.

SHVACHKIN, N. KH. 1966. Development of phonemic speech perception in early childhood. *Izvestiya Akad. Pedag. Nauk RSFSR,* 1948, Vyp. 13. Abstracted by D. I. Slobin in Smith, Frank, and G. A. Miller, eds., *Genesis of Language.* Cambridge: M.I.T. Press, pp. 381–82.

SIMNER, MARVIN. 1969. Response of the newborn infant to the cry of another infant. Paper presented at meeting of the Society for Research in Child Development. Santa Monica, Calif., March 1969.

SKINNER, B. F. 1957. *Verbal Behavior.* New York: Appleton-Century-Crofts, p. 3.

SLOBIN, D. I. 1964. Some thoughts on the relation of comprehension to speech. Paper presented at American Speech and Hearing Association meeting, San Francisco, Calif., November 1964.

———. 1966a. Grammatical transformations and sentence comprehension in childhood and adulthood. *Journal of Verbal Learning and Verbal Behavior,* **5**: 219–27.

———. 1966b. Soviet Psycholinguistics. In O'Connor, N., ed., *Present Day Russian Psychology: A Symposium by Seven Authors.* Oxford, England: Pergamon Press, p. 138.

———. 1966c. Comments on "Developmental Psycholinguistics." In Smith, Frank, and G. A. Miller, eds., *The Genesis of Language.* Cambridge: M.I.T. Press, pp. 85–91.

———, ed. 1967. *A Field Manual for Cross Cultural Study of the Acquisition of Communicative Competence.* University of California, Berkeley, July 1967.

———. 1968. Recall of full and truncated passive sentences in connected discourse. *Journal of Verbal Learning and Verbal Behavior,* **7**: 876–81.

———. In Press. Early grammatical development in several languages with special attention to Soviet research. In Bever, T., and W. Weksel, eds., *The Structure and Psychology of Language.*

———, and C. A. WELSH. 1967. Elicited imitation as a research tool in developmental psycholinguistics. Unpublished Manuscript, Department of Psychology, University of California, Berkeley.

SMITH, C. S. 1966. Two studies of the syntactic knowledge of young children. Paper presented at Linguistics Colloquium, Massachusetts Institute of Technology.

SMITH, M. E. 1926. An investigation of the development of the sentence and the extent of vocabulary in young children. *Child Welfare.* Iowa City: University of Iowa.

SNOW, KATHERINE. 1963. A detailed analysis of the articulation responses of normal first grade children. *Journal of Speech and Hearing Research,* **6**: 277–90.

SOKOLOV, E. N. 1960. Neuronal models and the orienting reflex. In Brazier, M. A. B., ed., *The Central Nervous System and Behavior.* New York: The George Macy Companies, Inc., pp. 187–276.

STAATS, A. W. 1967. Emotions and images in language: a learning analysis of their acquisition and function. In Salzinger, K., and S. Salzinger, eds., *Research in Verbal Behavior and Some Neurophysiological Implications.* New York: Academic Press, pp. 123–48.

STEVENS, KENNETH N., and ARTHUR S. HOUSE. In Press. Speech perception. In Tobias, J., and E. Schubert, eds., *Foundations of Modern Auditory Theory.*

STEWART, WILLIAM A. 1967.   Sociolinguistic factors in the history of American Negro Dialects. *The Florida FL Reporter*, **5**: No. 2.

STOKOE, W. 1960.   *Sign Language Structure: An Outline of Visual Communication Systems of the American Deaf.* Washington, D.C.: Gallaudet College.

TANNENBAUM, P. H., and F. WILLIAMS. 1968.   Generation of active and passive sentences as a function of subject or object focus. *Journal of Verbal Learning and Verbal Behavior*, **7**: 246–50.

TELFORD, CHARLES W., and JAMES M. SAWREY. 1967.   *The Exceptional Individual: Psychological and Educational Aspects.* Englewood Cliffs, N.J.: Prentice-Hall, Inc.

TONKOVA-YAMPOL'SKAYA, R. V. 1969.   Development of speech intonation in infants during the first two years of life. Translated in *Soviet Psychology*, **7**: 48–54.

TRAVIS, L. E., ed. 1957.   *Handbook of Speech Pathology.* New York: Appleton-Century-Crofts.

TRUBY, H. M., J. F. BOSMA, and J. LIND. 1965.   Newborn infant cry. *Acta Paediatrica Scandinavica*, Supplement 163.

TURNER, E. A., and R. ROMMETVEIT. 1968.   Focus of attention in recall of active and passive sentences. *Journal of Verbal Learning and Verbal Behavior*, **7**: 543–48.

VERNON, McKAY. 1967.   Relationship of language to the thinking process. *Archives of General Psychiatry*, **16**: 325–33.

VON BEKESY, GEORG, and WALTER ROSENBLITH. 1951.   The mechanical properties of the ear. In Stevens, S. S., ed., *Handbook of Experimental Psychology.* New York: John Wiley & Sons, Inc., p. 1075.

VYGOTSKY, L. S. 1962.   *Thought and Language.* Cambridge: M.I.T. Press.

WALES, R. J., and J. C. MARSHALL. 1968.   The organization of linguistic performance. In Lyons, J., and R. J. Wales, eds., *Psycholinguistic Papers.* Chicago: Aldine, pp. 29–80.

WALSH, E. GEOFFREY. 1964.   *Physiology of the Nervous System.* Boston: Little, Brown and Co.

WERNER, H., and EDITH KAPLAN. 1950.   Development of word meaning through verbal context: an experimental study. *Journal of Psychology*, **29**: 251–57.

WERNER, H., and BERNARD KAPLAN. 1964.   *Symbol Formation.* New York: John Wiley & Sons, Inc.

WHORF, B. L. 1956.   *Language, Thought and Reality.* Cambridge: M.I.T. Press.

WILLIAMS, F., and A. C. NAREMORE. 1969.   Social class differences in children's syntactic performance. *Journal of Speech and Hearing Research*, **12**: 778–93.

WILLIAMS, F., and B. S. WOOD. In Press.   Negro children's speech: some social class differences in word predictability. *Language and Speech.*

WINITZ, H., and O. C. IRWIN. 1958.   Syllabic and phonetic structure of infants' early words. *Journal of Speech and Hearing Research*, **1**: 250–56.

YENI-KOMSHIAN, GRACE, R. A. CHASE, and R. L. MOBLEY. 1967.   Delayed auditory feedback studies in the speech of children between 2 and 3 years. Annual Report, Neurocommunications Laboratory, Johns Hopkins University School of Medicine, pp. 165–88.

YOUNISS, JAMES, and H. G. FURTH. 1963.   Reaction to a placebo: the mediational deficiency hypothesis. *Psychological Bulletin*, **60**: 499–502.

INDEX

A

Addition, 126, 139
Adjective, 112, 142
Ambiguity, 164
Aphasoid, 208–9
Articulation defect, 201
Auditory mechanism, 39–44, 52, 252
  structure of, 39
Auditory signal:
  infants' responses, 42–44
  neonates' responses, 39–42
Auxiliary verb, 105, 106, 108, 113, 122

B

Babbling:
  comprehension during, 166–71
  function, 54–56, 69
  general characteristics of, 55–56, 59, 88
  segmental features of, 64–69
    in perception, 68–69, 89
    in production, 66–68, 89, 90
  syllabic features of, 63–64
Base structure rules:
  early expansion, 109–111, 122
  in early sentences, 133–34

Base structure rules (*cont.*):
  in expansion of NP and VP, 135–39
  linguistic descriptions of, 128–29
Bilingualism, 219
Brain (of man):
  association cortex, 31
  dominant hemisphere, 30, 31, 34, 36–38
  functioning of and language, 30, 32–34, 51–52, 251
  maturation of, 34–35, 51, 250–51
  structural differences, 30–35, 51, 251–52
  weight of, 31, 36

C

Capacities for language acquisition:
  central capacities (summary), 37–38, 50–52
  as a human being, 28–30, 250–53, 254–55
  peripheral capacities (summary), 50–52
Cloze procedure, 227–30
Cognition and language:
  in cognitive tasks, 6–15, 51–52
  in linguistic tasks, 235–43